THE ELEMENTS OF GRAPHING DATA

THE ELEMENTS
OF GRAPHING
DATA

William S. Cleveland
AT&T Bell Laboratories

WADSWORTH ADVANCED BOOKS AND SOFTWARE

Monterey, California

Wadsworth Advanced Book Program
A Division of Wadsworth, Inc.

Printed in the United States of America
3 4 5 6 7 8 9 10 — 89 88 87 86

Library of Congress Cataloging in Publication Data

Cleveland, William S., 1943–
    The elements of graphing data.

    Bibliography: p.
    Includes index.
    1. Graphic methods. I. Title.
QA90.C54 1985   511'.5   85–10603

ISBN 0-534-03729-1 CLOTH

ISBN 0-534-03730-5 PAPER

To Lisa, Robert, and Scott

ACKNOWLEDGEMENTS

To John Tukey, for ingenious inventions and applications of graphical data analysis.

To many colleagues at Bell Labs, for creating an optimal environment to study graphical data analysis.

To Marylyn McGill, for relentlessly pursuing perfection in experimenting with graphical displays and in managing the production of this book.

To Bob McGill, for our experiments in graphical perception and our many experiments with graphical inventions.

To Elsie Edelman, for the considerable word processing skills that were needed to produce the text.

To Lisa Cleveland, for days of proofreading in Summit and Abcoude.

To John Kimmel, for a near perfect author-editor relationship.

To many who commented on the manuscript, for helping greatly to steer the revisions - Paul Anderson, Jon Bentley, John Chambers, Lisa Cleveland, Arnold Court, Mary Donnelly, Bob Futrelle, Colin Mallows, Bob McGill, Brad Murphy, Richard Nuccitelli, James Palmer, Arno Penzias, and John Tukey.

CONTENTS

PREFACE

This book is about graphing data in science and technology. It contains graphical methods and principles that are powerful tools for showing the structure of data. The material is relevant for data *analysis*, when the analyst wants to study data, and for data *communication*, when the analyst wants to communicate data to others.

Many of the methods and principles in the book are new; many others are old, but not widely known. The first few decades of the 20th century were an exceptionally fertile time for the invention of *numerical* statistical procedures. Statistical scientists invented methods and approaches to data analysis that eventually permeated all of science and technology. The period since about 1960 has been an exceptionally fertile time in statistical science for the invention of *graphical* procedures for data analysis. An infusion of this graphical methodology into science and technology will raise the effectiveness of data analysis just as confidence intervals and hypothesis tests did decades ago.

The prerequisites for understanding the book are minimal. A few topics require a knowledge of the elementary concepts of probability and statistical science, but these topics can be skipped without affecting comprehension of the remainder of the book.

The book was meant to be read from the beginning and to be enjoyed. However, it is possible to read here and there. Winding its way through the book is a summary of the material: the figures and their legends. Reading this summary can help readers direct themselves to specific items.

Except for one small section, there is nothing in this book about computer graphics. The basic ideas, the methods, and the principles of the book transcend the medium used to implement them, but the reality is that the computer looms behind the book content because it is the medium of the present for many and of the future for almost all. The graphs of the book that are not copies of other people's graphs were computer generated. The software used was the S system for data analysis and graphics [9] developed by Richard Becker and John Chambers of AT&T Bell Laboratories, and GRAP [13], a very recent system developed by Jon Bentley and Brian Kernighan, also of Bell Labs.

Many graphical methods are missing from this book. I included only those that had promise for application to the most commonly occurring types of data and that would be relevant for all areas of science and technology. Many specialized methods, important as they are, are omitted.

The graphs in this book are communicating information about fascinating subjects, and I have not hesitated to describe the subjects in some detail when needed. In many cases some knowledge of the subject is required to understand the purpose of a graphical analysis or why a graph is not doing what was intended or what a new graphical method can show us about data. I hope the reader will share with me the excitement of experiencing the increased insight that graphical data display brings us about these subjects.

1

INTRODUCTION

1.1 THE CONTENTS OF THE BOOK

Chapter 2: Principles of Graph Construction

Figure 1.1 graphs an estimate of average temperature in the Northern Hemisphere following a nuclear war involving 60% of the world's arsenal of nuclear weapons. The data are from a *Science* article, "Nuclear Winter: Global Consequences of Multiple Nuclear Explosions," by Turco, Toon, Ackerman, Pollack, and Sagan [127]. The temperatures are computed from a series of physical models that describe a script for the nuclear war, for the creation of particles, for radiation production, and for convection. Figure 1.1 shows that the predicted temperature drops to about −25 °C and then slowly increases toward the current average ambient temperature in the Northern Hemisphere, which is shown by the dotted line on the graph.

In Figure 1.1 the data region is enclosed by a rectangle, the tick marks are outside of the rectangle, the size of the rectangle is set so that no values of the data are graphed on top of it, and there are tick marks on all four sides of the graph. Principles of graph construction such as these are the topic of Chapter 2. The focus is on the basic elements: tick marks, scales, legends, plotting symbols, reference lines, keys, labels, and markers. These details of graph construction are critical controlling factors whose proper use can greatly increase the information gotten from a graph.

Chapter 3: Graphical Methods

Figure 1.2 is a graphical method called a *dot chart*, which was invented in 1981 to display data in which each value has a label associated with it that we want to show on the graph [28]. The large dots convey the values and the dotted lines enable us to visually connect each value with its label. The dot chart has several different forms depending on the nature of the data and the structure of the labels.

The data in Figure 1.2 are the number of speakers for 21 of the world's languages [138, p. 245]. Only languages spoken by at least 50 million people are shown. The data are graphed on a log base 2 scale, so values double in moving left to right from one tick mark to the next.

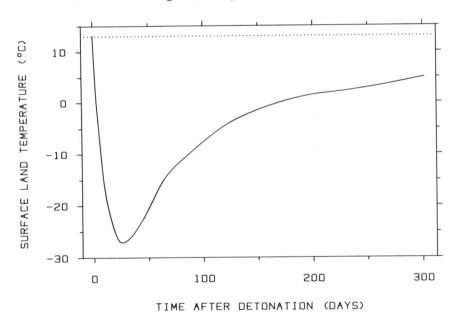

Figure 1.1   PRINCIPLES OF GRAPH CONSTRUCTION. The graph shows model predictions of average temperature in the Northern Hemisphere following a 10,000 megaton nuclear exchange. On the graph, the data region is enclosed by a rectangle, the tick marks are outside of the rectangle, the size of the rectangle is set so that no values of the data are graphed on top of it, and there are tick marks on all four sides of the graph. Chapter 2 is about principles of graph construction such as these.

Figure 1.3 is a graph of ozone against wind speed for 111 days in New York City from May 1 to September 30 of 1973. The graph shows that ozone tends to decrease as wind speed increases due to the increased ventilation of air pollution that higher wind speeds bring. However, because the pattern is embedded in a lot of noise, it is difficult to see more precise aspects of the pattern, for example, whether there is a linear or nonlinear decrease. In Figure 1.4 a smooth curve has been added to the graph of ozone and wind speed. The curve was computed by a method called *robust locally weighted regression*, often abbreviated to *lowess*, that was invented in 1977 [26]. Lowess provides a graphical summary that helps our assessment of the dependence; now we can see that the dependence of ozone on wind speed is nonlinear. One

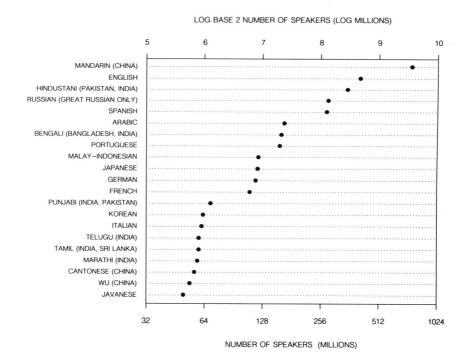

Figure 1.2   GRAPHICAL METHODS. The figure shows a graphical method called a dot chart, which can be used to show data where each value has a label. The data are the number of speakers for the world's 21 most spoken languages. The data are graphed on a log base 2 scale, so values double in moving left to right from one tick mark to the next.

important property of lowess is that it is quite flexible and can do a good job of following a very wide variety of patterns.

Chapter 3 is about graphical methods such as the dot chart, lowess, and graphing on a log base 2 scale. Some of the graphs are methods by virtue of the design of the visual vehicle used to convey the data; the dot chart is an example. Other methods use the standard Cartesian graph as the visual vehicle, but are methods by virtue of the quantitative information that is shown on the graph; graphing a lowess curve is an example of such a method.

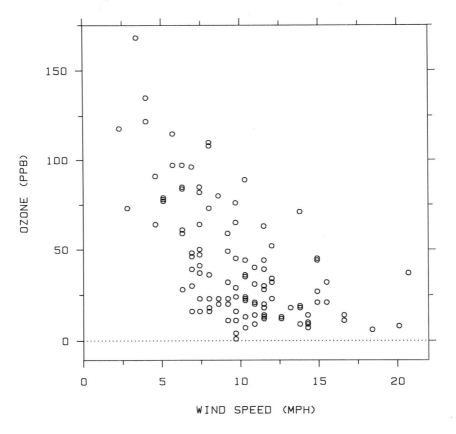

Figure 1.3 GRAPHICAL METHODS. An air pollutant, ozone, is graphed against wind speed. From the graph we can see ozone tends to decrease as wind speed increases, but judging whether the pattern is linear or nonlinear is difficult.

Chapter 4: Graphical Perception

When a graph is constructed, quantitative and categorical information is *encoded*, chiefly through position, size, symbols, and color. When a person looks at a graph, the information is visually *decoded* by the person's visual system. A graphical method is successful only if the decoding process is effective. No matter how clever and how technologically impressive the encoding, it is a failure if the decoding

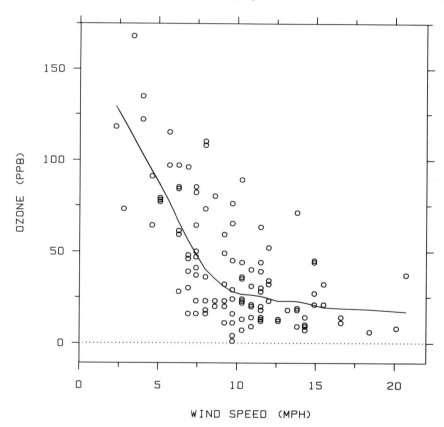

WIND SPEED (MPH)

Figure 1.4   GRAPHICAL METHODS. A method of smoothing data called lowess was used to compute a curve summarizing the dependence of ozone on wind speed. With the curve superposed, we can now see that the dependence of ozone on wind speed is nonlinear. Chapter 3 is about graphical methods such as lowess, dot charts, and graphing on a log base 2 scale.

process is a failure. Informed decisions about how to encode data can be achieved only through an understanding of the visual decoding process, which is called *graphical perception*.

Consider the top panel of Figure 1.5 which graphs the values of imports and exports between England and the East Indies. The data were first shown in 1786 on a graph of William Playfair [108] that will

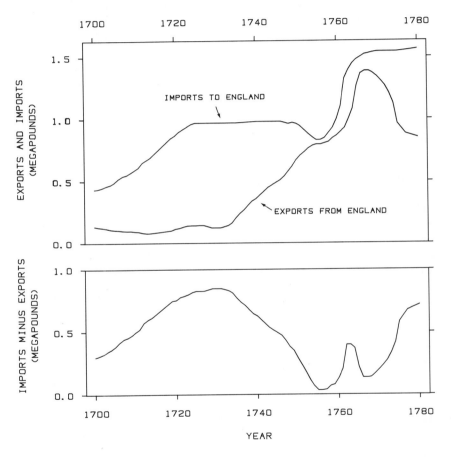

Figure 1.5 GRAPHICAL PERCEPTION. The top panel is a graph of exports and imports between the East Indies and England. The data are from a graph published by William Playfair in 1786. It is difficult to visually decode imports minus exports, which are encoded by the vertical distances between the curves. Imports minus exports are graphed directly in the bottom panel, and now we can see that their behavior just after 1760 is quite different from what we visually decode in the top panel. Chapter 4 deals with issues of graphical perception such as this.

be discussed in Chapter 4. To visually decode the import data we can make judgments of *positions* along the vertical scale; the same is true of exports. Another important set of quantitative values on this graph is the amounts by which imports exceed exports; to decode these values we must judge the vertical *distances* between the two curves.

There is a problem with the top panel of Figure 1.5. It is exceedingly difficult for our visual system to judge vertical distances between two curves when there is a large change in the slopes; we tend to judge minimum distances, which lie along perpendiculars to the tangents of the curves. For example, from the top panel of Figure 1.5 the visual impression is that imports minus exports do not change by much during the period just after 1760 when both series are rapidly increasing. This visual impression is quite incorrect. Imports minus exports are graphed directly in the bottom panel of Figure 1.5 so that the values can be decoded visually by judgments of position along a common scale, and now we can see there is a rapid rise and fall just after 1760.

Chapter 4 is about issues of graphical perception such as this. A *paradigm* for graphical perception is presented. ("Paradigm" is used here in the sense of Thomas S. Kuhn to mean a framework that organizes information [84].) Elementary graphical-perception tasks that people perform in visually decoding quantitative information from graphs are identified. Then, using both the theory of visual perception and experiments in graphical perception, the tasks are ordered based on how accurately people perform them. Also, the roles of detection and distance in graphical perception are investigated. The paradigm has an important application: data should be encoded on graphs so that the visual decoding involves tasks as high in the ordering as possible. This is illustrated by many examples. One result is that new methods are developed and some of the most-used graphical forms are set aside.

1.2 THE POWER OF GRAPHICAL DATA DISPLAY

The premise of this book is that infusing the new knowledge about graphical data display into science and technology will lead to a deeper understanding of the data that arise in scientific studies. Graphs are exceptionally powerful tools for data analysis. The reason is nicely encapsulated in a sentence from a 1982 letter written to me by W. Edwards Deming: "Graphical methods can retain the information in the data." Numerical data analytic procedures — such as means, standard deviations, correlation coefficients, and t-tests — are essentially data reduction techniques. Graphical methods complement such numerical techniques. Graphical methods tend to show data sets as a whole, allowing us to summarize the general behavior and to study detail. This leads to much more thorough data analyses.

One reason why graphical displays can retain the information in the data is that a large amount of quantitative information can be displayed *and* absorbed. This is illustrated in Figure 1.6. Panel 1 (the top panel) is a graph of monthly average atmospheric carbon dioxide concentrations measured at the Mauna Loa Observatory in Hawaii [75]. The panel shows two striking phenomena. One is the persistent long-term rise in CO_2 concentrations due to the burning of fossil fuels. This rise, if continued unabated, will produce the famous greenhouse effect: global temperatures will rise, the polar ice caps will melt, the coastal areas of the continents will be put under water, and the climates of different regions of the earth will change radically [57, 85].

The second phenomenon is the yearly rise and fall of the CO_2 concentrations. This is due largely to vegetation in the Northern Hemisphere. When the foliage grows in the spring, plant tissue absorbs CO_2 from the atmosphere, and atmospheric concentrations decline. When the foliage decreases at the end of the summer, CO_2 returns to the atmosphere, and the atmospheric concentrations increase.

We can get substantial insight into the variation in the CO_2 data by a combination of numerical and graphical procedures. Panels 2 and 3 in Figure 1.6 show numerical descriptions of the long-term trend in the concentrations and of the seasonal oscillations. These trend and seasonal components were computed by a complicated algorithm called SABL [29]. Panel 4 of Figure 1.6 is the variation in the CO_2 that is neither seasonal nor trend; this remainder is just the CO_2 data minus the trend component and minus the seasonal component. On the vertical scales of the four panels of Figure 1.6 the number of units per cm varies. The bars on the right help to show the relative scaling by portraying changes of the same magnitude on the four panels.

Panel 1 of Figure 1.6 allows us to see the overall behavior of the CO_2 data; the bottom three panels allow us to see more detailed behavior. The trend panel shows that the rate of the CO_2 increase is increasing since the slope of the trend curve increases through time; the global CO_2 increase is worsening.

The seasonal panel shows that the seasonal oscillations are getting slightly bigger. For a long time it was thought that these seasonal oscillations were stable and not changing through time, but then around 1980 three groups — one at CSIRO in Australia [106]; a second at Scripps Institution of Oceanography in California [6]; and a third at

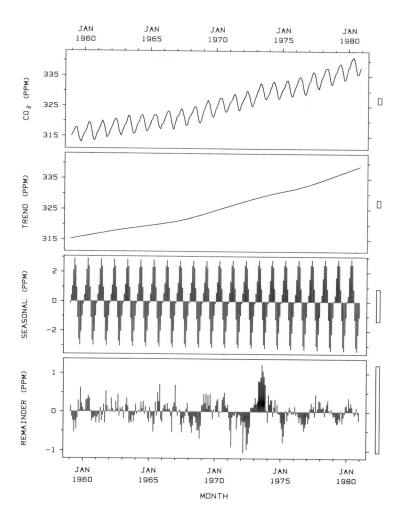

Figure 1.6   THE POWER OF GRAPHICAL DATA DISPLAY. Panel 1 (the top panel) shows monthly average CO_2 concentrations from Mauna Loa, Hawaii. Panel 2 shows a numerical description of the long-term trend in the concentrations, caused by the burning of fossil fuels. Panel 3 shows a numerical description of the seasonal oscillations, which are caused by the increase and decrease of foliage on the earth during the year. Panel 4 displays the CO_2 concentrations minus the trend component and minus the seasonal oscillations. The bars on the right portray changes of the same magnitude on the four panels. A graph like this enabled one group to discover that the amplitudes of the CO_2 seasonal fluctuations are increasing. This visual display shows 2112 numbers. No vehicle other than a graph is capable of conveying so much quantitative information so readily.

AT&T Bell Laboratories in New Jersey [30] — independently discovered the small, but persistent change in the Mauna Loa seasonal oscillations. No one yet has a good understanding of what is causing the change, but a number of scientists are working to determine if it is due to a slow change in the seasonal rise and fall of foliage on the earth or some other mechanism. This small change could well be the harbinger of an important change in the way the earth is working.

Panel 4 of Figure 1.6 shows the effect of another global phenomenon. The values of the remainder show slow oscillations of several years in length; this is revealed by stretches in which the remainder is predominantly above or below zero. These changes in the CO_2 concentrations are correlated with changes in the Southern Oscillation index, which is a measurement of the difference in atmospheric pressure between Easter Island in the South Pacific and Darwin, Australia [5]. Changes in the index are also associated with changes in climate. For example, when the index drops sharply, the trade winds are reduced and the temperature of the equatorial Pacific increases. This warming, which has important consequences for South America, often occurs at Christmas time and is called El Niño — the child [77].

Figure 1.6 conveys a large amount of information about the CO_2 concentrations. We have been able to summarize overall behavior and to see very detailed information. It may come as a surprise just how much quantitative information is shown; there are 1104 data points on this graph and each data point specifies a concentration and a time; thus 2208 numbers are displayed. No vehicle other than a graph could convey so much quantitative information so readily.

1.3 THE CHALLENGE OF GRAPHICAL DATA DISPLAY

Graphical data display is surprisingly difficult. Even the most simple matters can easily go wrong. This will be illustrated by two examples where seemingly straightforward graphical tasks ran into trouble.

Aerosol Concentrations

Figure 1.7 is a graphical method called a *percentile comparison graph* which will be discussed in detail in Chapter 3; the figure shows the graph as it originally appeared in 1974 in a *Science* report written by T. E. Graedel, Beat Kleiner, Jack Warner, and me [31]. (As with almost all of the reproduced graphs in this book, the size of the graph is the same as that of the source.) The display compares Sunday and workday concentrations of aerosols, or particles in the air. First, the graph has a construction error: the 0.0 label on the horizontal scale should be 0.6. Unfortunately, the error makes it appear that the left corner is the origin; many readers probably wondered why the line $y = x$, which is drawn on the graph, does not go through the origin. A second problem is that the scales on the graph are poorly chosen; comparison of the Sunday and workday values would have been enhanced by making the horizontal and vertical scales the same. (Scale issues such as these are discussed in Chapter 2.) Finally, because in 1974 many of the principles of graphical perception that are discussed in Chapter 4 had not yet been formulated, it did not occur to us then that it is not easy to compare the vertical distances of the points from the line $y = x$; the solution to this problem is a graphical method called the *Tukey sum-difference graph*, which will be discussed in Chapters 3 and 4.

Brain Masses and Body Masses of Animal Species

Figure 1.8 is a graph from Carl Sagan's intriguing book, *The Dragons of Eden* [113]. The graph shows the brain masses and body masses, both on a log scale, of a collection of animal species. We can see that log brain mass and log body mass are correlated, but this was not the main reason for making the graph.

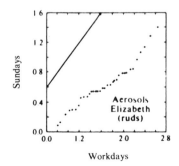

Figure 1.7   THE CHALLENGE OF GRAPHICAL DATA DISPLAY. This graph, made in 1974, compares Sunday and workday concentrations of aerosols. The line shown is $y = x$. The graph has problems. There is a construction error: the 0.0 label on the horizontal scale is wrong and should be 0.6. The horizontal and vertical scales should be the same but are not. Furthermore, it is hard to judge the deviations of the points from the line $y = x$.
Figure republished from [31]. Copyright 1974 by the AAAS.

What Sagan wanted to describe was an intelligence scale that has been investigated extensively by Harry J. Jerison [68]. Sagan writes that this measure of intelligence is "the *ratio* of the mass of the brain to the total mass of the organism." Later he adds, referring the reader to the graph, "of all the organisms shown, the beast with the largest brain mass for its body weight is a creature called *Homo sapiens*. Next in such a ranking are dolphins."

The first problem is that Sagan has made a mistake in describing the intelligence measure; it is not the ratio of brain to body mass but rather is (brain mass)/(body mass)$^{2/3}$. If we study a group of related species, such as all mammals, brain mass tends to increase as a function of body mass. The general pattern of the data is reasonably well described by the equation

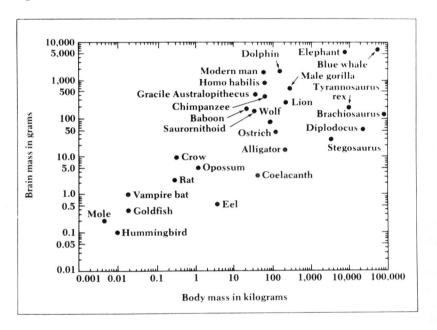

Figure 1.8   THE CHALLENGE OF GRAPHICAL DATA DISPLAY. This graph shows brain and body masses of animal species. The intent was for viewers to judge an intelligence measure; this requires comparing values of $y - 2/3\,x$ for the graphed points, which is difficult to do.

$$\text{brain mass} = c \, (\text{body mass})^{2/3} \; .$$

Since the densities of different species do not vary radically, we may think of the masses as being surrogate measures for volume, and volume to the 2/3 power behaves like a surface area. Thus the empirical relationship says that brain mass depends on the surface area of the body; Stephen Jay Gould conjectures that this is so because body surfaces serve as end points for so many nerve channels [53, pp. 182-183]. Now suppose a given species has a greater brain mass than other species with the same body mass; what this means is that (brain mass)/(body mass)$^{2/3}$ is greater. We might expect that the big-brained species would be more intelligent since it has an excess of brain capacity given its body surface. This idea leads to measuring intelligence by (brain mass)/(body mass)$^{2/3}$.

Let us now return to Figure 1.8 and consider the graphical problem, which is a serious one. How do we judge the intelligence measure from the graph? Suppose two species have the same intelligence measure; then both have the same value of

$$\frac{(\text{brain mass})}{(\text{body mass})^{2/3}} = r \; .$$

Thus

$$\log(\text{brain mass}) = 2/3 \, \log(\text{body mass}) + \log{(r)}$$

for both species. This means that in Figure 1.8, the two equally intelligent species lie on a line with slope 2/3. Suppose one species has a greater value of r than another; then the smarter one lies on a line with slope 2/3 that is to the northwest of the line on which the less intelligent one lies. In other words, to judge the intelligence measure from Figure 1.8 we must mentally superpose a set of parallel lines with slope 2/3. (If we attempt to judge Sagan's mistaken ratios, we must superpose lines with slope 1.) This mental-visual task is simply too hard.

Figure 1.8 can be greatly improved, at least for the purpose of showing the intelligence measure, by graphing the measure directly on a log scale, as is done in the dot chart of Figure 1.9. Now we can see strikingly many things not so apparent from Figure 1.8. Happily, modern man is at the top. Dolphins are next; interestingly, they are ahead of our ancestor *homo habilis*. We can also see that this intelligence measure should be regarded as a rough one since it suggests that a goldfish is smarter than a wolf.

It should be emphasized that for some purposes, Figure 1.8 is a useful graph. For example, it shows the values of the brain and body masses and gives us information about their relationship. The point is that it does a poor job of showing the intelligence measure.

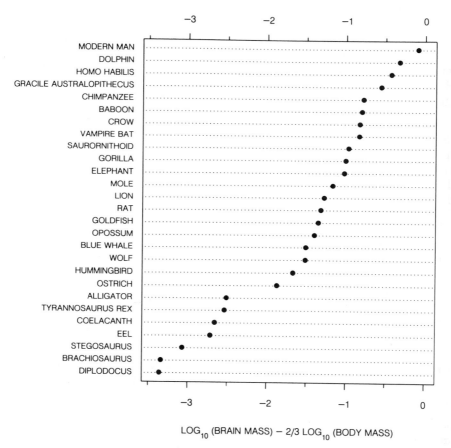

$$LOG_{10} \text{ (BRAIN MASS)} - 2/3 \, LOG_{10} \text{ (BODY MASS)}$$

Figure 1.9   DOT CHART. The intelligence measure, log (brain mass) − 2/3 log (body mass), is shown directly by a dot chart. (Both masses are expressed in grams for this computation.) The values of the measure can be judged far more readily than in Figure 1.8. For example, we can see modern man is at the top, even ahead of our very clever fellow mammals, the dolphins.

1.4 SOURCES AND GOALS

Principles of Graph Construction

In 1980 I began a study of graphs in scientific publications. Many people were working hard to develop graphical methods for data analysis, and it seemed reasonable to suppose that buried in the geophysics literature or in the electrical engineering literature or in the literature of many other subjects were clever ideas for displaying data. Indeed, some good ideas were uncovered, but they were a few bright lights standing out in what was mostly a dark picture. In the main, instead of inventiveness, there were errors, poorly explained graphs, graphs where the data could not be seen, graphs where different elements could not be visually disentangled, graphs where the method of display was poorly selected, and graphs that seemed to beg for more or different quantitative information to be shown [79].

In one study, I read the articles and reports of the 1980 Volume 207 of *Science*; there were 249 articles and reports and 67% of them had graphs. I analyzed the 377 graphs, and recorded types, problems, purposes, unconventional practice, possible methods of improvement, and a number of other variables [27]. 30% of the graphs in the volume had at least one of four types of specific problems:

(1) *Explanation* (15.4%) — Something on the graph was not explained.

(2) *Discrimination* (10.1%) — Items on the graph, such as different symbol types, could not be easily distinguished due to the design or size of the graph.

(3) *Construction* (6.4%) — A mistake was made in the construction of the graph such as tick marks incorrectly spaced, mislabeling, items omitted, and wrong scales.

(4) *Degraded Image* (6.4%) — Some aspect of the graph was missing or partially missing due to poor reproduction.

If the only problems uncovered in these studies were those just described, the response could be a few simple guidelines that would eliminate them. But there were deeper problems. First, in many cases the basic graphical form showing the data was poorly chosen. Second, and even more fundamentally, the quantitative information shown on many graphs was poorly chosen. The response to the problems of construction, both superficial and deep, is the principles of graph construction of Chapter 2.

In developing the principles of Chapter 2, I attempted to focus on the basics, to avoid being arbitrary, and to eliminate any principle that was just a matter of style or personal preference. It is a continual challenge in developing principles for graphs not to degenerate into simply expressing personal preferences. William Strunk Jr., prophet of generations of writers and co-author of *The Elements of Style* [120], knew well the tension between freedom and rules. E. B. White writes [120, p. xv]: "Style rules of this sort are, of course, somewhat a matter of individual preference, and even the established rules of grammar are open to challenge. Professor Strunk, although one of the most inflexible and choosy of men, was quick to acknowledge the fallacy of inflexibility and the danger of doctrine." I have tried hard to avoid inflexibility and doctrine in Chapter 2.

Graphical Methods

In the 1960s John Tukey, a renowned statistical scientist and Renaissance man of science, turned his attention to graphical data analysis [126]. Tukey invented a multitude of graphical methods and employed graphs heavily in his book *Exploratory Data Analysis* [125], demonstrating clearly the important role graphs can play in data analysis. This, and the computer graphics revolution, spawned a graphics movement in the field of statistical science, and interest in developing new graphical methods grew rapidly in the 1970s and 1980s [21, 123].

Chapter 3 of this book contains graphical methods that arose in this recent research movement in statistical science, methods from other areas of science and technology, and new methods. The methods selected for discussion in the chapter are useful for all of science and technology and have wide scope in terms of the types of data to which they can be applied. Many specialized methods, useful only in specific fields or only for specialized types of data, are not included. For example, there is a vast methodology for making statistical maps [14, 112] — showing how data vary as a function of geographical location — that is not treated here. Missing also are a number of graphical methods that serve as diagnostic tools for specialized numerical statistical methods [21].

Graphical Perception

In 1981 Robert McGill and I began a series of experiments to probe basic, elementary aspects of graphical perception. The experimentation, together with reasoning from the theory of visual perception, led to the formulation of initial paradigms in a paper in the *Journal of the American Statistical Association* [33] and in an article in *Science* [35]. The material in Chapter 4 draws heavily on these two sources.

Despite the importance of the visual decoding process in graphical data display, graphical perception received very little formal, scientific study in the past. Many have studied the process informally, but informal study is not good enough. Without controlled experiments and measurements there can be no science. Informal study, however, has its value. Intuition flowing from experience is a powerful tool in all areas of science, including graphical perception. We can profitably study graphical perception just by making a graph and looking at it, provided the look is genuinely critical. Certain aspects of the paradigm in Chapter 4 have been derived by researchers in graphical methods — for example, John Tukey [125], Edward R. Tufte [123], Jacques Bertin [14], and Karl G. Karsten [74] — using just such a process of making a graph and studying it.

But intuition and one-subject experiments where researchers study their own graphs can take us just so far. Different researchers will be led to different opinions, some issues are too subtle to submit to just looking, and some phenomena are different from what they seem once you have measured them. To understand graphical perception we need objective numerical measures of people's accuracy in performing graphical-perception tasks, just as measurements are needed in other areas of science. Such a process is behind the paradigm of Chapter 4.

Much of the small amount of experimentation in graphical perception that has been carried out in the past [82, 83] has not led very far because the focus has tended to be the direct comparison of two different types of graphs rather than the probing of basic, elementary aspects. When we visually decode data from a graph, a very complex set of perceptual and cognitive tasks are carried out. Thus, if the basic experimental units are different types of graphs, there is too much complexity and variation to make much progress. In the paradigm of Chapter 4, the complex tasks are broken up into simpler, elementary tasks that then become the focus of the experimentation and theory. Thus the paradigm is an attempt to identify the elementary particles of graphical perception and to describe their interactions and properties.

The more general topic of visual perception has been studied, of course, in great depth. Theories of vision, such as the textons of Bela Julesz [72] and the computational theory of David Marr [94], and the results of experiments in visual perception [8] are important for understanding graphical perception, but the general studies are by no means sufficient for a good understanding of the more specialized topic.

In the past, lack of attention to issues of graphical perception has resulted in the use of data displays that convey quantitative information poorly and in graphical inventions that do not work. Here is one example. In the graphics movement that began in the 1960s in statistical science, much energy was devoted to inventing methods for displaying measurements of three or more variables. An example of such data is daily averages of seven variables — temperature, humidity, barometric pressure, rainfall, solar radiation, wind speed, and wind direction — at one site for 100 days; the data consist of 100 points in a seven-dimensional space. There were many inventions: Chernoff faces [24], Anderson metroglyphs [3], Cleveland-Kleiner weathervane plots [18], Diaconis-Friedman M and N plots [45], Tukey-Tukey dodecahedral views [124], Kleiner-Hartigan trees [78], Andrews curves [4], Tufte rug plots [123, pp. 135-136], and the scatterplot matrix, which is described in Section 6 of Chapter 3. All of the methods in the list, with the exception of the scatterplot matrix, failed in the sense that they almost never showed anyone anything about data that could not be seen more easily by other means. Peter Huber writes [61, p. 674]: "The mere multiplicity of the attempts to deal with more than three continuous dimensions by encoding additional variables into glyphs, Chernoff faces, stars, Kleiner-Hartigan trees, and so on indicates that each of them has met only with rather limited success."

Why did so many methods in the domain of multidimensional data display fail? The answer is that not enough attention was paid to graphical perception. Inventors generated ideas for encoding multidimensional data and did not worry about whether it was easy or hard to visually decode the quantitative information using the methods. Consider Chernoff faces. The values of one point in the space (e.g., the seven values of the meteorological variables mentioned above for one day) are shown by one face. Each variable is encoded by an aspect of the faces (e.g., nose length encodes temperature, the curvature of the mouth encodes humidity, and so forth). The encoding is enormously clever, but the method is of very limited usefulness. Visually decoding the quantitative information is just too difficult.

Chapter 4 is radical insofar as it calls upon us to approach graphs with a new concept: In using graphs and in inventing new graphical methods we should make explicit, conscious use of principles of graphical perception to guide what is used and what is invented.

2

PRINCIPLES OF
GRAPH CONSTRUCTION

This chapter is about the basic elements of graph construction — scales, legends, plotting symbols, reference lines, keys, labels, panels, markers, and tick marks. Principles of graph construction are given that can enhance the ability of a graph to show the structure of the data. The principles are relevant both for data *analysis*, when the analyst wants to study the data, and for data *communication*, when the analyst wants to present quantitative information to others.

In this chapter there are many examples of graphs from science and technology that have problems. Such problems are pervasive because graphing data is a complex task. (See Sections 3 and 4 of Chapter 1.) The principles are applied to the examples to show how the problems can be solved.

Section 2.1 defines terms. Section 2.2 gives principles that make the elements of a graph visually clear, and Section 2.3 gives principles that contribute to a clear understanding of what is graphed. Section 2.4 is about scales, and Section 2.5 discusses principles that are general strategies for graphing data. Finally, Section 2.6 lists the principles of graph construction given in the previous sections.

2.1 TERMINOLOGY

Terminology for graphical displays is unfortunately not fully developed and usage is not consistent. Thus, in some cases we will have to invent a few terms and in some other cases we will pick one of several possible terms now in use. Terminology is defined in Figures 2.1 and 2.2, which display the same data in two different ways; the words in boldface convey the terminology. For the most part, the terms are self-explanatory, but a few comments are in order.

In Figures 2.1 and 2.2 the data are the percent changes from 1950 in death rates in the United States due to cardiovascular disease and due to all other diseases [87]. In Figure 2.1 the two data sets are *superposed* and in Figure 2.2 they are *juxtaposed*. The *marker* along the horizontal scale on each graph shows the time of the first specialized cardiovascular care unit in a hospital in the United States. In Figure 2.1 the *data labels* are part of the *key*, but in Figure 2.2 they are in the *data regions*.

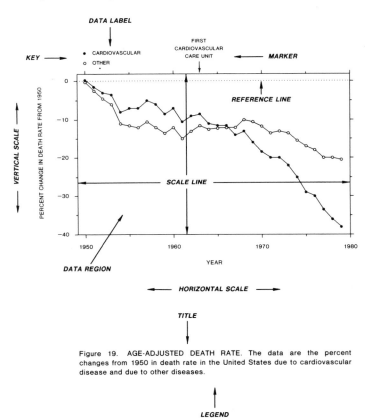

Figure 19. AGE-ADJUSTED DEATH RATE. The data are the percent changes from 1950 in death rate in the United States due to cardiovascular disease and due to other diseases.

Figure 2.1   TERMINOLOGY. This figure and the next define terminology. The two sets of data — death rates due to cardiovascular disease and death rates due to all other diseases — are superposed. The data labels are in the key on this graph.

Scale has two meanings in graphical data display. One is the ruler along which we graph the data; this is the meaning indicated in Figure 2.1. But scale is also used by some to mean the number of data

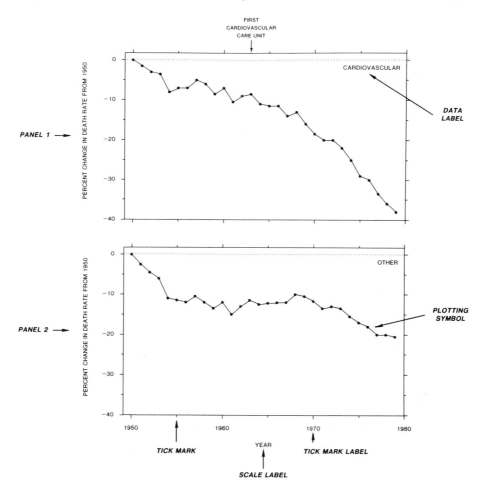

Figure 19. AGE-ADJUSTED DEATH RATE. The data are the percent changes from 1950 in death rate in the United States due to cardiovascular disease and due to other diseases.

Figure 2.2 TERMINOLOGY. This figure also defines the meaning of terms. The two sets of data are juxtaposed by using two panels. Each panel on this graph has a data label.

units per cm. This meaning will not be used in this book. Instead, the phrase, *number of units per cm*, will be used. Not every concept needs a single-word definition.

2.2 CLEAR VISION

Clear vision is a vital aspect of graphs. The viewer must be able to visually disentangle the many different items that appear on a graph. In this section elementary principles of graph construction are given to help achieve clear vision.

Make the data stand out. Avoid superfluity.

Make the data stand out and *avoid superfluity* are two broad strategies that serve as an overall guide to the specific principles that follow in this section.

The data — the quantitative and qualitative information in the data region — are the reason for the existence of the graph. The data should stand out. It is too easy to forget this. One of the major problems uncovered in the studies of graphs in scientific publications described in Section 4 of Chapter 1 was the data not standing out. There are many ways to obscure the data, such as allowing other elements of the graph to interfere with the data or not making the graphical elements encoding the data visually prominent. Sometimes different values of the data can obscure each other.

We should eliminate superfluity in graphs. Unnecessary parts of a graph add to the clutter and increase the difficulty of making the necessary elements — the data — stand out. Edward R. Tufte puts it aptly; he calls superfluous elements on a graph *chartjunk* [123].

Let us look at one example of implementing these two general principles where the result is increased understanding of the data. Figure 2.3 shows data on a !Kung woman and her baby [80]. The !Kung are an African tribe of hunter-gatherers from Botswana and Namibia whose present culture provides a glimpse into the history of man. One interesting feature of their procreation is that there is a long interval between births; a mother will typically go three years after the birth of a child before having the next one. This was puzzling since abortion or other forms of birth control are not used.

In 1980 two Harvard anthropologists, Melvin Konner and Carol Worthman, put forward a likely solution to the puzzle [80]. They argued that it was the very frequent nursing of infants by their mothers during the first one to two years of life that produces the long inter-birth interval. The nursing results in the secretion of the hormone prolactin into the mother's blood, which in turn reduces the functions of the gonads. This acts as a birth control mechanism.

Konner and Worthman used the graph in Figure 2.3 to show the frequency of nursing and other activities of one !Kung woman and her baby. The open bars and tall vertical lines are nursing times; the closed bars show times when the baby is sleeping; F means fretting; and slashed lines represent the time held by the mother with arrows for picking up and setting down. A major problem with Figure 2.3 is that the data do not stand out. It is hard to get a visual summary of the extent and variability of each activity and it is difficult to remember which symbol goes with which activity, so that constant referring to the legend is necessary. A minor problem with Figure 2.3 is that the arrows for picking up and setting down are superfluous.

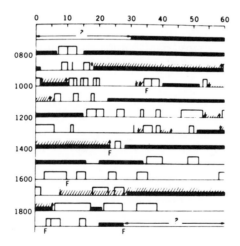

Figure 2.3   SUPERFLUITY AND STANDING OUT. The graph shows the activities of a !Kung woman and her baby. The open bars and tall vertical lines are nursing times; the closed bars show times when the baby is sleeping; F means fretting; and slashed lines are intervals when the baby is held by the mother, with arrows for picking up and setting down. The data do not stand out on this graph.
Figure republished from [80]. Copyright 1980 by the AAAS.

Figure 2.4 is an improved graph of Figure 2.3. The data stand out and there are no superfluous elements. The constant referring to the legend is not necessary and we get a much better idea of the extent of the activities and their interactions. Figure 2.4 shows clearly the frequency and duration of the nursing bouts for this two-week-old boy. To Western eyes the frequency of the bouts is astonishing. It turns out that this high frequency is needed to make the prolactin birth control mechanism work, since the hormone has a half-life in the blood stream of only 10 to 30 minutes. The figure also shows clearly that nursing and holding infrequently occur together; presumably feeding is done in some prone position.

The specific principles that follow in this section will allow us to achieve the two general goals of making the data stand out and avoiding superfluity.

Use visually prominent graphical elements to show the data.

On the graph in Figure 2.5 [25] the data do not stand out. The plotting symbols are not visually prominent, and in the bottom panel we cannot tell how many data values make up the black blob in the lower left corner.

A good way to help the data to stand out is to show them with a graphical element that is visually prominent. This is illustrated in Figure 2.6; the data from Figure 2.5 are regraphed. The symbols showing the data stand out, and now the data can be seen. The symbols that look like the spokes of a wheel represent multiple points; each spoke is one point. For example, the spoked symbol in the Lorne Lavas panel represents four data values.

There are other problems with Figure 2.5 that have been corrected in Figure 2.6. First, in the top panel of Figure 2.5, two tick mark labels, 0.725 and 0.735, have been interchanged. Also, it is hard to compare data on the three graphs in Figure 2.5 because the scales are different; scales issues such as these will be discussed in Section 2.4.

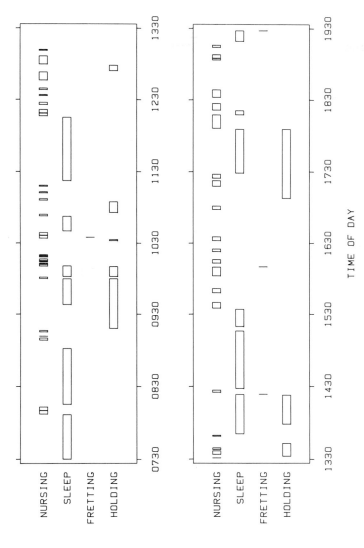

Figure 2.4 SUPERFLUITY AND STANDING OUT. *Make the data stand out. Avoid superfluity.* These are two broad principles that guide the specific principles to follow in this section. The data from Figure 2.3 are regraphed. It is now easier to see the activity times and their interactions, constant referring to the legend is not necessary, and there are no superfluous graphical elements.

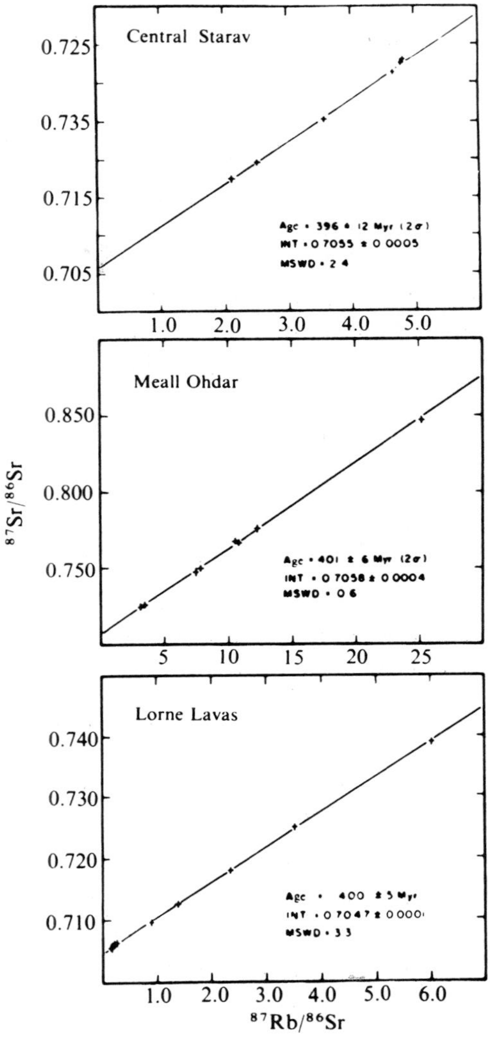

Figure 2.5 VISUAL PROMINENCE. The data do not stand out.
Figure republished by permission from Nature [25]. Copyright © 1983 Macmillan Journals Limited.

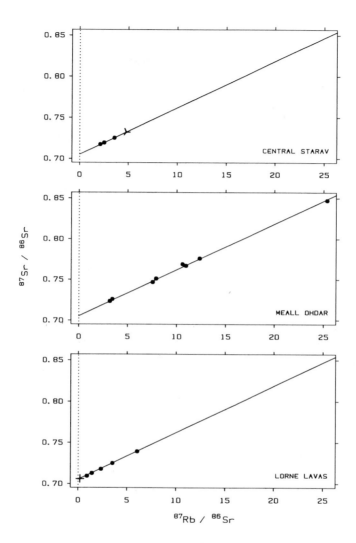

Figure 2.6 VISUAL PROMINENCE. *Use visually prominent graphical elements to show the data.* Now the data from Figure 2.5 can be seen. The symbols that look like the spokes of a wheel represent multiple points; each spoke is one observation.

When plotting symbols are connected by lines, the symbols should be prominent enough to prevent being obscured by the lines. In Figure 2.7 the data and their standard errors are inconspicuous, in part because of the connecting lines [17]. In Figure 2.8 visually prominent filled circles show the data. These large, bold plotting symbols make the data amply visible and ensure that the connecting of one datum to the next by a straight line does not obscure the data. The connection is useful since it helps us to track visually the movement of the values through time.

The data in Figure 2.8 are from observations of nesting sites of bald eagles in northwestern Ontario [56]. The graph shows good news: After the ban on the use of DDT, the average number of young per site began increasing.

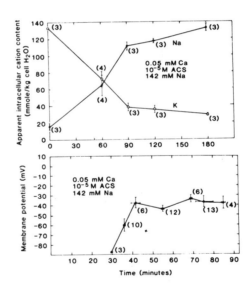

Figure 2.7   VISUAL PROMINENCE. The data on this graph do not stand out because the graphical elements showing the observations and their standard errors are not prominent enough to prevent being obscured by the connecting lines.
Figure republished from [17]. Copyright 1983 by the AAAS.

Use a pair of scale lines for each variable. Make the data region the interior of the rectangle formed by the scale lines. Put tick marks outside of the data region.

Data are frequently obscured by graphing them on top of scale lines. One example is Figure 2.9 where points are graphed on top of the vertical scale line. The graph and data of Figure 2.9 are from an

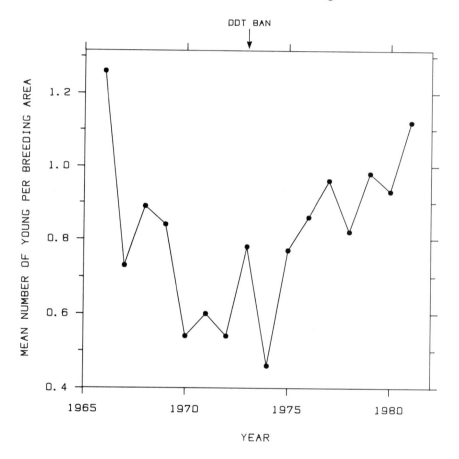

Figure 2.8   VISUAL PROMINENCE. The plotting symbols on this graph are prominent enough to prevent being obscured by the connecting lines.

interesting experiment run by four Harvard anatomists — Charles
Lyman, Regina O'Brien, G. Cliett Greene, and Elaine Papafrangos [89].
In the experiment, the researchers observed the lifetimes of 144 Turkish
hamsters (*Mesocricetus brandti*) and the percentages of their lifetimes that
the hamsters spent hibernating. The goal of the experiment was to
determine whether there is an association between the amount of
hibernation and the length of life; the hypothesis is that increased
hibernation *causes* increased life. Hamsters were chosen for the
experiment since they can be raised in the laboratory and since they
hibernate for long periods when exposed to the cold. Certain species of
bats also hibernate for long periods in the cold but, as the experimenters
put it, "their long life-span challenges the middle-aged investigator to
see the end of the experiment."

The graph in Figure 2.9 suggests that hibernation and lifetime are
associated; while this does not *prove* causality it does support the
hypothesis. The graph also shows one deviant hamster that spent a

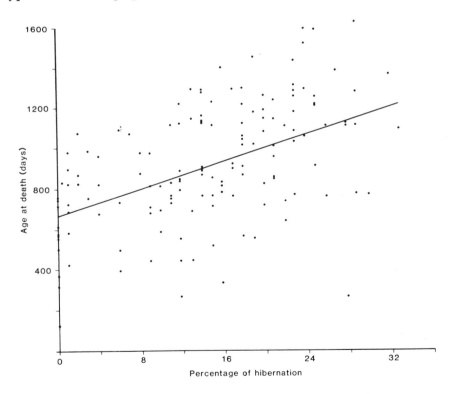

Figure 2.9   SCALE LINES AND THE DATA REGION. The data for zero
hibernation are obscured by the left vertical scale line.
Figure republished from [89]. Copyright 1981 by the AAAS.

large fraction of its life hibernating but nevertheless died at a young age. Hibernation cannot save a hamster from all of the perils of life.

One unfortunate aspect of Figure 2.9 is that the data for hamsters with zero hibernation are graphed on top of the vertical scale line. This obscures the data to the point where it is hard to perceive just how many points there are. No data should be so obscured. One way to avoid this is shown in Figure 2.10. The data region — the place where the symbols representing the data are allowed to be — is in the interior of the rectangle formed by the scale lines. Now the values with zero hibernation can be seen clearly.

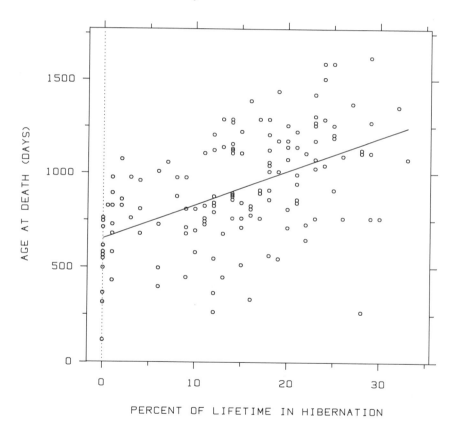

Figure 2.10   SCALE LINES AND THE DATA REGION. *Use a pair of scale lines for each variable. Make the data region the interior of the rectangle formed by the scale lines. Put tick marks outside of the data region.* This format prevents data from being obscured. Using two scale lines for each of the two variables on this graph, instead of the more usual one, allows easier judgment of the values of data on the top or on the right of the graph.

Ticks are put outside the data region in Figure 2.10 because ticks can obscure data, as is illustrated in the upper panels of Figure 2.11 [64].

Four scale lines are used in Figure 2.10 rather than the two of Figure 2.9. Judging the value of a point by judging its position along a scale line is easier as the distance of the point from the scale line decreases. The consequence of one vertical scale line on the left is that the vertical scale values of data to the right are harder to assess than those of data to the left because the rightmost values are further from

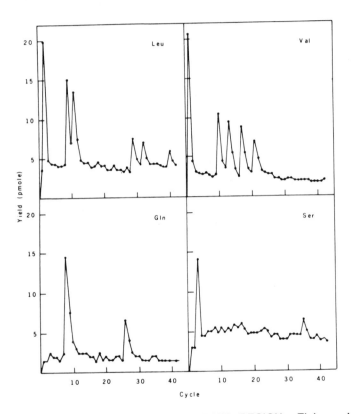

Figure 2.11   SCALE LINES AND THE DATA REGION.   Tick marks can obscure data.

Figure republished from [64]. Copyright 1980 by the AAAS.

the line; similarly, when there is just one horizontal scale line, the horizontal scale values of data at the top are harder to assess than those at the bottom. By using four scale lines, the graph treats the data in a more nearly equitable fashion.

The four scale lines also provide a clearly defined region where our eyes can search for data. With just two, data can be camouflaged by virtue of where they lie. This is true for the data in Figure 2.12 [139]; it is easy to overlook the three points hidden in the upper left corner. In Figure 2.13 the graph has four scale lines and the three points are more prominent.

Making the data region the entire interior of the rectangle formed by the scale lines means the plotting symbol for a data point could just touch a scale line. But just touching has the potential to camouflage points. So it is probably best to interpret "interior" as a rectangle slightly inside the scale line rectangle.

Do not clutter the data region.

Another way to obscure data is to graph too much. It is always tempting to show everything that comes to mind on a single graph, but graphing too much can result in less being seen and understood. This

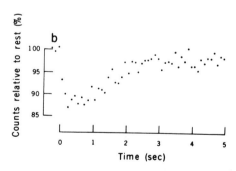

Figure 2.12   SCALE LINES AND THE DATA REGION. The three points in the upper left are camouflaged.
Figure republished from [139]. Copyright 1980 by the AAAS.

is illustrated in Figure 2.14 [122]. The data are particle counts from an exciting scientific exploration: the passage of the Pioneer II spacecraft by Saturn. Inside the data region we have reference lines, a label, arrows, a key, symbols showing the data, tick marks, error bars, and smooth curves. The graph is cluttered, with the result that it is hard to visually disentangle what is graphed. It is unfortunate to have any of these valuable data obscured.

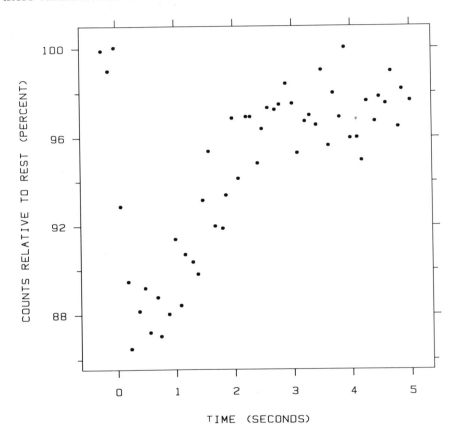

Figure 2.13   SCALE LINES AND THE DATA REGION. The four scale lines provide a clearly defined region for our eyes to look for data. Now, none of the data from Figure 2.12 are in danger of being overlooked.

The data are shown again in Figure 2.15. The clutter in the data region has been alleviated, in part, by removing the error bars. It would be prudent to convey accuracy for these data numerically rather than graphically; on a log scale the error bars decrease radically and disappear from sight as the counts increase. (It is possible that accuracy is nearly constant on a scale of $(counts/sec)^{1/2}$ since count data of this sort tend to have a Poisson distribution. Thus accuracy might be conveyed more readily on the square root scale rather than on the log scale.) Other removals have taken place. The plethora of tick marks on the vertical scale has been reduced, as well as the number of tick mark labels on the top horizontal scale line. Also, the top horizontal scale line is labeled in Figure 2.15, but not in Figure 2.14.

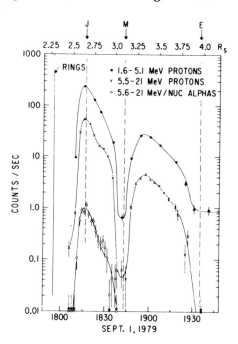

Figure 2.14   CLUTTER. This graph is cluttered. The result is that different graphical elements in the data region obscure one another.
Figure republished from [122]. Copyright 1980 by the AAAS.

The clutter in the data region also has been reduced by some alterations. The key is outside the data region, the label for rings is outside the data region, the arrows showing values below 0.01 counts/sec in Figure 2.14 have been replaced by a separate panel, and the wandering curves have been replaced by straight lines connecting successive data points. These changes have reduced interference between different elements of the graph and thus have reduced the clutter.

Figure 2.16 [81] is also cluttered; the error bars interfere with one another so much that it is hard to see the values they portray. One

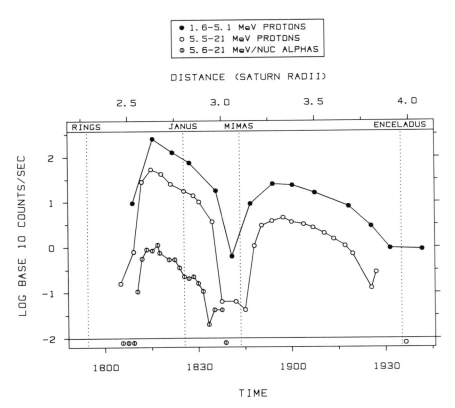

Figure 2.15   CLUTTER. *Do not clutter the data region.* The clutter of Figure 2.14 has been removed by alteration and excision. For example, the number of tick marks has been reduced.

solution is shown in Figure 2.17. In the top three panels the three data sets are juxtaposed and in the bottom panel they are superposed, but without the error bars. The juxtaposition allows us to see clearly each set of data and its error bars; the superposition allows us to compare the three sets of data more effectively.

Do not overdo the number of tick marks.

A large number of tick marks is usually superfluous. From 3 to 10 tick marks are generally sufficient; this is just enough to give a broad sense of the measurement scale. Copious tick marks date back to a time when numerical values were communicated on graphs more than they are today. In our high-tech age we have photocopies of tables, computer tapes, disk packs, and telecommunications networks to transfer data. Every aspect of a graph should serve an important purpose. Any superfluous aspects, such as unneeded tick marks, should be eliminated to decrease visual clutter and thus increase the visual prominence of the most important element — the data.

Figure 2.18 [113] has too many tick marks. The filled circles show the number of bits of information (horizontal scale) in the DNA of various species when they emerged and the time of their emergence (vertical scale). The open circles show, in the same way, the bits of

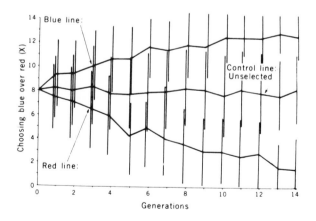

Figure 2.16   CLUTTER. This graph is also cluttered.
Figure republished from [81]. Copyright 1980 by the AAAS.

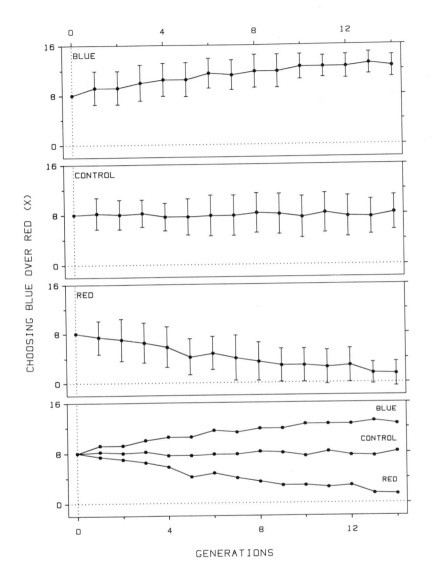

Figure 2.17   CLUTTER. The clutter of Figure 2.16 has been eliminated by graphing the data on juxtaposed panels. The bottom panel is included so that the values of the three data sets can be more effectively compared.

information in the brains of various species. On a first look at this graph, the bottom scale line makes it easy to think there are two horizontal scales. This is not so. The labels of the form 3×10^k are showing, approximately, the values of the midpoints of the numbers of the form 10^k. For example, midway between 10^7 and 10^8 on a log scale is $10^{7.5} = 10^{0.5} \, 10^7 \approx 3 \times 10^7$. The large number of tick marks and labels needlessly clutters the graph, and the approximation can easily lead to confusion.

In Figure 2.19 the brain and DNA data are graphed again with fewer tick marks and labels; the horizontal and vertical scales have been interchanged so that time is now on the horizontal scale with earlier times on the left and later times on the right.

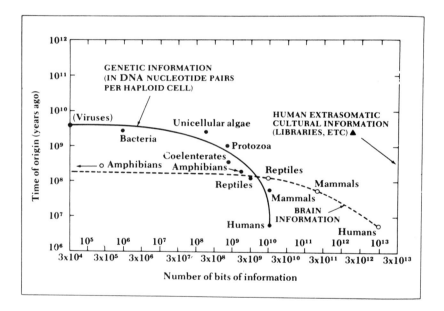

Figure 2.18 TICK MARKS. There are too many tick marks and tick mark labels on this graph. Using tick mark labels of the form 3×10^k as an approximation of $10^{k+0.5}$ is confusing.

Figure republished from *The Dragons of Eden: Speculations on the Evolution of Human Intelligence*, by Carl Sagan, p. 26. Copyright © 1977 by Carl Sagan. Reprinted by permission of Random House, Inc.

Use a reference line when there is an important value that must be seen across the entire graph, but do not let the line interfere with the data.

Reference lines are used in Figure 2.20. The data are the weights of the Hershey Bar, the famous American candy bar. (These data, and

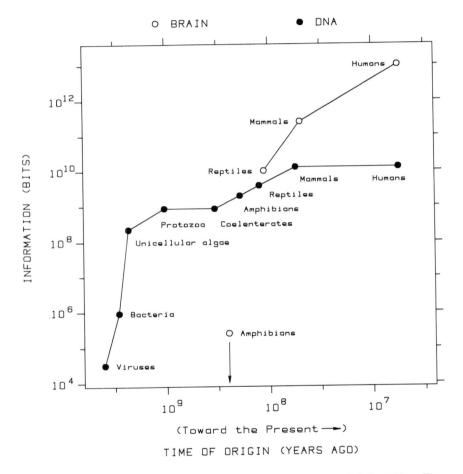

Figure 2.19 TICK MARKS. *Do not overdo the number of tick marks.* The vertical axis of this graph, previously the horizontal axis of Figure 2.18, has a sensible number of tick marks and labels.

Stephen Jay Gould's analysis of them [54], are discussed in detail in Section 4 of Chapter 3.) The vertical reference lines, which show times of price increases, cross the entire graph and let us see what happened to weight exactly at the times of the price increases. Except for the change from 30¢ to 35¢, all price increases were accompanied by a size increase.

In Figure 2.21 only a marker is used to show the time of the first cardiovascular care unit since the high precision of a reference line is not needed. We can see the position clearly enough to perceive that somewhere after that point, the death rate for cardiovascular disease decreased more rapidly; a reference line is avoided since we want, as always, to reduce the visual burden in the data region.

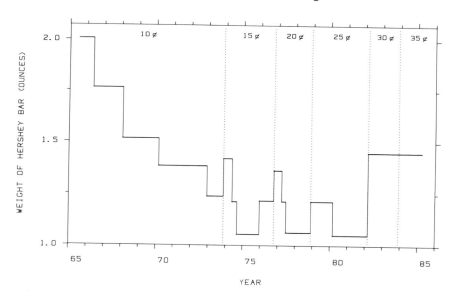

YEAR

Figure 2.20   REFERENCE LINES. *Use a reference line when there is an important value that must be seen across the entire graph, but do not let the line interfere with the data.* The weight of the Hershey Bar is graphed against time. The vertical reference lines divide time up into price epochs; prices are shown just below the top vertical scale. The precision of the reference lines is needed to show us exactly where the price increases occur.

***Do not allow data labels in the data region to interfere with the
quantitative data or to clutter the graph.***

Figure 2.22 shows the relationship between the average number of
bad teeth in 11 and 12 year old children and the per capita sugar
consumption per year for 18 countries and the state of Hawaii [101].
When it is important to convey the names for the individual values of a
data set, data labels in the data region are generally unavoidable. In so
doing we should attempt to reduce the visual prominence of the labels
so that they interfere as little as possible with our ability to assess the
overall pattern of the quantitative data.   This has been done in
Figure 2.22 through the use of several methods: the plotting symbol is
visually very different from the letters of the labels, the letters of the
labels are small, and when possible a label has been placed outside of
the region formed by the point cloud rather than inside.

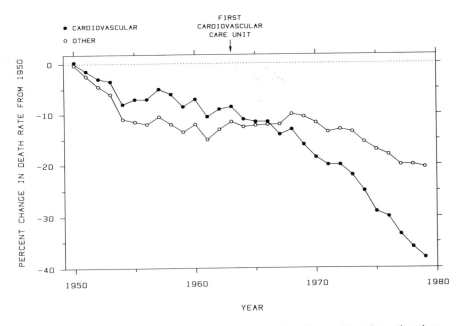

Figure 2.21   REFERENCE LINES. Only a marker is used to show the time
of the first cardiovascular care unit since the high precision of a reference
line is not needed.

In Figure 2.23 [113] the plotting symbols are not sufficiently visually distinguishable from the labels. The result is that the point cloud is camouflaged by the labels.

Figures 2.22 and 2.23 show one type of data label; each value in the data set has its own name. Sometimes the quantitative information on a

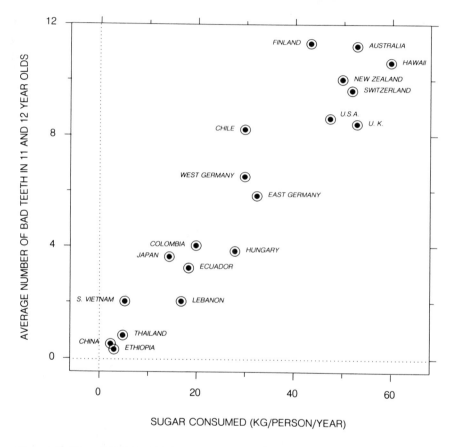

Figure 2.22   DATA LABELS. *Do not allow data labels in the data region to interfere with the quantitative data or to clutter the graph.* The data labels on this graph are needed to convey the names. The visual impact of the labels has been lessened so that they interfere as little as possible with our assessment of the overall pattern of the quantitative data.

graph consists of different data sets where each data set has a name that we want to convey. This is illustrated in Figure 2.24, which shows life expectancies for four groups of people: black females, black males, white females and white males [129, p. 71]. Four data labels in the data region convey the data set names without obscuring the data or cluttering the data region.

Sometimes a key with the data labels is needed to identify data sets, either because data labels in the data region would add too much clutter or because the values for each data set cannot be identified without using different plotting symbols for the different data sets. A key is used in Figure 2.25 for both reasons. On this graph the data labels are long and the data region is already host to many things. Furthermore, a key is needed because there is no other convenient way to allow identification of the values below $-2\ \log_{10}$ (counts/sec), which are shown at the bottom of the graph.

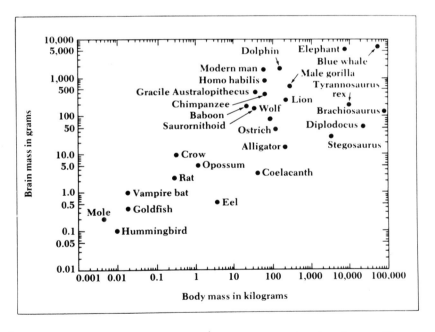

Figure 2.23   DATA LABELS. The data labels interfere with our assessment of the overall pattern of the quantitative data.

Figure republished from *The Dragons of Eden: Speculations on the Evolution of Human Intelligence*, by Carl Sagan, p. 39. Copyright © 1977 by Carl Sagan. Reprinted by permission of Random House, Inc.

Avoid putting notes, keys, and markers in the data region. Put keys and markers just outside the data region and put notes in the legend or in the text.

We should approach the data region with a strong spirit of minimalism and try to keep as much out as possible. Not doing so can jeopardize our relentless pursuit of making the data stand out. There is no reason why markers, keys, and notes need to appear in the data region.

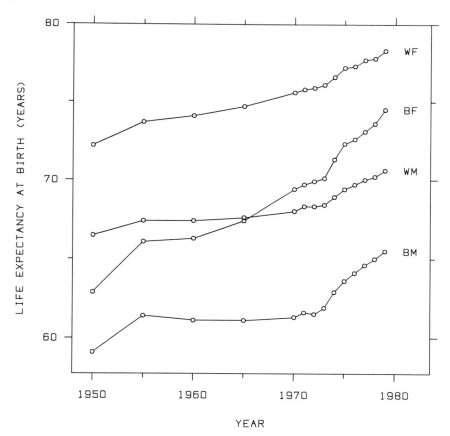

Figure 2.24 DATA LABELS. Groups of data values often can be identified by data labels in the data region. The labels are abbreviations in which B = black, W = white, M = male, and F = female.

Keys and markers can go outside the data region and notes can go in the text or the legend. This has not been done in Figure 2.26 [133] and the result is needless clutter and a confusing graph. The main graph (not including the inset) shows release rates of xenon-133 from the Three Mile Island nuclear reactor accident in 1979 and concentrations of xenon in the air of Albany, N.Y. during the same time period. The purpose of the graph is to show that in Albany, about 500 km from Three Mile Island and downwind during the period of the accident, xenon concentrations rose after the accident.

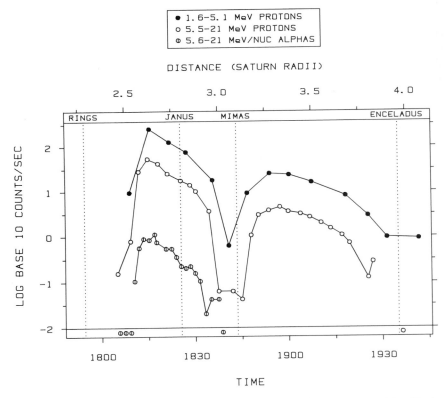

Figure 2.25   DATA LABELS. Groups of data values also can be identified by a key. One disadvantage, compared with data labels in the data region, is that identification is slightly harder because we must look back and forth between the key and the quantitative data. One advantage over data labels in the data region, an important one in this example, is that clutter in the data region is reduced. Furthermore, a key is needed in this example because there is no other convenient way to allow identification of the values below $-2 \log_{10}$ (counts/sec), which are shown at the bottom of the graph.

Figure 2.26 has a number of problems arising from some unusual and unexplained conventions and from putting too much in the data region. The writing in the data region is really two scale labels, complete with units. The top label describes two types of Albany air concentration measurements. The bottom label describes the Three Mile Island release rates. Part of the difficulty in comprehending this graph is that three Albany air samples are below the label for release rates, which gives an initial incorrect impression that they are air samples measuring the release rates. The ambient air measurements are shown in a somewhat unconventional way. The two solid rectangles are averages over two intervals; the width shows the averaging interval and a good guess is that the height, which is not explained, shows an average ±2 sample standard deviations. The triangles with "LT" above them indicate other ambient air measurements which are "less than" the values indicated. The inset, which impinges on the data region, has very little additional information; it shows two averages and repeats 5 of

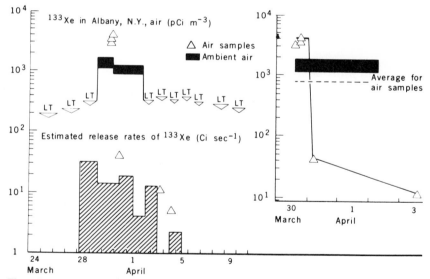

Fig. 1. Xenon-133 activity (picocuries per cubic meter of air) in Albany, New York, for the end of March and early April 1979. The lower trace shows the time-averaged estimates of releases (curies per second) from the Three Mile Island reactor (2). The inset shows detailed values for air samples (gas counting) and concurrent average values for ambient air (Ge diode). Abbreviation: *LT*, less than.

Figure 2.26 NOTES, KEYS, AND MARKERS. Everything — including the scale labels, a key, "LT" (meaning less than), and an inset — has been thrown into the data region of this graph. The result is confusing.
Figure republished from [133]. Copyright 1980 by the AAAS.

the air sample measurements. There is an inaccuracy somewhere; for the three largest air sample values, the times shown on the inset do not agree with the times shown on the main graph. The two averages in the inset do not convey any important information.

These data deserve two panels and deserve less in the data region to make completely clear what has been graphed. This has been done in Figure 2.27; the writing, key, and LT's have been removed from the data region and the inset has been deleted. The bottom panel shows the release rates of xenon from Three Mile Island; the horizontal line segments show averages over various time intervals. The top panel shows the Albany measurements; the horizontal line segments show intervals over which some measurements were averaged, the error bars show plus and minus two sample standard deviations (if the guess about Figure 2.26 was correct), and an arrow indicates the actual value was less than or equal to the graphed value. Furthermore, the labels for the two types of measurements have been corrected. Both are ambient air measurements and both are from air samples. The terms "continuous monitor" and "grab samples" correctly convey the nature of the two types.

Overlapping plotting symbols must be visually distinguishable.

Unless special care is taken, overlapping plotting symbols can make it impossible to distinguish individual data points. This happens in several places in Figure 2.28 [23]. The data are from an experiment on the production of mutagens in drinking water. For each category of observation (free chlorine, chloramine, and unchlorinated) there are two observations for each value of water volume. That is, duplicate measurements were made. But two values do not always appear because of exact or near overlap. For example, for the unchlorinated data only one observation appears for water volume just above 0.5 liters.

This problem of visual clarity is a surprisingly tough one. Several solutions are given in Section 4 of Chapter 3.

Superposed data sets must be readily visually discriminated.

It is very common for graphs to have two or more data sets superposed within the same data region. We already have encountered many such graphs in Chapters 1 and 2. The studies reported in Section 4 of Chapter 1 revealed that one of the most serious

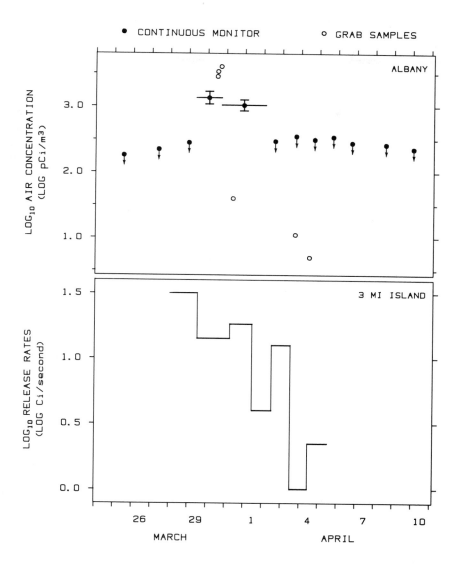

Figure 2.27 NOTES, KEYS, AND MARKERS. *Avoid putting notes, keys, and markers in the data region. Put keys and markers just outside the data region and put notes in the legend or in the text.* The graph in Figure 2.26 has been improved by the following actions: removing the writing, the key, and the inset from the data region; showing the two data sets on separate panels; removing the idiosyncrasies; correcting the labels describing the two types of measurement.

shortcomings in graphs in science and technology was poor visual discrimination of the different data sets on graphs employing superposition.

In Figure 2.29 [95] it is difficult to visually disentangle the solid squares, circles, and triangles; such plotting symbols are in general visually similar, but in Figure 2.29 the problem is exacerbated by the symbols not being crisply drawn. In Figure 2.30 [50] the different

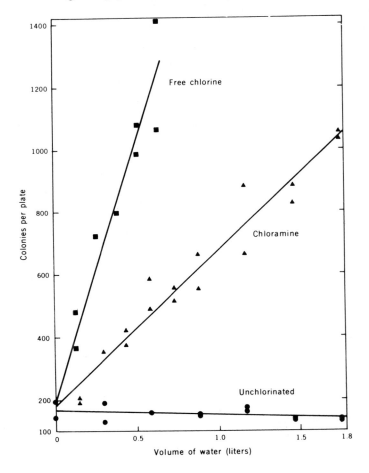

Figure 2.28   OVERLAPPING PLOTTING SYMBOLS. *Overlapping plotting symbols must be visually distinguishable.* On this graph, because of exact and near overlap, some of the data cannot be seen. Methods for combatting overlap are given in Chapter 3.

Figure republished from [23]. Copyright 1980 by the AAAS.

curves are hard to disentangle in many places and impossible in others. For example, on the left of the graph between 8 and 16 hours, curves E1 and E3 merge and then join CDC in a triple junction; a little later one curve splits off, but it is impossible to tell which it is. More copious labeling might help but it still would require a concentrated and highly

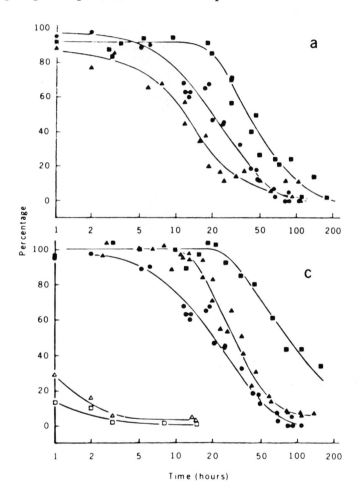

Figure 2.29 SUPERPOSED DATA SETS. *Superposed data sets must be readily visually discriminated.* One of the pervasive problems of graphs in science and technology is the lack of visual discrimination of different data sets superposed in the same data region. On this graph we cannot easily visually discriminate the circles, squares, and triangles.
Figure republished from [95]. Copyright 1980 by the AAAS.

cognitive mental effort to follow each curve visually, rather than the rapid, easy discrimination that we should strive for when data sets are superposed. We do not want to have to visually follow a curve on a graph the way we have to visually follow a twisting secondary road on a detailed map; rather, we want to be able to see a single curve as a whole, mentally filtering out the other curves.

Graphs that fail to allow effective visual discrimination are pervasive because the problem is a difficult one to solve. Solutions will be given in Section 5 of Chapter 3.

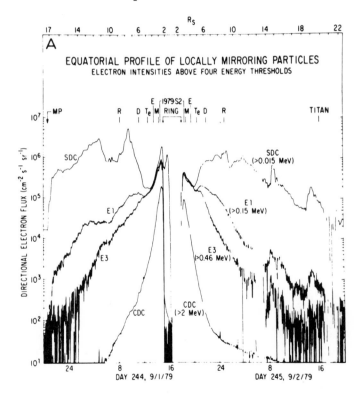

Figure 2.30   SUPERPOSED DATA SETS. The curves on this graph merge, in going from left to right, and then separate with their identities lost. Methods for graphing different data sets and maintaining visual discrimination are given in Chapter 3.
Figure republished from [50]. Copyright 1980 by the AAAS.

Visual clarity must be preserved under reduction and reproduction

Graphs that communicate data to others often must undergo reduction and reproduction; these processes, if not done with care, can interfere with visual clarity. In Figure 2.31 [60] the ghostly image in the background should be a shaded area representing immunoreactivity, but the shading is barely visible due to poor reproduction. Figure 2.31 has other problems. The scales are poorly constructed. The right vertical scale shows a break; in fact it is not a break in the usual sense of a gap in the scale, but rather the number of units per cm suddenly changes. The same type of change occurs on the left vertical scale, but the authors have chosen not to flag this one. The graphed data move through the data region as if nothing is happening to the scales.

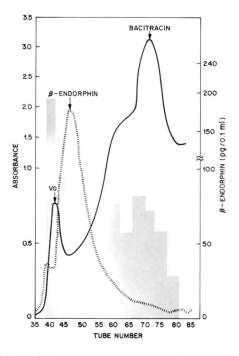

Figure 2.31   REDUCTION AND REPRODUCTION. *Visual clarity must be preserved under reduction and reproduction.* This did not happen on this graph. The ghostly image in the background was supposed to represent immunoreactivity.

Figure republished from [60]. Copyright 1980 by the AAAS.

In Figure 2.32 [98] the lines that are supposed to connect the labels with the curves are washed out. Lines, curves, and lettering must be heavy enough and symbols must be large enough to withstand reduction and reproduction.

One good test to check the ability of a graph original to stand up to both reduction and reproduction is to put it through a reducing photocopier. If a reduction to 2/3 is available, copy the original and then copy the copy. If the second copy, which is a reduction to $(2/3)^2 = 4/9$, is still visually clear, then it is likely that the original will withstand most reduction and reproduction processes. Clearly other strategies, depending on the photocopy equipment available and on the way the graph original will be utilized, can be tailored to each situation.

2.3 CLEAR UNDERSTANDING

Graphs are powerful tools for communicating quantitative information in, for example, technical reports and journal articles. The principles of this section, which are oriented toward the task of communication, contribute to a clear understanding of what is graphed.

Put major conclusions into graphical form. Make legends comprehensive and informative.

Communication of the results of scientific and technological studies, when the results involve quantitative issues, can be greatly enhanced by graphs that speak to the essence of the results. Graphs and their

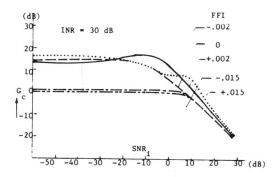

Figure 2.32   REDUCTION AND REPRODUCTION. The lines from the curves to their labels are washed out.
Figure republished from [98]. © 1983 IEEE.

legends can incisively communicate important data and important conclusions drawn from the data. One good approach is to make the sequence of graphs and their legends as nearly independent as possible and to have them summarize evidence and conclusions. This book has been constructed in this way; the graphs and their legends summarize the ideas, and the text has been written around the sequence of graphs. This is to be expected of a book on graphs, but it is also an effective device for other writings in science and technology.

For a graph to be understood clearly, there must be a clear, direct explanation of the data that are graphed and of the inferences drawn from the data. Here is a framework for figure *legends* that can contribute to such a clear explanation:

1. Describe everything that is graphed.

2. Draw attention to the important features of the data.

3. Describe the conclusions that are drawn from the data on the graph.

The framework is illustrated in the legend of Figure 2.33. The data are involved in an astounding discovery that sounds more like science fiction than a highly supportable scientific hypothesis. Sixty-five million years ago extraordinary mass extinctions of a wide variety of animal species occurred, marking the end of the Cretaceous period and the beginning of the Tertiary. The dinosaurs died out along with the marine reptiles and the flying reptiles such as the ichthysaur. Many marine invertebrates also became extinct; ocean plankton almost disappeared completely.

What could have caused such a calamity? In 1980 Luis Alvarez, Walter Alvarez, Frank Asaro, and Helen Michel at Berkeley discovered unusually high levels of iridium right at the K-T (Cretaceous-Tertiary) boundary in sediments from Italy, Denmark, and New Zealand [2]. It is likely that the high iridium levels have an extraterrestrial cause; asteroids and meteors are rich in iridium while the earth's crust is not because this heavy element sank to the core during the earth's molten years. From these data and other information, the four hypothesized that an asteroid, 10 ± 4 km in diameter, struck the earth and sent a dust cloud into the atmosphere that blocked sunlight for a period of several months or even years. The loss of light interfered with food chains and led to the mass extinctions. As the dust from the asteroid settled it deposited an iridium-rich layer on the surface of the earth.

The asteroid hypothesis has been supported by subsequent measurements. Among them are measurements of pollen, fern spores, and iridium in New Mexico [104]. These data are shown in Figure 2.33.

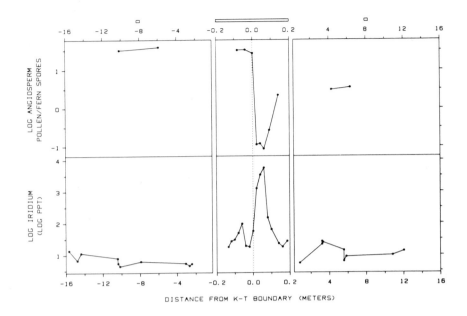

Figure 2.33   EXPLANATION. *Put major conclusions into graphical form.*
Make legends comprehensive and informative. Describe everything that is
graphed and convey the conclusion drawn from the data. The following is a
legend, including the title, that might accompany this graph in its original
subject matter context:
ANGIOSPERM-FERN RATIO AND IRIDIUM NEAR THE *K–T* BOUNDARY. The
graph shows measurements of a core from northeastern New Mexico. The
horizontal scale is in meters from the boundary between the Cretaceous and
the Tertiary periods; negative values are below the *K–T* boundary so time
goes from earlier to later in going from left to right. The widths of the three
rectangles at the top of the graph show the same number of meters on the
horizontal scales of the three panels. The upper panel shows the ratio of
angiosperm pollen to fern spores on a log base 10 scale; the *K–T* boundary
is taken to be the time point at which these values begin to decrease. The
bottom panel shows concentrations of iridium, also on a log base 10 scale;
the concentrations begin a dramatic rise and fall at the boundary. Since the
principal source of iridium is extraterrestrial, its rise and fall supports the
hypothesis that an asteroid struck the earth causing a cloud of dust in the
upper atmosphere; this is argued to have darkened the earth for months or
years, leading to the large number of extinctions, including the dinosaurs,
that occurred at the beginning of the Tertiary period.

The horizontal scale is distance in the sediment from the K-T boundary. Distance, of course, is just a surrogate for time, which goes from earlier to later as we go from left to right. The point at which the ratio of pollen to fern spores begins to decrease is taken to be the K-T boundary because at the beginning of the Tertiary period angiosperms declined relative to ferns. At this boundary there is a corresponding peak in the iridium concentrations, shown in the bottom panel.

The legend of Figure 2.33 follows the three-step guidelines presented earlier. The graph and its legend can nearly stand alone as a document that conveys the basic idea of the asteroid-impact hypothesis and the quantitative information that gives it credence.

The interplay between graph, legend, and text is a delicate one that requires substantial judgment. No complete prescription can be designed to allow us to proceed mechanically and to relieve us of thinking hard. However, a viewer is usually well served by a legend that makes a graph as self-contained as possible. If there are several graphs, the legends collectively can be an independent piece; for example, a detailed description of a data set described in one graph legend does not need to be repeated in a subsequent graph legend.

It is possible, though, to overdo a comprehensive legend. Putting a description of the experimental procedure in the legend — conventional in medical and biological writings and mandatory in some circles — seems to go too far. It burdens the graph and makes what should be a concise summary into a tome. Figure 2.34 [139] is an example. The ratio of legend area to graph area is 2.8; this is too much detail. The details of an experimental procedure must be communicated, but surely there is a better place than a figure legend, which is a summary.

Too little detail, however, occurs more frequently in graphs in science and technology than too much detail. The studies of graphs in scientific publications described in Section 4 of Chapter 1 revealed an alarming percentage of graphs containing elements not explained either in the text or in the legend. Figure 2.35 [39] is an example. The bars and error bars are not explained anywhere. One good guess is that they are sample means and estimates of the standard errors of the means; guessing should not be necessary.

Error bars should be clearly explained.

Error bars are a convenient way to convey variability in data. Unfortunately, terminology is so inconsistent in science and technology that it is easy for an author to say one thing and a viewer to understand something else.

Error bars can convey one of several possibilities:

(1)   The *sample standard deviation* of the data.

(2)   An *estimate of the standard deviation* (also called the *standard error*) of a statistical quantity.

(3)   A *confidence interval* for a statistical quantity.

Fig. 2. Tension and the intensity of the 42.9-nm layer line during 1-second tetanus at the sarcomere length of 2.2 μm. (a) Tension record averaged over the 40 tetanic contractions required for obtaining the time course of the layer-line intensity. A sartorius muscle was dissected from *Rana catesbeiana* and tetanized for 1 second at 2-minute intervals. The horizontal line represents the period of stimulation. Tension was recorded with an isometric tension transducer (Shinkoh, type UL). (b) Intensity of the first-order myosin layer line at 42.9 nm. The x-ray source was a rotating-anode generator (Rigaku FR) with a fine focus (1.0 by 0.1 mm) on a copper target. This was operated at 50 kV with a tube current of 70 mA; such a high power was possible with an anode of a large diameter (30 cm) rotating at a high speed (9000 rev/min). A bent-crystal monochromator was used at a source-to-crystal distance of 25 cm with a viewing angle of 6°. The intensity of the myosin layer line was measured with a scintillation counter combined with a mask; the mask had apertures at the positions of the off-meridional parts of the first-order

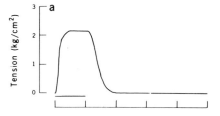

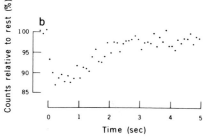

layer line. The meridional reflection at 14.3 nm is known to be slightly displaced during contraction, suggesting a minute change in the myosin periodicity (*1, 3*). It is, therefore, possible that the 42.9-nm layer line is also slightly displaced. However, the possible displacement (14 μm at the position of the mask) would be insignificant compared with the width of each aperture (0.8 mm). The intensity measured at the resting state was 1400 count/sec. The intensities during and after tetanus were expressed as percentages of the resting intensity and plotted against time after the first stimulus of each set of stimuli. Each point represents the intensity averaged over a 100-msec period. The first three points represent the measurements made before stimulation.

Figure 2.34   EXPLANATION. It is possible to overdo the explanation in a legend. The complete description of the experimental procedure in this legend is too much detail. The ratio of the legend area to the graph area is 2.8.

As an example, let us consider a particular case, also the most frequent one. Suppose the data are $x_1, ..., x_n$ and the statistical quantity being graphed is the sample mean,

$$\bar{x} = \frac{1}{n} \sum_{i=1}^{n} x_i .$$

The sample standard deviation of the data is

$$s = \left[\frac{1}{(n-1)} \sum_{i=1}^{n} (x_i - \bar{x})^2 \right]^{\frac{1}{2}} .$$

An estimate of the standard error of the mean is

$$s/n^{\frac{1}{2}} .$$

If the data are from a normal distribution then a 95% confidence interval for the population mean is $(\bar{x} - k\, s/n^{\frac{1}{2}}, \bar{x} + k\, s/n^{\frac{1}{2}})$, where k is a value that depends on n; if n is larger than about 60, k is approximately 1.96.

Error bars are used in Figure 2.36 [66]. In the last sentence of the figure legend we are told that the graphed values "represent means of

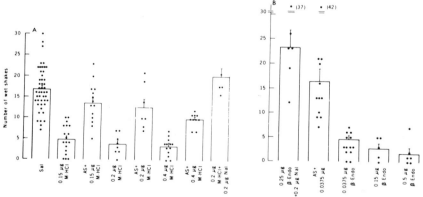

Fig. 1. Inhibitory effect of morphine hydrochloride (A) and β-endorphin (B) on wet-shake behavior in rats. Antagonism was by antibody to cerebroside sulfate (AS). A volume of 2 μl was delivered into the PAG in 1-μl increments with a 1-minute interval in between. The control consisted of saline (Sal). Morphine HCl (M-HCl) and β-endorphin were preceded by saline, AS, or naloxone (Nal) as indicated. The dose of morphine HCl and naloxone refers to the chloride salt. Each point is the datum for one animal. The AS + morphine HCl groups are all significantly different (t-test, P < .005) from the corresponding morphine HCl groups alone (A). The group receiving AS + 0.0375 μg of β-endorphin is also significantly different (P < .005) from the group receiving 0.0375 μg of β-endorphin (B).

Figure 2.35 EXPLANATION. The more common problem of scientific data display is too little explanation, rather than too much. The bars and error bars on this graph are not explained in the text or in the legend.
Figure republished from [39]. Copyright 1980 by the AAAS.

three to four mice ± the standard deviation." What are we being shown? Is it (1) or (2) above? It is probably (1), but we should not have to deal with probability in understanding what is graphed.

Error bars should be unambiguously described. For the three cases cited above, the following is some terminology that can prevent ambiguity:

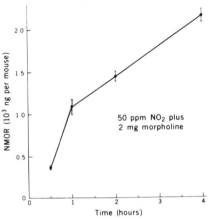

Fig. 1. Time course of NMOR biosynthesis in mice. Groups of three to four male ICR mice were gavaged with freshly prepared solutions of 2 mg of MOR (Aldrich Chemical) in 0.2 ml of distilled water and immediately placed in exposure chambers (Nalge desiccators, modified for gas inflow from the bottom and exhaust from the top). Mice were then exposed to 50 ppm of NO_2 (three to four mice per chamber, 5 cubic feet per hour, 20 volume changes per hour) at intervals of from 0.5 to 4 hours. The required concentrations of NO_2 were produced by mixing stock NO_2 (custom grade, Union Carbide) with air at an appropriate flow rate, prior to introduction into the chambers; we checked the accuracy of the exposure mixtures by periodically monitoring and analyzing the NO_2 in the exhaust from the chambers, using the Griess-Saltzman reaction (19). Concurrent controls consisted of two mice exposed in separate chambers to NO_2 alone for 4 hours, additional controls were gavaged with 2 mg of MOR or 0.2 ml of distilled water and exposed to air for identical periods in separate chambers. After exposure to NO_2, the mice were killed by freezing in liquid nitrogen and blended to a fine powder (20). Two or three aliquots (approximately 8 g each) were taken from each mouse powder and blended with 75 ml of ice-cold 35 percent aqueous methanol in a Waring Blendor (5 minutes, medium speed); a known amount of a nitrosamine standard [152 ng of di-n-propylnitrosamine (DPN), Aldrich] was then added, and blending continued for 1 to 2 minutes. Homogenates were divided in half and centrifuged (5000g, 25 minutes, 5°C; swinging bucket), supernatant was removed, and the pellets were extracted again with cold 35 percent methanol. The pooled supernates were extracted (twice) with an equal volume (total, 150 ml) of dichloromethane [(DCM), Burdick and Jackson] (21), and the organic layer was dried by passage through a cotton gauze (Ex-tube, Analytichem International) and concentrated to 2 ml in a Kuderna Danish concentrator (Kontes, 250 ml) kept in a 65°C bath. Aliquots (20 μl) of the concentrates from each of two or three powder samples were injected into the thermal energy analyzer-gas chromatograph (Thermo Electron modified model TEA-502) (22) for NMOR analysis. Peaks were identified and quantitated by comparison with the retention time and response of reference nitrosamines (23). The plotted values are corrected for any background control NMOR levels and for the DPN standard recoveries and represent means of three to four mice ± the standard deviation.

Figure 2.36   ERROR BARS. *Error bars should be clearly explained.* It is important to distinguish between the sample standard deviation and an estimate of the standard deviation of the sample mean (the standard error of the mean). It is not clear from the explanation of this graph which of these two statistics the error bars portray.

Figure republished from [66]. Copyright 1980 by the AAAS.

(1)   The error bars show plus and minus one sample standard deviation of the data.

(2)   The error bars show plus and minus an estimate of the standard deviation (or one standard error) of the statistic that is graphed.

(3)   The error bars show a confidence interval for the statistic that is graphed.

Unambiguous description is only one issue with which we need to concern ourselves in showing error bars on graphs. A second important issue is whether they convey anything meaningful. This statistical issue is discussed in Section 7 of Chapter 3.

When logarithms of a variable are graphed, the scale label should correspond to the tick mark labels.

The dot chart in Figure 2.37 shows death rates for the leading causes of death of people in the age group 15 to 24 years in the United States [99]. The logarithms of the data are graphed; that is, equal increments on the horizontal scale indicate equal increments of the logarithm of death rate. On the top horizontal scale line the tick mark labels show the values of the data on the original scale. The scale label describes the variable and its units on the original scale, to correspond to the tick mark labels. The bottom horizontal scale line uses another method for labeling; the tick mark labels and the scale labels correspond, but both are describing the variable on the log scale.

Proofread graphs.

Graphs should be proofread and carefully checked for errors. In the study of the graphs in the journal *Science* described in Section 4 of Chapter 1, construction errors were uncovered in 6.4% of the graphs. Any of them could have been detected by careful proofreading. Figure 2.38 [115] shows such an error for a graph of measurements of Saturn's magnetic field made by the Pioneer II spacecraft; the exponents for the tick mark labels on the vertical scale line are missing. This is quite unfortunate since the magnitude of the magnetic field is of much interest. The authors write about the graph: "This is shown in Figure 1.1, which presents an overview of the encounter as evident in the magnitude of the ambient magnetic field." It is unfortunate to have a graph error degrade the communication of such exciting, high-quality scientific work.

Strive for clarity.

Strive for clarity is really a summation of the principles presented so far; in Section 2.2 the principles contribute to making a graph visually clear and in Section 2.3 the principles contribute to a clear understanding of what is graphed. Striving for clarity should be done consciously. We should ask of every graph, "Are the data portrayed clearly?" and "Are the elements of the graph clearly explained?" Let us consider one example.

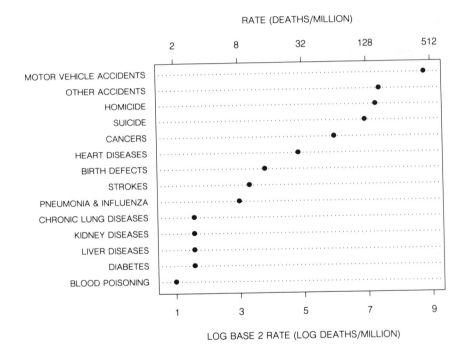

Figure 2.37   LABELS FOR LOGS. *When logarithms of a variable are graphed, the scale label should correspond to the tick mark labels.* The logarithms of the data are graphed on this dot chart. On the top horizontal scale line the tick mark labels are in the units of the data on the original scale, so the scale labels describe the data on the original scale. On the lower scale line the tick mark labels are expressed in log units of the data, so the scale label describes the logarithms of the data.

The data in Figure 2.39 [132] are percentages of degrees awarded to women in several areas of science and technology during three time periods. The elements of the graph are not fully explained; little is said in the text, so we must rely on the labeling and the legend to understand what is graphed. At first glance the labels suggest the graph is a standard divided bar chart with the length of the bottom division of each bar showing the percentage for doctorates, the length of the middle division showing the percentage for master's, and the top division showing the bachelor's. This is not so. (It would imply that in most cases the percentage of bachelor's degrees given to women is generally lower than the percentage of doctorates.) A little detective work makes it clear that the total distance from the zero baseline to the top encodes the percentage for bachelor's, the total distance from the baseline to the top of the middle division encodes the percentage for master's, and the length of the bottom division encodes doctorate's. This type of graph works only because the percentages decrease in going from bachelor's degrees to master's degrees to doctorates for every category.

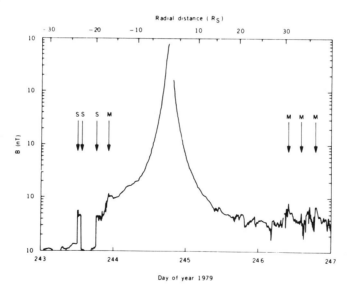

Figure 2.38 PROOFREAD. *Proofread graphs.* Graphs should be proofread, just as we do text. On this graph, lack of careful proofreading resulted in missing exponents on the tick mark labels of the vertical scale.
Figure republished from [115]. Copyright 1980 by the AAAS.

There are other problems with this graph. Only two bars are shown for computer science, with no explanation. One can only assume, since majoring in computer science is a new phenomenon, that the 1959-1960 time period is missing. There is a construction error; the horizontal line for doctorates in all science and engineering in 1969-1970 is missing. Another difficulty with the graph is visual; the bar chart format makes it hard to visually connect the three values of a particular degree for a particular subject.

In Figure 2.40 the data from Figure 2.39 are regraphed. There has been a striving for clarity. It is clear how the data are represented, and the design allows us to see easily the values of a particular degree for a particular subject through time. Finally, the figure legend explains the graph in a comprehensive and clear way.

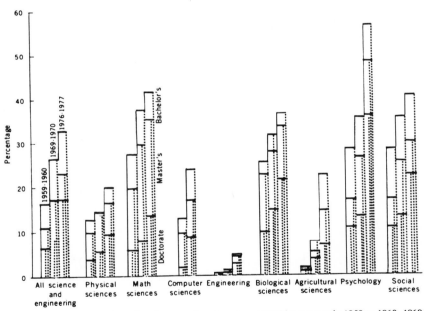

Fig. 1. Proportion of degrees in science and engineering earned by women in 1959 to 1960, 1969 to 1970, and 1976 to 1977 (6). Included in the social science degrees are anthropology, sociology, economics, and political science.

Figure 2.39   CLARITY. This graph fails both in clarity of vision and clarity of explanation.
Figure republished from [132]. Copyright 1980 by the AAAS.

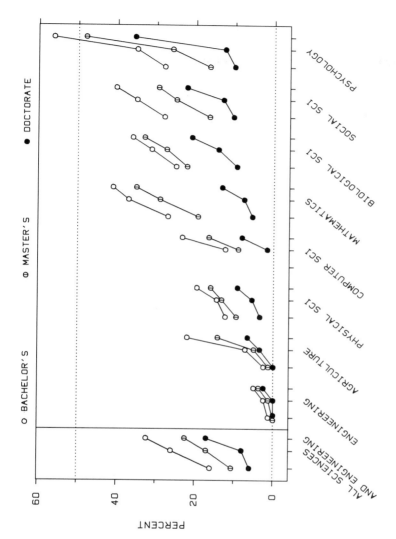

Figure 2.40 CLARITY. *Strive for clarity.* This is a summation of the principles in Sections 2.2 and 2.3. This graphing of the data from Figure 2.39 strives for clarity. It shows the percentage of degrees earned by women for three degree categories, three time periods, and nine categories of subjects. For each subject category the three tick marks indicate the years 1959-1960, 1969-1970 and 1976-1977.

2.4 SCALES

Scales are fundamental. A graph is a graph, in part, because it has one or more scales. Graphing data would be far simpler if these basic, defining elements of graphs were straightforward, but they are not; scale issues are subtle and difficult. This section is about constructing scale lines, comparing scales, including zero, taking logarithms, and breaking a scale.

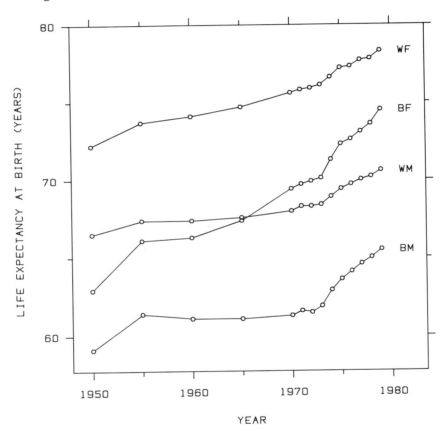

Figure 2.41   RANGES. *Choose the range of the tick marks to include or nearly include the range of the data.* The range of the values on the vertical scale are nearly contained within the range of the tick marks. On the horizontal scale the values are completely contained within the range of the tick marks.

Choose the range of the tick marks to include or nearly include the range of the data.

The interval from the minimum to the maximum of a set of values is the range of the values. It is a good idea to have the range of the data on a graph be included or nearly included in the range of the tick marks to allow an effective assessment of all of the data. In Figure 2.41 the range of the data on the horizontal scale is included in the range of the tick marks, and the data on the vertical scale are nearly included in the range.

Subject to the constraints that scales have, choose the scales so that the data fill up as much of the data region as possible.

There are a number of constraints that affect the choice of scales on graphs. One, just discussed, is that the range of the tick marks should encompass or nearly encompass the range of the data. Another is that we do not want data to be graphed on scale lines. Also, in some cases we want a particular value to be included in the scale; the most common example is showing a zero value. (More will be said later about including zero.) Finally, when different panels of a graph are compared, we will often want the scales to be the same on all panels.

But subject to these constraints, we should attempt to use as much of the data region as possible. This is not done in Figure 2.42 [121].

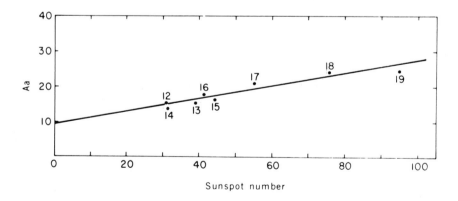

Figure 2.42 FILLING THE DATA REGION. Only 26% of the vertical scale is used by the data.

Figure republished from [121]. Copyright 1980 by the AAAS.

Only 26% of the vertical scale is taken up by the data. Space is wasted on this graph. In contrast, Figure 2.43 utilizes the data region more efficiently. The data span most of the range of the scales without getting too close to the frame. The data are the number of cigarettes consumed daily by a smoker in a 28-day program to quit smoking; after the 28 days the smoker quit altogether. A "day" is defined as starting at 6:00 a.m. and ending 24 hours later. The open circles are the days Monday to Friday and the closed circles are Saturdays and Sundays.

It is sometimes helpful to use the pair of scale lines for a variable to show two different scales.

The two scale lines for a variable on a graph provide an opportunity to show two different scales for the variable; the additional

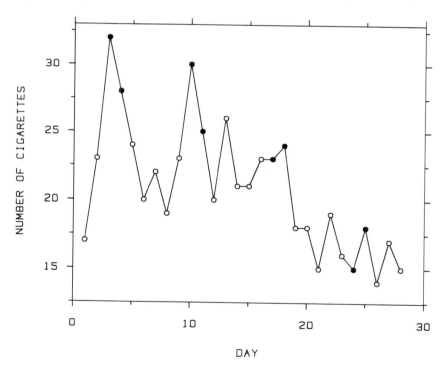

Figure 2.43   FILLING THE DATA REGION. *Subject to the constraints that scales have, choose the scales so that the data fill up as much of the data region as possible.*

information of a second scale often can be helpful. One example is Figure 2.44. The data, which are from the 1980 census [130], are the number of people in the United States in 1980 for each age from 0 to 84. The bottom horizontal scale line shows the age and the top horizontal scale line shows the year of birth.

When the logarithms of data are graphed there is an opportunity to use two scales. In Figure 2.45 the death rates for people 15 to 24 years

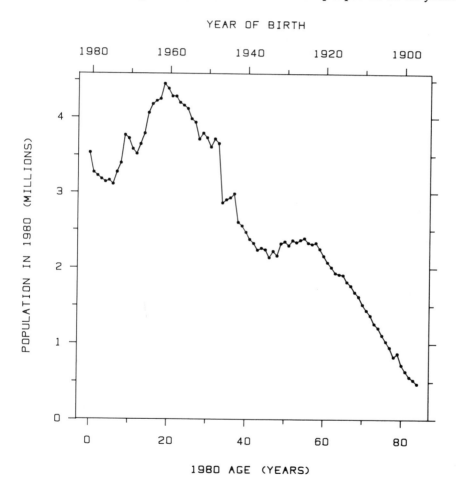

Figure 2.44 TWO SCALES. *It is sometimes helpful to use the pair of scale lines for a variable to show two different scales.* The bottom horizontal scale line shows age and the top horizontal scale line shows year of birth.

old are graphed on a log scale. The bottom horizontal scale line shows log death rate in log deaths/million. The tick mark labels on this scale line allow us to see quickly by how much two values of the data differ in multiples of two. For example, the death rate due to automobile accidents is four times larger than that for suicide. The top scale line shows death rate on the original scale in deaths/million. This scale is added to allow an assessment of the magnitudes of the death rates without having to take powers of two in our heads.

When magnitudes are shown on a graph we can use two scales to show the data in their units of measurement and to show percent change from some baseline value. Figure 2.46 is a graph of averages of

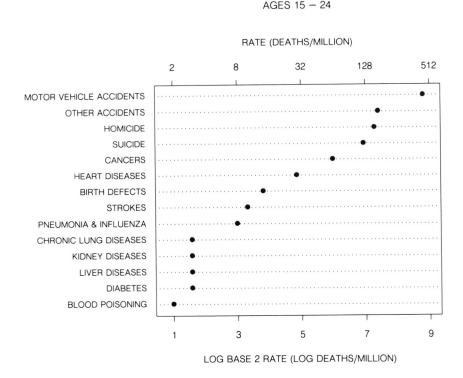

DEATH RATES FOR PEOPLE
AGES 15 – 24

Figure 2.45   TWO SCALES. The bottom horizontal scale line shows log death rate in log deaths/million and the top horizontal scale line shows death rate in deaths/million.

the mathematics Scholastic Aptitude Test scores for selected years from 1967 to 1982 [131, p. 158]. The left vertical scale line shows the scores and the right vertical scale line shows percent change from 1967. Without the right scale it takes some mental arithmetic to determine the percent changes, for example, to see that the change from 1967 to 1982 was about 5%.

Choose appropriate scales when graphs are compared.

Figure 2.47 shows data from an experiment on graphical perception [33] that will be discussed in Section 3 of Chapter 4. A group of 51 subjects judged 40 pairs of values on bar charts and the same 40 pairs on pie charts; each judgment consisted of studying the

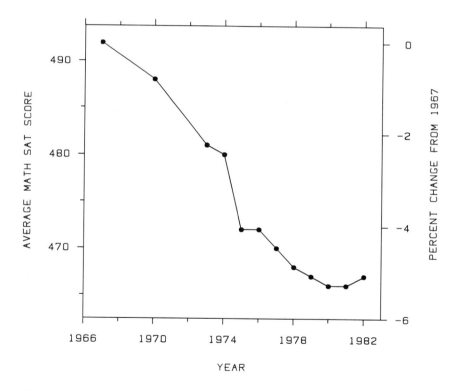

Figure 2.46   TWO SCALES. The left vertical scale line shows SAT score and the right vertical scale line shows percent change from 1967.

two values and visually judging what percent the smaller was of the larger. The left panel of Figure 2.47 shows the 40 average judgment errors (averaged across subjects) graphed against the true percents for the 40 pie chart judgments. The right panel shows the same variables for the bar chart judgments. The two smooth curves were computed using the lowess procedure that will be described in Section 4 of Chapter 3. To enhance the comparison of the bar chart and pie chart values, the scales on the two panels are the same; this allows us to see very clearly that the pie chart judgments are less accurate than the bar chart judgments. One result of the common scale is that the data do not fill either panel; we should always be prepared to forego the fill principle to achieve an effective comparison. But note that if all of the data were put on one of the panels, the data would fill the data region.

Unfortunately, scales cannot always be made the same; we must forego equal scales when the result is poor resolution. The next best thing is to have the same number of units per cm; this is illustrated in Figure 2.48. The data are the winning times of four track races at the Olympics from 1900 to 1984 [22, 138, p. 833]. The four lines have the same slopes but different intercepts and were fit to the data using least squares. If the vertical scales had been the same, the wide variation in

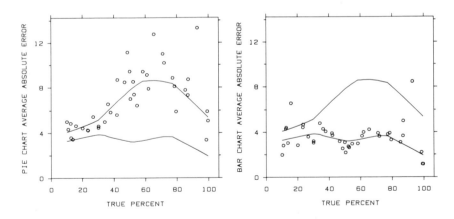

Figure 2.47   COMPARISON. *Choose appropriate scales when graphs are compared*. Scales on different panels should be made as commensurate as possible when the data on the different panels are compared. On this graph the scales on the left panel are the same as those on the right.

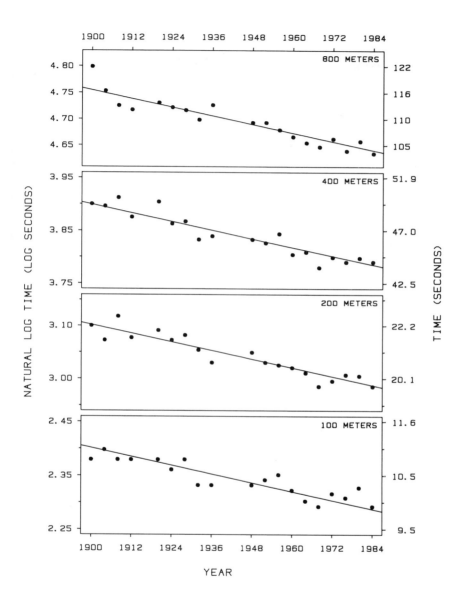

Figure 2.48   COMPARISON. Sometimes making scales identical ruins the resolution of one or more panels. The next best thing is illustrated on this graph — the number of units per cm is the same on the four vertical scales. The four lines on the panels have the same slope.

the times for the different races would have ruined the resolution. Instead, the number of log seconds per cm is the same. This allows us to compare changes in the data on different panels. For example, we can see that the overall rate of decrease through time for the four sets of data is about the same. Since logs are graphed, this means that the percent reduction in the running times for the four distances has been the same. Our ability to see this easily comes from having the same number of log units per cm on the vertical scales of the four panels.

Sometimes even the number of units per cm cannot be the same without ruining the resolution. In Figure 2.49 the data in the top panel are the monthly measurements of atmospheric CO_2 concentrations that were discussed in Section 2 of Chapter 1. The remaining panels are statistical descriptions of the trend in the data, the seasonal variation in the data, and all other variation. The range of the data and of the trend are very similar, so the vertical scales of the top two panels are the same. The variation of the data in the bottom two panels is much less than that in the top panels; if the number of units per cm were the same on the vertical scales of all panels, the resolution in the bottom two panels would be degraded. One way to appreciate how the scales change on the four panels is to study the tick mark labels and the distances between them, but this is a difficult mental-visual task. To make appreciation of the scale change easier in Figure 2.49, rectangles have been put to the right of the panels. The vertical lengths of the rectangles represent equal changes in parts per million on the four panels.

Do not insist that zero always be included on a scale showing magnitude.

When the data are magnitudes, it is helpful to have zero included in the scale so we can see its value relative to the value of the data. But the need for zero is not so compelling that we should allow its inclusion to ruin the resolution of the data on the graph.

There has been much polemical writing about including zero when graphs are used to communicate quantitative information to others. Too frequently zero has been endowed with an importance it does not have. Darrell Huff in his book *How to Lie with Statistics* [62, pp. 64-65] goes so far as to say that a graph of magnitudes without a zero line is dishonest. Referring to Figure 2.50 he writes:

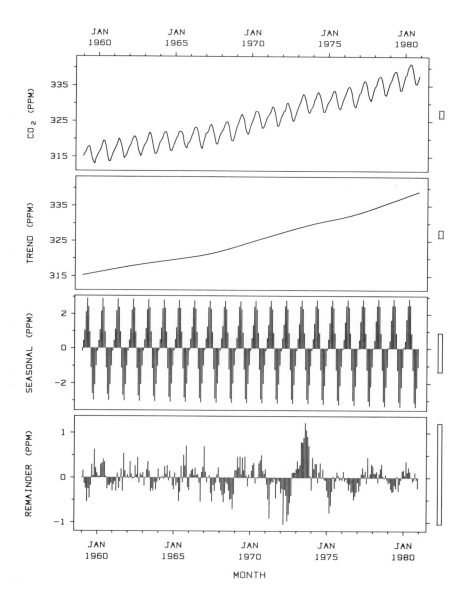

Figure 2.49   COMPARISON. Sometimes keeping the number of units per cm the same also ruins the resolution. On this graph the number of units per cm on the vertical scales varies. The rectangles on the right help to show the relative scaling; the vertical lengths portray changes of the same magnitudes on the four panels.

An editorial writer in *Dun's Review* in 1938 reproduced a chart from an advertisement advocating advertising in Washington, D.C., the argument being nicely expressed in the headline over the chart: GOVERNMENT PAY ROLLS UP! The line in the graph went along with the exclamation point even though the figures behind it did not. What they showed was an increase from about $19,500,00 to $20,000,000. But the red line shot from near the bottom of the graph clear to the top, making an increase of under four percent look like more than 400. The magazine gave its own graphic version of the same figures alongside — an honest red line that rose just four percent, under this caption: GOVERNMENT PAY ROLLS STABLE.

Huff's presumption is that viewers will not look at scale labels and apply the most trivial of quantitative reasoning. The result, the graph

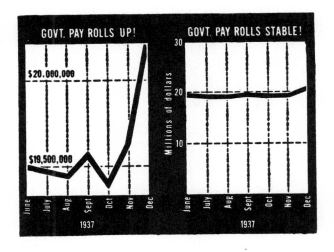

Figure 2.50 ZERO. The compulsion to include zero on a scale has ruined many graphs. Darrell Huff in *How to Lie With Statistics* argues the left graph is misleading, but the right graph is a waste of space that shows very little quantitative information beyond what could be conveyed in one sentence.

on the right in Figure 2.50, is a waste of space because the resolution is so poor; the simple statement, "government payrolls were 19.5 million dollars in June and rose by about 4% from June to December" is much more incisive and efficient. The graph on the left in Figure 2.50 conveys more quantitative information; for example, we can determine from the left graph that the rise is roughly 4%, but not from the right.

For graphical communication in science and technology *assume the viewer will look at the tick mark labels and understand them.* Were we not able to make this assumption, graphical communication would be far less useful. If zero can be included on a scale without wasting undue space, then it is reasonable to include it, but never at the expense of resolution.

The data in Figure 2.51 [69] are emission signals in the λ_L channel from Saturn and were measured by the Pioneer II spacecraft. Including zero on the vertical scale in Figure 2.51 has degraded the visual resolution of the data. It is quite unlikely that a graph of these data with the vertical scale going from 4.0 to 5.5, which includes the range of the data, would lead space physicists to think the percent variation in the emission signals is larger than it really is.

Resolution has been ruined in Figure 2.52; including zero is ludicrous. The graph shows the CO_2 data and trend curve that were graphed in Figure 2.49. Figure 2.53 shows the data in the sensible way; now the changes in CO_2 through time can be seen far more clearly.

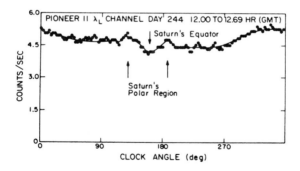

Figure 2.51   ZERO. The resolution of this graph is degraded by including zero.

Figure republished from [69]. Copyright 1980 by the AAAS.

Use a logarithmic scale when it is important to understand percent change or multiplicative factors.

There are some who feel that including a zero line on a graph helps us to better understand percent change and multiplicative factors. Darrell Huff [62, pp. 61-62] states that a graph with a zero baseline is beneficial "because the whole graph is in proportion and there is a zero line at the bottom for comparison. Your ten percent *looks* like ten percent."

It may well be that a zero line contributes a little to such judgments, but our ability to judge percents and factors is at best

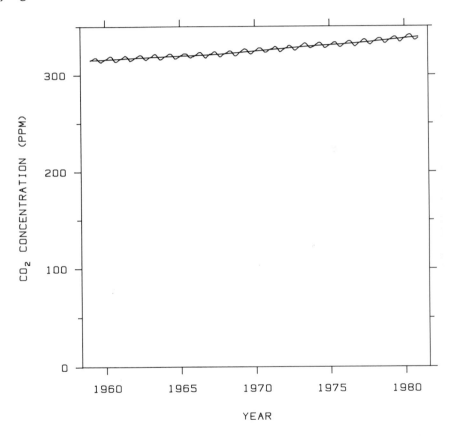

Figure 2.52   ZERO. Including zero here is ludicrous. It is reasonable to include zero if, unlike this graph, it does not ruin the resolution.

extremely poor. If we want to make such judgments it is far better to take logarithms. Suppose $a, b, c,$ and d are all positive numbers with

$$\frac{a}{b} = \frac{c}{d}$$

and b a few times bigger than d. Then on a graph of the four numbers it is quite hard to judge that the ratios are equal because on the graph, b is further from a than c is from d. This is illustrated in Figure 2.54. The data are the number of telephones in the U.S. from 1935 to 1970

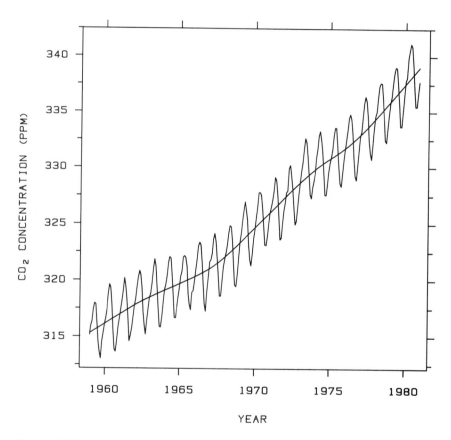

Figure 2.53   ZERO. *Do not insist that zero always be included on a scale showing magnitude.* This graph conveys much more quantitative information than Figure 2.52.

[128, p. 783]. The zero line is there, but it is very difficult to judge percents. Consider the following basic question: How is the percent increase in phones changing through time? For example, how does the percent change from 1935 to 1953, the middle of the time period, compare with the percent change from 1953 to 1970? It is very difficult to judge from Figure 2.54 without reading off values from the vertical scale and doing arithmetic.

When magnitudes are graphed on a logarithmic scale, percents and factors are easier to judge since equal multiplicative factors and percents

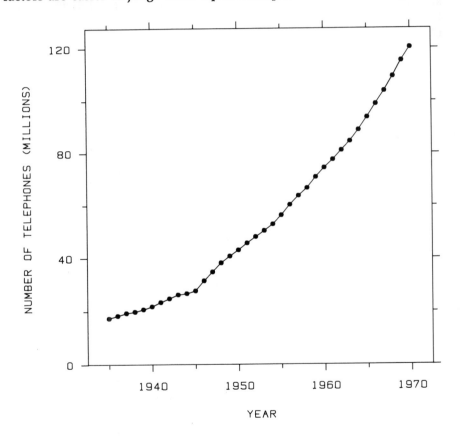

Figure 2.54   LOGS FOR FACTORS. The data are the number of telephones in the United States each year from 1935 to 1970. It is nearly impossible to judge whether the percentage increase is constant, decreasing, or increasing.

result in equal distances throughout the entire scale. For our four numbers above,

$$\log(b) - \log(a) = \log(c) - \log(d) .$$

So $\log(b)$ is the same distance along the log scale from $\log(a)$ as $\log(c)$ is from $\log(d)$. This is illustrated in Figure 2.55. A log base 2 scale is used on the vertical axis for the telephone data. Now we can see that the percent increase in telephones through time has been roughly stable, since the trend in the data is roughly linear. Now we can see easily that telephones increased from 1935 to 1953 by about the same factor ($2^{1.5} \approx 2.8$) as they did from 1953 to 1970.

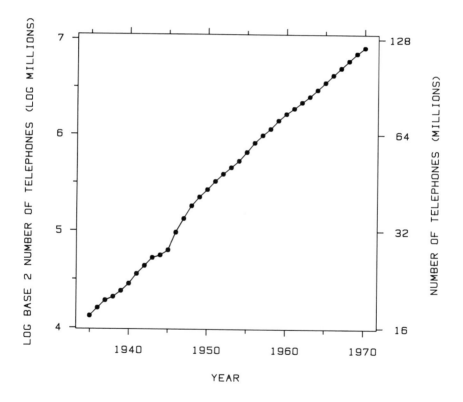

Figure 2.55   LOGS FOR FACTORS. *Use a logarithmic scale when it is important to understand percent change or multiplicative factors.* The data in Figure 2.54, are graphed by taking logarithms base 2. Now it is clear that the percentage increase in telephones was roughly stable from 1935 to 1970.

Showing data on a logarithmic scale can improve resolution.

It is common for positive data to be *skewed to the right*: some values bunch together at the low end of the scale and others trail off to the high end with increasing gaps between the values as they get higher. Such data can cause severe resolution problems on graphs, and the common remedy is to take logarithms. Indeed, it is the frequent success of this remedy that partly accounts for the large use of logarithms in graphical data display.

An example of skewed data is given in Figure 2.56. The graph shows the 14 most abundant elements in stone meteorites [48]; the data are the average percent of each of the elements. The resolution on the graph is poor because the ten smallest percents vary over a very small range. Figure 2.57 shows the data on a log scale; now the distribution is much more nearly uniform and the resolution is greatly improved.

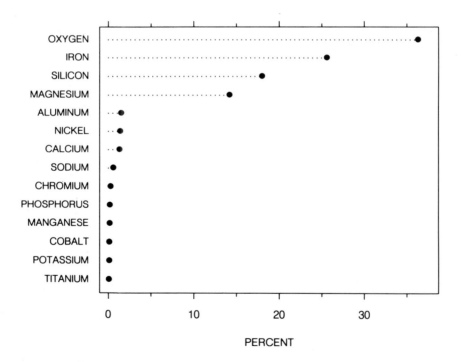

Figure 2.56   LOGS FOR RESOLUTION. Because the data on this graph are skewed to the right, the resolution of the majority of the values on the horizontal scale is poor.

Use a scale break only when necessary. If a break cannot be avoided, use a full scale break. Do not connect numerical values on two sides of a break.

Figure 2.58 shows the iridium data discussed earlier in Figure 2.33. Two *full scale breaks* are used to signal changes on the horizontal scale. The middle panel has a much smaller number of data units (meters) per cm; the widths of the rectangles at the top of the graph portray the same number of horizontal scale units (meters) on the panels. A full break shows a change or gap in a scale about as forcefully as possible.

In science and technology today the convention for indicating a change or gap in the scale of a graph is a *partial scale break*: two short

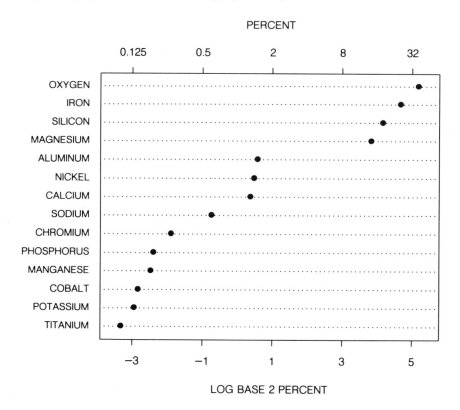

Figure 2.57   LOGS FOR RESOLUTION. *Showing data on a logarithmic scale can improve resolution.* The logs of the data in Figure 2.56 are graphed and the resolution has improved substantially.

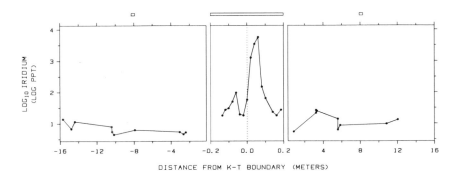

Figure 2.58 SCALE BREAKS. *Use a scale break only when necessary. If a break cannot be avoided, use a full scale break. Do not connect numerical values on two sides of a break.* This graph uses full scale breaks on the horizontal scale to signal changes in the number of units per cm. The full breaks show the scale breaks forcefully. Without the breaks, the data in the center panel would lie very nearly on a vertical line and there would be no time resolution. The rectangles at the top of the graph portray the same number of horizontal scale units on each panel.

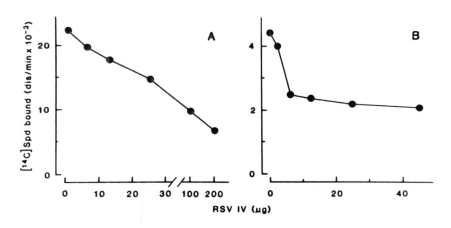

Figure 2.59 SCALE BREAKS. The partial scale break on the horizontal scale of the left panel does not give a forceful indication of a break. The connection of numerical values across the break gives the misleading impression that the data are roughly linear.
Figure republished from [105]. Copyright 1984 by the AAAS.

wavy parallel curves or two short parallel line segments breaking a scale line. This is illustrated on the horizontal scale line of the left panel in Figure 2.59 [105]. But the partial scale break is a weak indicator that the reader can fail to appreciate fully; visually, the graph is still a single panel that invites the viewer to see patterns between the two scales.

Numerical values should not be connected across a break. In the left panel of Figure 2.59, the connection across the break gives the misleading impression that the data are roughly linear across the entire horizontal scale; in fact the slope of the values decreases as the variable on the horizontal scale increases, as shown by Figure 2.60, which graphs the data with no scale break.

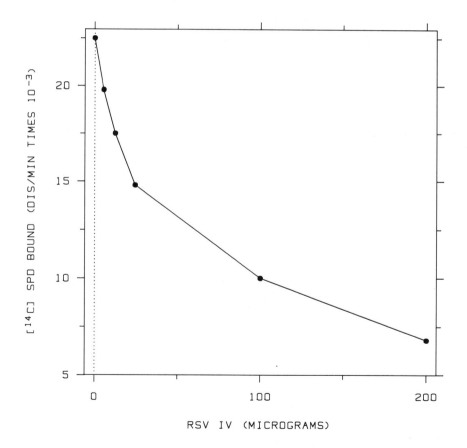

Figure 2.60   SCALE BREAKS. The data from the left panel of Figure 2.59 are graphed without a scale break. Now it is clear that the data are not roughly linear and that the slope decreases as the variable on the horizontal axis increases.

The problem in Figure 2.59 is not rare. The studies of graphs in scientific publications discussed in Section 4 of Chapter 1 revealed widespread problems caused by scale breaks. Figures 2.61 and 2.62 are other examples. Figure 2.61 [92] gives a misleading impression because the continuation of the lines across the break has no meaning. The tick marks on the horizontal scale are labeled 3, 10, and 30; since the logarithms of these values are nearly equally spaced, the authors presumably intended a horizontal log scale. The three lines give the impression that the pattern of each data set is linear through the origin. But a value of zero U/ml of interferon is off at minus infinity on the horizontal log scale, so the three lines could not possibly go through the origin. In Figure 2.62 [116] bars and error bars are allowed to barge right through two scale breaks. This renders meaningless the bar lengths and areas, important and prominent visual aspects of the graph.

Full scale breaks should be used only when necessary. Figure 2.60 shows the break of Figure 2.59 is not needed. Taking logarithms of the data can often relieve the need for a scale break. Figure 2.63 shows data

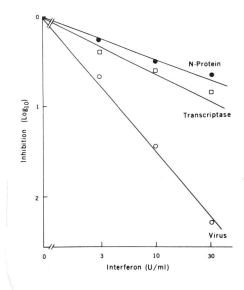

Figure 2.61   SCALE BREAKS. Scale breaks are a major cause of problems for graphs in science and technology. On this graph the lines drawn through the partial scale break have no meaning and give the misleading impression that the pattern of the data goes linearly through the origin. Since the horizontal scale is logarithmic, zero is actually at minus infinity.
Figure republished from [92]. Copyright 1980 by the AAAS.

from William Playfair's *Statistical Breviary* [109], published in 1801. The data are the populations of 22 European cities. Without a break, most of the data would be forced into a small region of the scale, which would degrade the resolution. (The dotted lines are allowed to cross the break because they carry no quantitative information that is distorted by the break.) The log scale in Figure 2.64 also improves the resolution. For most purposes a log scale is preferable to a broken one; all data can be readily compared with the log scale, whereas values on different panels of a broken scale can only be compared by the highly cognitive task of looking at the tick mark labels, reading off the values, and comparing them by doing mental arithmetic.

2.5 GENERAL STRATEGY

Graphing is much like writing. Our written language has grammatical and syntactical rules that govern the details of word and sentence construction; most of the graphical principles in the previous sections — Clear Vision, Clear Understanding, and Scales — are analogous to these rules. But there are also more general guidelines — that is, overall strategies — for writing; these are more nebulous rules aimed at producing clear, interesting prose. For example, William Strunk Jr. and E. B. White [120, p. 21, p. 72] encourage clarity by "Use definite, specific, concrete language," and encourage brevity by "Do not

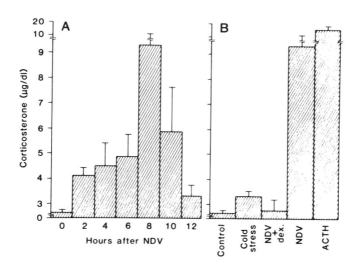

Figure 2.62   SCALE BREAKS. The lengths of the bars that barge right through the scale breaks have no meaning.
Figure republished from [116]. Copyright 1982 by the AAAS.

overwrite." The first two principles of this chapter — make the data stand out and avoid superfluity — are general strategies for graphs. (Note the similarity between the two Strunk and White principles and these two general graphical principles. Edward R. Tufte once made the insightful remark that Strunk and White's book on the elements of writing is one of the best treatises on graphing data.) In this section several general strategies for graphing data are discussed.

A large amount of quantitative information can be packed into a small region.

In the past, the number of values that could be put on a graph was limited by the graph having to be made by hand. Computer graphics has removed these shackles. Now the number of values is limited only by the resolution of graphics devices and the perceptual ability of our visual system.

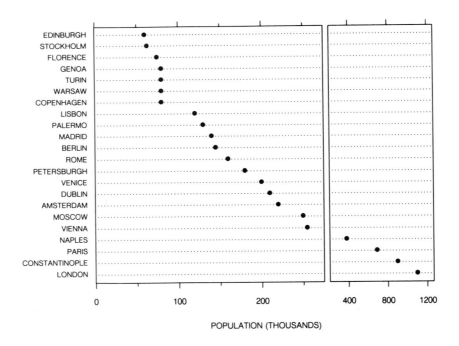

Figure 2.63   SCALE BREAKS. Without the scale break used on this graph, most of the data would be forced into a small region of the graph, which would degrade the resolution.

Previous principles in this chapter have stipulated that graphs should not be cluttered and should not have superfluous elements, but this does *not* preclude a large amount of quantitative information being shown on a graph, even a small graph. It is possible to put a large dataset on a graph in an uncluttered way. Figure 2.65, the graph of the CO_2 data and its three components that we have seen before, is an example. There are 276 monthly data points on each of the panels of this graph, which is 1104 points altogether. Each data point consists of two numbers, a value on the horizontal scale and a value on the vertical scale. Thus 2208 numbers are shown on this graph.

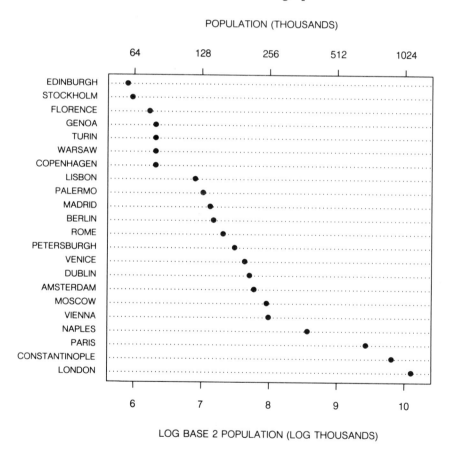

Figure 2.64   SCALE BREAK. The data from Figure 2.63 are graphed on a log scale, which relieves the need for a scale break.

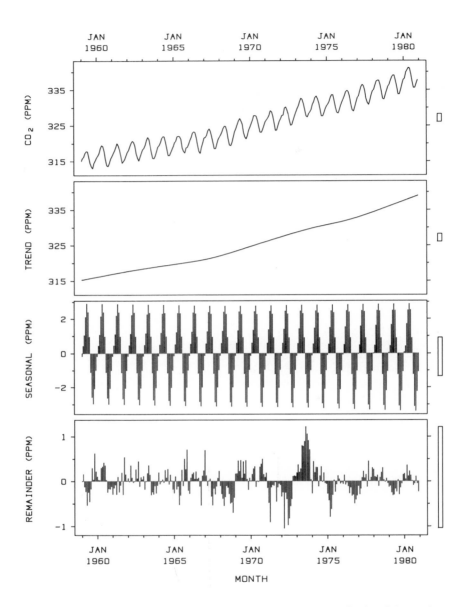

Figure 2.65 PACKING DATA. *A large amount of quantitative information can be packed into a small region.* The computer graphics revolution has given us the capability to graph a large amount of quantitative information in a small space. There are 1104 data points on this graph; each portrays two numerical values, so 2208 numbers are shown.

Graphing data should be an iterative, experimental process.

Iteration and experimentation are important for all of data analysis, including graphical data display. In many cases when we make a graph it is immediately clear that some aspect is inadequate and we regraph the data. In many other cases we make a graph, and all is well, but we get an idea for studying the data in a different way with a different graph; one successful graph often suggests another.

In part, graphing data needs to be iterative because we often do not know what to expect of the data; a graph can help discover unknown aspects of the data, and once the unknown is known, we frequently find ourselves formulating a new question about the data. Even when we understand the data and are graphing them for presentation, a graph will look different from what we had expected; our mind's eye frequently does not do a good job of predicting what our actual eyes will see.

Figure 2.66 is a simulation of an actual graph session and its iteration of graph making as it might have occurred in real life. The data are the number of doctorates in the physical sciences and in the mathematical sciences in the United States each year from 1960 to 1981 [100].

The first try, Graph 1, is a reasonable one and shows each data set graphed against time. We can see similar trends in both series; there is a rise to a peak just after 1970 and then a decline. The rise and decline for the physical sciences is greater, but the number of doctorates in the physical sciences is greater. This prompts asking how the percent changes in the two series compare; the response is Graph 2, where the logarithms of the data are shown. The graph suggests that in the early years the percent increases in the mathematical science degrees are greater, but that starting in the late 1960s the percent changes are similar.

Graph 2 allows us to study percent change between any two values. However, if we want to see just year-to-year percent change, graphing these values directly can give us a more incisive look. This has been done in Graph 3. The values confirm our impression of the overall trend in yearly percent change shown in Graph 2, but they also show more precise quantitative values — for example, we can see that the yearly increases in physical science doctorates oscillated around 10% in the early years.

One problem with Graph 3 is a large amount of year-to-year fluctuation that interferes somewhat with our ability to judge the overall trends. One solution is to smooth the data. Graph 4 shows the data after smoothing by a numerical procedure called lowess that will be described in Section 4 of Chapter 3. The distracting fluctuations have been removed and now we can see that in 1960 the percent increase in mathematical science doctorates was about double that for the physical sciences, but that the trends in the two sets of rates grew closer and became virtually identical after about 1975.

This depiction in Figure 2.66 of graph iterations is actually oversimplified. It is likely that in a real-life graphing of these data the choice of plotting symbols, the placement of the data labels, and the choice of the amount of smoothing would require several more iterations. (In fact, the real-life graphing that produced Figure 2.66 did require more iterations.)

Graph data two or more times when it is needed.

A corollary of the previous principle on iteration is that, whether we are in the mode of analyzing data or presenting data to others, we should not hesitate to make two or more graphs of the same data. Two different ways of graphing data sometimes bring out aspects that only one way cannot. For example, in a presentation of the doctorate degree data of Figure 2.66, it would be entirely sensible to use Graph 2 and Graph 4; both show interesting aspects of the data. Figure 2.67 is another example. Each of the three sets of data is shown twice. Graphing each data set separately in the top three panels allows the error bars to be perceived without interfering with one another. Graphing the three data sets together in the bottom panel allows them to be more effectively compared.

Many useful graphs require careful, detailed study.

There are some who argue that a graph is a success only if the important information in the data can be seen within a few seconds. While there is a place for rapidly-understood graphs, it is too limiting to make speed a requirement in science and technology, where the use of graphs ranges from detailed, in-depth data analysis to quick presentation. The next two graphs illustrate these extremes.

Cyril Burt was a giant in psychology until his world began to crumble in 1974, three years after his death. Burt was one of the leading proponents of the theory that intelligence, as measured by IQ scores, is largely inherited. Burt's data strongly supported this view — too strongly, as it turns out. In 1974 suspicions were raised about the authenticity of some of Burt's data and his analyses [73]. For five years doubts about Burt's integrity grew, culminating in a biography by Hearnshaw who concluded, as others already had, that Burt faked much of his data, invented collaborators, and sent letters to journals from fictitious people who supported his work [58].

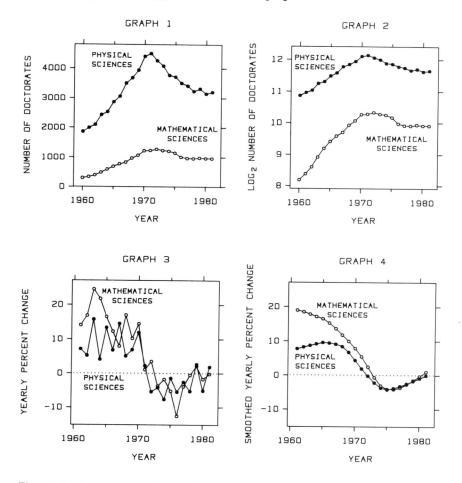

Figure 2.66   ITERATION.   *Graphing data should be an iterative, experimental process.* The four graphs in this figure are four successive looks at the data; each of the last three is inspired by its predecessor.

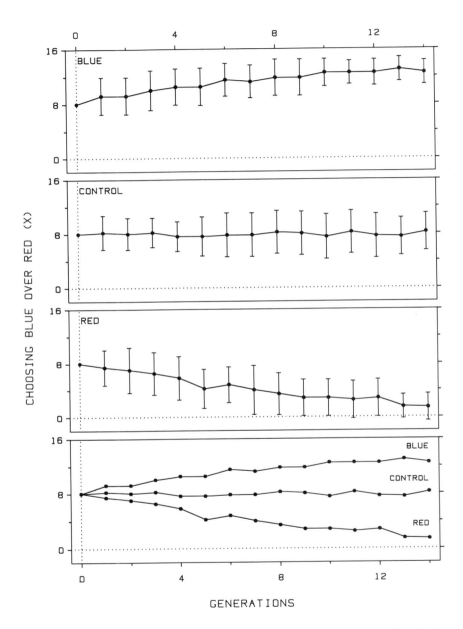

Figure 2.67 REGRAPHING. *Graph data two or more times when it is needed.* Each data set is graphed twice, once in one of the three top panels to allow an unobstructed view of the error bars and once in the bottom panel to allow an effective comparison of the data sets.

Table 2.1 shows data that Burt published in 1961 in the *British Journal of Statistical Psychology* [20]. The numbers are part of a larger data set that were widely quoted in subsequent scientific work until D. D. Dorfman, a psychologist at the University of Iowa, gave a convincing argument in 1978 that the numbers were made-up, either in whole or in part [46]. The values in Table 2.1 were purported to be mean IQ scores of 40,000 father-child pairs divided into six social classes.

Table 2.1   CYRIL BURT DATA. The data are means of adult IQ scores and means of child IQ scores for six social classes. The means were computed from IQ scores for 40,000 father-child pairs.

	Adult Mean IQ	Child Mean IQ
Higher Professional	139.7	120.8
Lower Professional	130.6	114.7
Clerical	115.9	107.8
Skilled	108.2	104.6
Semiskilled	97.8	98.9
Unskilled	84.9	92.6

The data in Table 2.1 look innocent enough until they are graphed. Figure 2.68 is a graph of the mean scores for the children against the corresponding values for adults. The impugnment of these data is based, in part, on the notion that the mean scores are simply too good to be true. In 1959, J. Conway [38] had put forward the equation

$$\text{child score} - 100 = \frac{1}{2}(\text{adult score} - 100)$$

as a method for predicting the mean IQ score of children in a given class from the mean IQ score of the fathers in the class; this predictive line is shown in Figure 2.68. The line lies extraordinarily close to the data. Thus for Burt's data, Conway's predictive method, with its mathematically elegant coefficient of 0.5, makes nearly perfect predictions.

Figure 2.68 requires only a quick look to absorb the important quantitative information. The main message — that the mean scores are very close to the line — can be absorbed almost instantaneously.

Some graphs, however, require long and detailed scrutinizing. This is entirely reasonable. The important criterion for a graph is not simply how fast we can see a result; rather, it is whether through the use of the graph we can see something that would have been harder to see otherwise or that could not have been seen at all. If a graphical display requires hours of study to make a discovery that would have gone undetected without the graph, then the display is a success.

Figure 2.69 is a graph that requires detailed study. The graphical method used in the figure, an exceedingly useful one called a *scatterplot matrix*, will be discussed in Section 6 of Chapter 3. The data in Figure 2.69 are measurements of four variables: wind speed, temperature, solar radiation at ground level, and concentrations of the air pollutant, ozone [18]. There is one measurement of each variable on each of 111 days.

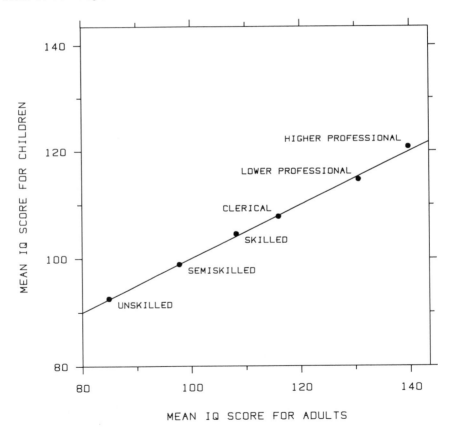

Figure 2.68   DETAILED STUDY. The important information on this graph, that Cyril Burt's fictitious data lie very close to the line, can be extracted with just a quick look.

Each panel of Figure 2.69 is a scatterplot of one variable against another. For the three panels in the second row, the vertical scale is ozone, and the three horizontal scales are solar radiation, temperature, and wind speed. So the graph in position (2,1) in the matrix — that is, the second row and first column — is a scatterplot of ozone against solar radiation; position (2,3) is a scatterplot of ozone against temperature; position (2,4) is a scatterplot of ozone against wind speed.

The scatterplot matrix reveals much about the four variables. A discussion of what is seen, since it is long and detailed, will be postponed to the full discussion of scatterplot matrices in Chapter 3; it

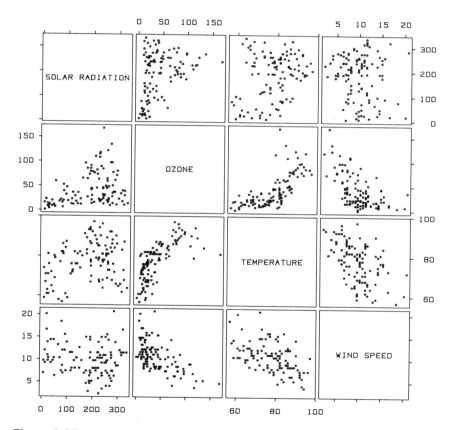

Figure 2.69 DETAILED STUDY. *Many useful graphs require careful, detailed study.* Compared with that needed for Figure 2.68, this scatterplot matrix of ozone and meteorological measurements requires lengthy study to extract the information. But the lengthy study reveals information that would be very difficult or impossible to get by other means.

suffices to say here that the revelations come only after careful, detailed study of the graph. It might well be expected that a graph with 1332 points on it, each encoding two numbers for a total of 2664 numbers, would require careful study.

2.6 A LISTING OF THE PRINCIPLES OF GRAPH CONSTRUCTION

Clear Vision

Make the data stand out. Avoid superfluity.

Use visually prominent graphical elements to show the data.

Use a pair of scale lines for each variable. Make the data region the interior of the rectangle formed by the scale lines. Put tick marks outside of the data region.

Do not clutter the data region.

Do not overdo the number of tick marks.

Use a reference line when there is an important value that must be seen across the entire graph, but do not let the line interfere with the data.

Do not allow data labels in the data region to interfere with the quantitative data or to clutter the graph.

Avoid putting notes, keys, and markers in the data region. Put keys and markers just outside the data region and put notes in the legend or in the text.

Overlapping plotting symbols must be visually distinguishable.

Superposed data sets must be readily visually discriminated.

Visual clarity must be preserved under reduction and reproduction.

Clear Understanding

Put major conclusions into graphical form. Make legends comprehensive and informative.

Error bars should be clearly explained.

When logarithms of a variable are graphed, the scale label should correspond to the tick mark labels.

Proofread graphs.

Strive for clarity.

Scales

Choose the range of the tick marks to include or nearly include the range of data.

Subject to the constraints that scales have, choose the scales so that the data fill up as much of the data region as possible.

It is sometimes helpful to use the pair of scale lines for a variable to show two different scales.

Choose appropriate scales when graphs are compared.

Do not insist that zero always be included on a scale showing magnitude.

Use a logarithmic scale when it is important to understand percent change or multiplicative factors.

Showing data on a logarithmic scale can improve resolution.

Use a scale break only when necessary. If a break cannot be avoided, use a full scale break. Do not connect numerical values on two sides of a break.

General Strategy

A large amount of quantitative information can be packed into a small region.

Graphing data should be an iterative, experimental process.

Graph data two or more times when it is needed.

Many useful graphs require careful, detailed study.

3

GRAPHICAL METHODS

This chapter is about graphical methods: types of graphs and ways of encoding quantitative information on graphs. The methods allow us to analyze both the overall structure of the data and the detail of the data.

Section 3.1 discusses two methods, logarithms and residuals. These are general purpose tools that are useful in all areas of graphical data analysis.

Section 3.2 is about graphing one or more sets, or categories, of measurements of one quantitative variable. Suppose we have measurements of the brain weights of three groups of animals: gorillas, orangoutangs, and chimpanzees. In this example we have one quantitative variable, brain weight, and a categorical variable, animal species. The graphical methods of the section let us study and compare the data distributions: where the sets of data lie along the measurement scale.

Section 3.3 is about dot charts, which are used to show measurements of a quantitative variable in which each measurement has a label associated with it that we want to display on the graph. An example is the distances of the planets from the sun; each measured object, a planet, has a distance and a name. Several different forms of the dot chart are described; the different forms accommodate different measurement scales and different structures of the measurement labels.

Section 3.4 is about graphing two quantitative variables to study their relationship; for example, the methods could be used to study how brain weights of gorillas are related to their body weights.

In Section 3.5 the setting is similar to Section 3.4, but now there are two or more categories of measurements of two quantitative variables. For example, we might have measurements of brain weights and body weights of gorillas, orangoutangs, and chimpanzees. The section presents methods of superposition and juxtaposition of the different categories of data that allow us to study the relationship of the two variables and to identify the categories.

Section 3.6 deals with measurements of three or more quantitative variables; an example is measurements of blood pressure, heart rate, weight, height, age, and sodium intake for a group of people. Understanding such multidimensional data is difficult, but the use of graphical methods in the section can often increase our understanding.

Section 3.7 is about statistical variation. There is a general discussion of the empirical variation in data and the sample-to-sample variation of a statistic computed from data. Two-tiered error bars are introduced for showing sample-to-sample variation.

3.1 GENERAL METHODS: LOGARITHMS AND RESIDUALS

Logarithms

Logarithms are one of man's most useful inventions. They are indispensable in science and technology and are a vital part of graphical methods. Their usefulness has been amply illustrated earlier in the book — for improving resolution and for showing data where percents and factors are important.

In Figure 3.1, logarithms of the maximum amounts of solar radiation penetrating ocean water at various ocean depths are graphed against depth [88]. Until 1984 it was presumed that living things did not exist in the ocean below about 200 meters because of low light intensity. In 1984 scientists at the Smithsonian Institution in Washington, D.C. and the Harbor Branch Foundation in Florida discovered an alga at a depth of 268 meters in waters off the coast of San Salvador Island in the Bahamas. The filled circles in Figure 3.1 are measurements of radiation that the discoverers presented in their paper and the open circles are values that they extrapolated from the measured values. The line on the graph is the least squares line fitted to the measured values.

Logarithms are useful here because radiation changes by five powers of ten from about 10^3 at sea level to about 10^{-2} at 268 meters. Also, it is natural to use a log scale because we would expect attenuation of the solar radiation, if the transmission properties of the ocean water are relatively constant, to be multiplicative as a function of depth; if s is the radiation at sea level and f is the fraction of radiation remaining after passing through one centimeter of ocean water, then the radiation at a depth of one centimeter is $r(1) = fs$, at two centimeters is $r(2) = f^2 s$, and at d centimeters is $r(d) = f^d s$. On a log scale, radiation is

$$\log(r(d)) = d \, \log(f) + \log(s)$$

and is thus a linear function of d. Figure 3.1 shows such an attenuation process is commensurate with the log measurements, which are roughly

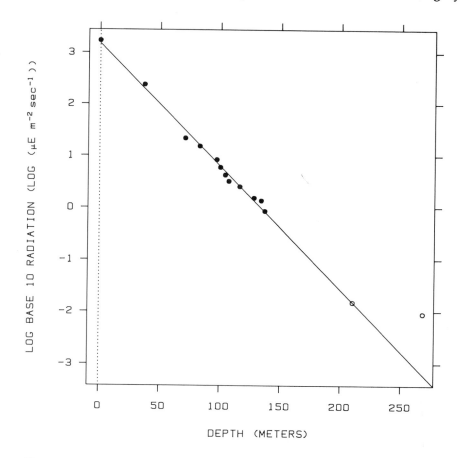

Figure 3.1   LOG BASE 10. Graphing data on a log base 10 scale is reasonable when the data go through many powers of 10, as on the vertical scale of this graph.

linear with depth. The extrapolated radiation value at 210 meters fits
the pattern of the measured values, but the extrapolated value at 268
meters does not; either the ocean water changes its properties or there
has been a faulty extrapolation.

Log Base 2 and Log Base e

Log base 10 is almost always used in scientific graphs for a log scale.
This is much too limiting. Log base 2 and log base e (natural
logarithms) should always be considered. Using a different base does
not change the pattern of the points but changes only the values at the
tick marks because the logarithm of one base is just a constant times the
logarithm of another base. The relationship between log base b and log
base c is

$$\log_c(x) = \log_b(x)/\log_b(c) \ .$$

Thus

$$\log_2(x) = \log_{10}(x)/\log_{10}(2)$$

and

$$\log_e(x) = \log_{10}(x)/\log_{10}(e) \ .$$

The choice of the base depends on the range of the data values that
need to be visually compared. Suppose the data go through many
powers of 10, as the radiation data in Figure 3.1 do. In such a case it is
reasonable to use log base 10. But suppose the data range over two
powers of 10 or less. This is the case in Figure 3.2; the data are the
number of telephones in the United States from 1935 to 1970 [128,
p. 783]. In such a case it is inevitable that equally spaced tick marks for
log base 10 will involve fractional powers of 10, as Figure 3.2 illustrates.
It is difficult to deal with such fractional powers. It is easy enough to
remember $10^{0.5}$ is a little bigger than 3, but to keep many fractional
powers of 10 in our heads and try to use them to study a graph is
cumbersome. In such a situation it makes sense to convert to log base 2
as in Figure 3.3. It is easier to deal with powers of 2 than fractional
powers of 10. For example, we can see that the number of phones
increased by a factor of about 4 from 1935 to 1960.

On a log base 2 graph it is often helpful to label one scale line on a log scale and the other scale line in the original units of the data. This reduces the amount of mental conversion from the log scale to the original scale. This second scale, however, does not completely eliminate mental conversion. Suppose there is a datum at 2^7 and a datum at 2^{13}; the second is greater by a factor of 2^6. In order to evaluate this factor, we must know $2^6 = 64$. Remembering powers of 2 up to 2^{10} is easy:

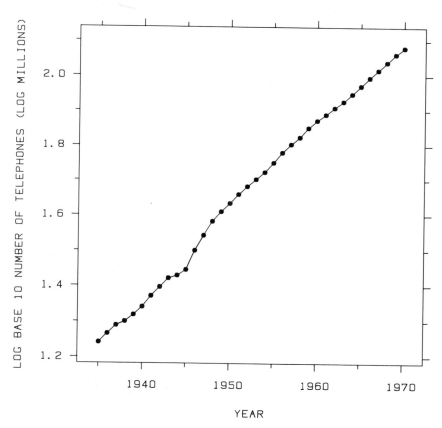

Figure 3.2   LOG BASE 10. The data, a time series of the number of telephones in the United States, are graphed on a log base 10 scale. When the data range through two or fewer powers of 10, the log base 10 scale is not as informative since we must deal with fractional powers of 10, as on this graph.

$$
\begin{array}{ll}
2^1 = 2 & 2^6 = 64 \\
2^2 = 4 & 2^7 = 128 \\
2^3 = 8 & 2^8 = 256 \\
2^4 = 16 & 2^9 = 512 \\
2^5 = 32 & 2^{10} = 1024 \; .
\end{array}
$$

The computer revolution has made it even easier to remember these powers. We can go even higher by using the computer scientists' trick: Let $k = 1000$ and approximate $1024 = 2^{10}$ by k so that

$$
2^{14} = 2^4 \times 2^{10} \approx 16k = 16,000
$$

and

$$
2^{24} = 2^4 \times 2^{20} \approx 16k^2 = 16,000,000 \; .
$$

Also, the following fractional powers of 2 are easy to remember because they are very close to simple numbers:

$$
\begin{array}{l}
2^{0.3} = 1.231 \approx 1.25 \\
2^{0.5} = 1.414 \approx 1.4 \\
2^{0.6} = 1.516 \approx 1.5 \\
2^{0.8} = 1.741 \approx 1.75 \; .
\end{array}
$$

A trick that can be used to keep the exponents on a log base 2 scale from getting too large — perhaps we can call it the statistical scientist's trick — is to take the original units to be in thousands, millions, or billions. For example, suppose the data range from 10^4 meters to 10^6 meters. The numbers on a log base two scale range from about 13 to 20. The trick is to think of the original units as kilometers; now the data range from 10 to 1000 kilometers and the numbers on the log base 2 scale range from about 3 to 10. This trick was employed in Figure 3.3, where the units of the vertical scale are log *millions* of telephones.

Logarithms base e are also useful because they have a wonderful property. Suppose u and v are values of the data. Let d be their difference on a natural log scale,

$$
d = \log_e(v) - \log_e(u) \; .
$$

Then if d lies between -0.25 to 0.25, the percent change in going from u to v, which is

$$
100 \left[\frac{v-u}{u} \right] ,
$$

is approximately equal to 100d%. In Figure 3.4 this approximation is illustrated with made-up data. A is larger than B by about 0.1 on the natural log scale, so A is about 10% larger than B; B is larger than C by about 0.25, so B is about 25% larger than C.

Let us see why this approximation works. Let

$$\frac{v}{u} = 1 + r$$

then the percent change in going from u to v is 100r%. Now

$$d = \log_e(v) - \log_e(u) = \log_e\left(\frac{v}{u}\right) = \log_e(1+r) .$$

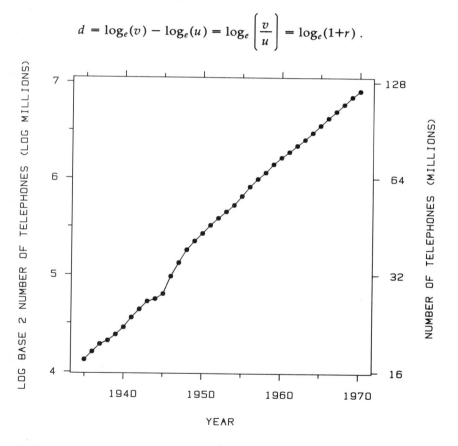

Figure 3.3   LOG BASE 2. When the data go through a small number of powers of 10, log base 2 often provides a useful scale. The left vertical scale line shows the data in log units and the right vertical scale line shows the original units.

But if d is small,

$$\log_e(1+r) \approx r$$

and therefore

$$d \approx r \, .$$

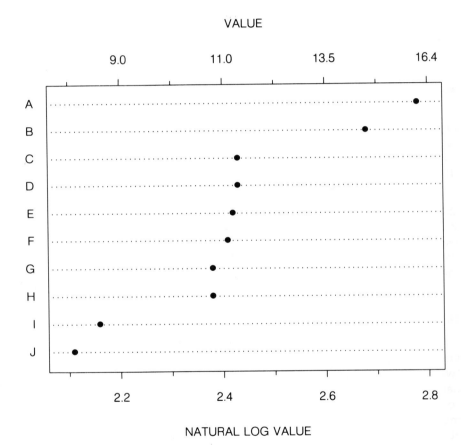

Figure 3.4   NATURAL LOGS. Logarithms base e are sometimes a good choice for a log scale. If two values on a natural log scale differ by d, where d is between −0.25 and 0.25, the percent difference of the values is to a good approximation $100d$%. On this graph, A is greater than B by about 0.1 log units, so A is about 10% bigger than B.

Here are several values of r and d:

$$\log_e(1+0.05) = 0.049 \qquad \log_e(1-0.05) = -0.051$$

$$\log_e(1+0.1) = 0.095 \qquad \log_e(1-0.1) = -0.105$$

$$\log_e(1+0.15) = 0.140 \qquad \log_e(1-0.15) = -0.163$$

$$\log_e(1+0.2) = 0.182 \qquad \log_e(1-0.2) = -0.223$$

$$\log_e(1+0.25) = 0.223 \qquad \log_e(1-0.25) = -0.288.$$

When d is greater than 0.25 or less than -0.25, the approximation is less accurate and is not as useful.

It is, of course, considerably harder to go back mentally to the original scale from a natural log scale than from base 2 or 10. We know readily what 2^3 and 10^3 are, but e^3 is harder. For this reason it is particularly important to use one scale line to show the original scale, as illustrated in Figure 3.4.

If all differences of the data on a natural log scale are between ±0.25, the approximation can be used, of course, for any two graphed values. This is illustrated in Figure 3.5. The conductivity of ocean water [88] is graphed against depth. The range of the data is about 0.15 natural log units, so no two measurements on the original scale differ by more than 15%.

Graphing Percent Change

When the maximum percent variation in the data is small, there is another way to graph the data that shows percent change between any two values. In Figure 3.6 the left vertical scale line shows the original data units and the right vertical scale shows percent change of conductivity from the sea-level value. The right scale shows that at 100 meters there is about a -5% change in conductivity from sea level and at 250 meters there is about a -15% change. Because these percent changes are small, the percent change in going from 100 meters to 250 meters is approximately $(-15\%) - (-5\%) = -10\%$. Thus, from the right vertical scale we can judge the percent change between *any* two values and not just between the baseline and another value; this approximation works well provided the percent changes of the two values from the baseline both lie between plus and minus 15%, which they always do in Figure 3.6. In general, a baseline value might be a value for some special condition, such as sea level in this example, or it might be the maximum value of the data, the minimum value, or a middle value.

Let us take a closer look at this approximation and why it works. Suppose b is the baseline value. Let $(1+s)b$ and $(1+t)b$ be two other values shown along the scale. The percent changes of the two values relative to the baseline are 100s% and 100t%, respectively; depending on the value of the baseline, s and t might be both positive, both negative, or have opposite signs. The percent change in going from $(1+s)b$ to $(1+t)b$ is

$$c = 100\left[\frac{(1+t)b - (1+s)b}{(1+s)b}\right] = 100\left[\frac{1+t}{1+s} - 1\right].$$

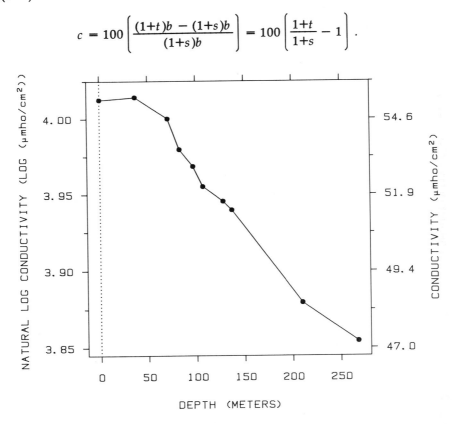

Figure 3.5 NATURAL LOGS. Conductivity is graphed on a natural log scale. Since the range of log conductivity is about 0.15, 100 times the difference of any two values can be interpreted as percent change.

If $|s|$ is small, then

$$\frac{1}{1+s} \approx 1 - s \ .$$

Thus

$$\frac{1+t}{1+s} \approx (1+t)(1-s) = 1 + t - s - ts \ .$$

If $|s|$ and $|t|$ are both small, then

$$ts \approx 0 \ .$$

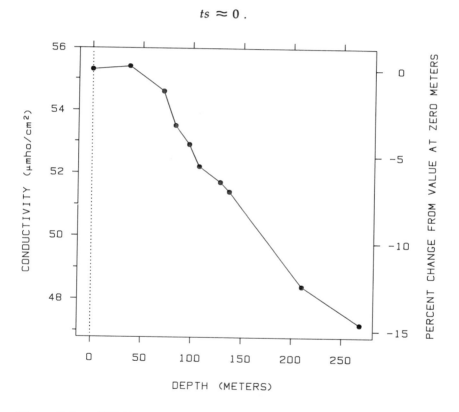

Figure 3.6   PERCENT CHANGE. The right vertical scale line shows percent change of conductivity from the sea-level value. Since the deviations from the baseline are all between ±15%, the right vertical scale line can be used to judge, to a good approximation, the percent change between any two values.

Thus

$$\frac{(1+t)}{(1+s)} \approx 1 + t - s .$$

This means that

$$c \approx 100t - 100s .$$

Here is one example of the approximation. Suppose the baseline is $b = 200$, and $u = 180$ and $v = 230$ are two other values. Then the change in u relative to b is -10% and the change in v relative to b is 15%. Thus the change in going from u to v is approximately 25%. The actual value, to one decimal place, is 27.8%.

Residuals

Figure 3.7 is a graph published in 1801 by William Playfair in his *Statistical Breviary* [109]. On the graph, the populations of 22 cities are encoded by the areas of the circles. Playfair, who was part statistical scientist and part political thinker, was the first person to study graphical data display and to experiment with graphical methods in a broad and serious way. In several brilliant strokes he invented many types of graphs that are in use today. His *Commercial and Political Atlas* of 1786 [108] and his subsequent publications contain time series graphs, bar charts, pie charts, and graphs with data encoded by circle areas and line lengths. However, some of Playfair's inventions did not work, as will be demonstrated in Chapter 4.

The graph in Figure 3.8 was made to see how accurately the circle areas of Playfair's graph encode the data; the analysis was inspired by the observation that the circle area for Turin is slightly less than that for Genoa, even though the population values recorded on the graph for these cities are equal. Let Y_i be the circle areas and let X_i be the populations. If the areas are to encode the data we should have

$$Y_i = KX_i \qquad \text{for } i = 1 \text{ to } 22 ,$$

which on a log scale is

$$\log_e(Y_i) = \log_e(X_i) + \log_e(K)$$

or

$$y_i = x_i + k .$$

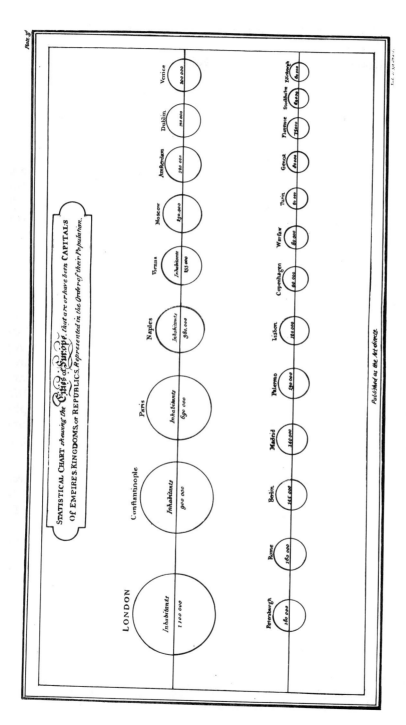

Figure 3.7   PLAYFAIR GRAPH. This graph, published by William Playfair in 1801, encodes the populations of European cities by circle areas.

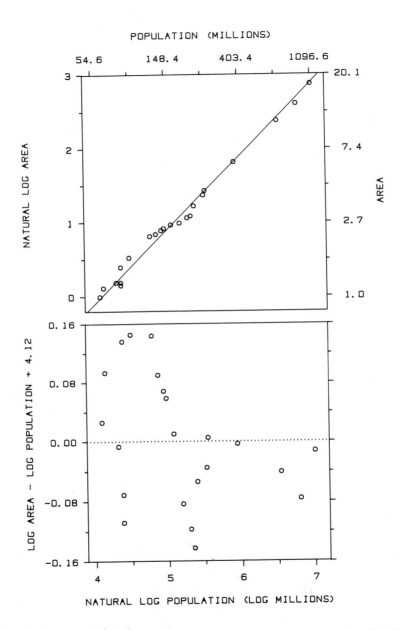

Figure 3.8   RESIDUALS. In the top panel, the areas of the circles in Playfair's graph are graphed against the populations, both on a natural log scale. The top panel shows that the points lie close to the line, but there is too little resolution to study the residuals, which are the vertical deviations. In the bottom panel the residuals are graphed against the populations and an interesting pattern in the deviations emerges.

In the top panel of Figure 3.8, y_i is graphed against x_i. Areas are relative to the area of the smallest circle in Figure 3.7, which shows the value for Edinburgh; that is, one unit of area on the vertical scale of the top panel in Figure 3.8 is equal to the area of the Edinburgh circle in Figure 3.7. Since

$$k = y_i - x_i \, ,$$

k was estimated by the mean of the 22 values of $y_i - x_i$; the estimate is −4.12. The line $y = x - 4.12$ is graphed in the top panel in Figure 3.8.

If the encoding by circle area were perfect, the points in the top panel of Figure 3.8 would lie exactly on the line. The vertical deviations of the points from the line, which are called *residuals*, tell us by how much the actual areas deviate from a perfect encoding. The values of the residuals are

$$y_i - (x_i - 4.12) = y_i - x_i + 4.12 \, , \quad \text{for } i = 1 \text{ to } 22 \, .$$

But it is difficult to assess the residuals because the points of the graph lie in a narrow band around the line, which results in poor resolution of the residuals.

The resolution of the residuals can be greatly improved by graphing them against x_i. This is done in the bottom panel of Figure 3.8. The residuals are now much more spread out since we have removed the overall linear effect. We can interpret the residuals as percent deviations, as discussed earlier in this section, because a log base e scale is used and because all residuals are between −0.25 and 0.25 log units. The largest residual is about 0.15, which means the area of the circle corresponding to the value is about 15% larger than the ideal area of the fitted line, and the smallest residual is about −0.15; thus the percent deviations of the actual areas from the ideal ones range between about −15% and 15%.

The graph of residuals in the bottom panel also shows an interesting pattern that is only barely discernible in the top panel. The residuals are not random as a function of the x_i but rather drift in a correlated way above and below zero. The tendency is for residuals corresponding to small populations to be positive and residuals for the larger populations to be negative; this means the circle areas for small populations tend to be too large and the circle areas for large populations tend to be too small. This drift in the residuals is curious.

If the deviation of the actual areas from an ideal encoding were a matter of measurement error, we would not expect, considering most mechanisms that might produce errors, to see the drift. More information about the production process and how the paper of the original graph has changed through time would be needed to solve the enigma.

Graphing residuals is an important method that has applications in all areas of graphical data analysis. We will look at several other examples.

Residuals can arise from comparing data with visual references other than fitted lines. The reference might be a curve, as in the top panel of Figure 3.9, which graphs made-up data. Judging the vertical deviations of the points from the curve is difficult because of the rapidly changing slope. (This issue of graphical perception is discussed in detail in Section 4 of Chapter 4.) The visual impression from the top panel is that the residuals are smaller on the right than on the left. The graph of residuals against x in the bottom panel shows that the opposite is the case.

Graphing residuals is also illustrated in Figure 3.10, again, by made-up data. Observations are compared to a theoretical value for each of eight groups. The two-tiered error bars show 50% and 95% confidence intervals for the observations. The residuals, which in this case are the data minus the theoretical values, are graphed in the bottom panel; the result is increased resolution of the deviations of the data from the theoretical values and a better comparison of where the theoretical values lie with respect to the confidence intervals for the data.

The Tukey Sum-Difference Graph

There is another situation where graphing residuals is helpful. Suppose y_i is graphed against x_i for $i = 1$ to n to see how close x_i and y_i are to one another. An example is shown in the top panel of Figure 3.11. The data on the vertical axis, y_i, are the logarithms of abundances of certain elements in rocks brought back from the moon's Mare Tranquillitatis by the Apollo 11 astronauts in 1969 [91, p. 27]. The data on the horizontal axis, x_i, are the logarithms of abundances of the same elements in basalt from the earth. The purpose of the graph is to see how the composition of the moon rocks compares with that of basalt.

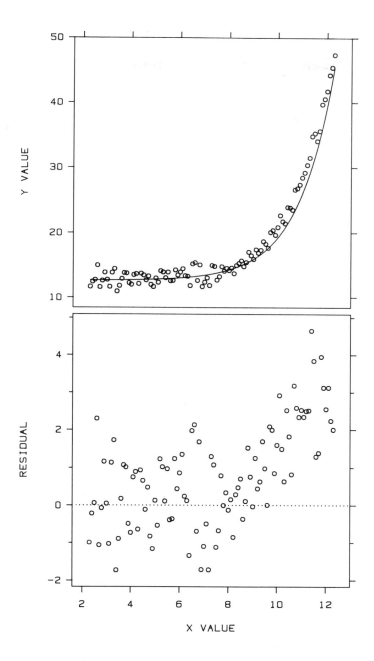

Figure 3.9   GRAPHING RESIDUALS. The visual impression from the top panel is that the vertical deviations of the points from the curve are greater for small *x* values than for large ones. The graph of residuals in the bottom panel shows the opposite is true.

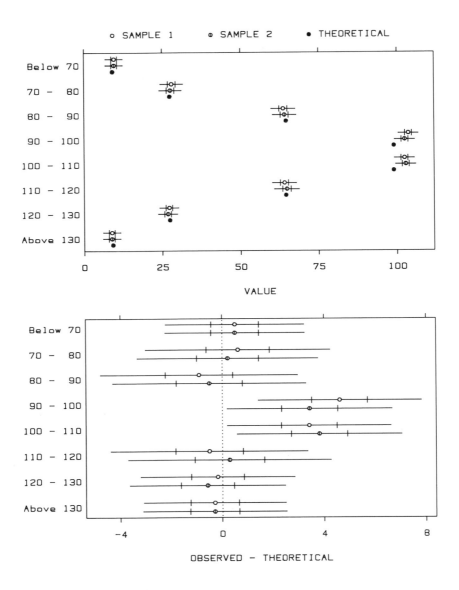

Figure 3.10   GRAPHING RESIDUALS. In the top panel made-up observations are compared with made-up theoretical values. The two-tiered error bars represent 50% and 95% confidence intervals. The residuals, which in this case are the data minus the theoretical values, are graphed in the bottom panel; the increased resolution allows us to compare more effectively where the theoretical values lie with respect to the confidence intervals.

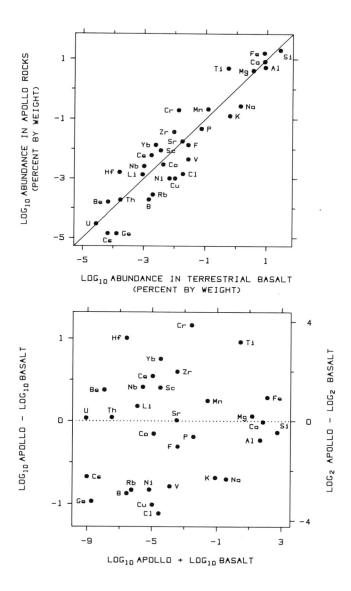

Figure 3.11   TUKEY SUM-DIFFERENCE GRAPH. In the top panel two sets of data with the same measurement scale are graphed to see how close the corresponding values are. The bottom panel is the Tukey sum-difference graph: $y_i - x_i$ is graphed against $y_i + x_i$. This graphical method, which is a 45° clockwise rotation of the top panel followed by an expansion of the vertical scale, allows us to study more effectively the deviations of the points from the line $y = x$.

In studying the composition data we would like to understand the values of $y_i - x_i$, the amounts by which the abundances differ. On the the top panel of Figure 3.11, $y_i - x_i$ is equal to the vertical deviation of the point (x_i, y_i) from the line $y = x$, and $x_i - y_i$ is equal to the horizontal deviation of (x_i, y_i) from the line. As with other graphs, however, it is difficult to assess the values of these deviations, or residuals, partly because the resolution of the residuals is poor.

In Figure 3.7, where we studied Playfair's data, our purpose was to see how the areas, y_i, *depend on* the population measurements, x_i. The variable y is a dependent variable and x is an independent variable. For the abundance data in the top panel of Figure 3.11 the situation is different. Neither variable is dependent or independent; we are seeking simply to see how the two variables are related, and by how much the abundances differ. We might look at residuals, in analogy with the Playfair data, by graphing $y_i - x_i$ against x_i. This, however, does not treat x_i and y_i equally, and we could just as well graph $y_i - x_i$ against y_i.

One way to graph $y_i - x_i$ that takes the equivalence of x_i and y_i into account is the *Tukey sum-difference graph*: $y_i - x_i$ is graphed against $y_i + x_i$, as illustrated in the bottom panel of Figure 3.11. The sum-difference graph can be thought of as the result of rotating the points in the top panel by 45° in a clockwise direction and then allowing the rotated points to expand in the vertical direction to fill the data region. To see this suppose

$$u_i = \frac{y_i + x_i}{\sqrt{2}}$$

and

$$v_i = \frac{y_i - x_i}{\sqrt{2}} .$$

If we graphed v_i against u_i and kept the number of data units per cm the same as on the graph of y_i vs. x_i, the points on the new graph would be exactly a 45° clockwise rotation of the points on the old one. The reader can rotate the book page 45° clockwise to see how the configuration of points on this new graph would appear. In the Tukey sum-difference graph there is no $\sqrt{2}$, which is a constant factor that does not affect the configuration of points; also, the number of data units per cm for $y_i - x_i$ is not forced to be the same as $y_i + x_i$, but rather the vertical scale is chosen so that the $y_i - x_i$ fill up the data region that is available.

In the bottom panel of Figure 3.11 the expansion of the scale for the $y_i - x_i$ now lets us assess these residuals far more effectively than in the top panel. The left vertical scale line shows differences of log base 10 abundances and the right vertical scale line shows differences of log base 2 abundances; the right vertical scale line helps us appreciate the factors since the differences vary only by about two powers of 10.

Figure 3.11 shows that titanium, which is one of the most abundant elements in both rock types, is higher in the moon rocks by about a factor of 10. Also, sodium is lower by a factor of about 5. This had already been discovered by the Surveyor spacecraft in 1967, which also measured composition in Mare Tranquillitatis. Surveyor landed on the moon, scooped up a lunar sample, measured abundances by alpha scattering, and sent the measurements back to earth as strings of zeros and ones. At the time, some doubted the reliability of the Surveyor results, in particular the high values of titanium and the low values of sodium. "Many doubting Thomases had to wait for the first Apollo landing on the Moon in July of 1969 to be convinced," wrote Anthony Turkevich, University of Chicago chemist and one of the developers of the Surveyor measurement methods [91, p. 23]. And convinced they were since the rock samples brought back by the Apollo missions showed the Surveyor measurements had been exceedingly accurate.

3.2 ONE OR MORE CATEGORIES OF MEASUREMENTS OF ONE QUANTITATIVE VARIABLE: GRAPHING DISTRIBUTIONS

Frequently, the goal of a data analysis is to study the distribution of one or more categories of measurements of a quantitative variable. That is, we want to study where the data for each category lie along the measurement scale.

An example of the study of distributions is shown in Figure 3.12. The data are from an experiment [51] on a special type of stereogram called a *random dot stereogram*, which was invented by Bela Julesz for studying visual perception [70, 71]. A viewer sees a three-dimensional object that is formed by a left and a right image, each of which has the appearance of tightly packed random dots. Typically, a viewer does not immediately see the object in such a stereogram, but after concentrating on the images for a while the object suddenly appears. The data in Figure 3.12 are the times taken by subjects to see a particular stereogram in which the viewed object was a spiral ramp pointing toward the viewer. Subjects were given varying types of prior information about what they were going to see, to determine if prior information can reduce appearance times. In Figure 3.12 there are two groups of measurements, where the grouping is based on the prior information given. The NV subjects received either *no* information or *verbal* information. The VV subjects received a combination of *verbal* and *visual* information. The NV group as whole received less prior information than the VV group, and the goal is to see if the distribution of the VV times is reduced compared with that for the NV times.

Point Graphs and Histograms

One standard way to show measurements of a variable or to compare different sets of measurements of a variable is to graph each set

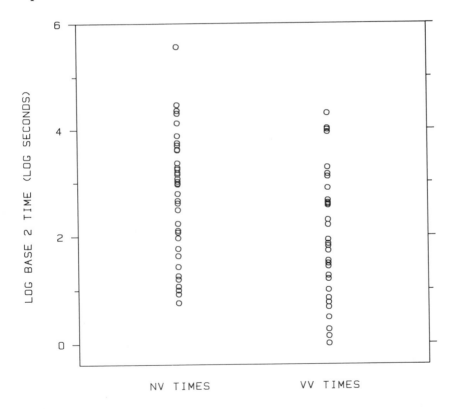

Figure 3.12   POINT GRAPH. The data are the times that two groups of people took to see a complex random dot stereogram. The goal is to compare the distributions of the two sets of data. In this figure two point graphs are used to make the comparison.

of values along a line. Such a *point graph* is used in Figure 3.12 to show the stereogram times.

Another standard method for studying distributions is the *histogram*, one of the staples of scientific graphics that has a long history going back at least to the 19th century. In Figure 3.13 the stereogram times are shown by histograms. The variable on the vertical scales is percent of counts — 100 times the number of counts in each interval divided by the total number of observations, which is 43 for the NV times and 35 for the VV times. Since the numbers of observations are different for the two groups, using the percent of counts in each interval rather than the counts themselves provides a more effective comparison of the two distributions.

A point graph is a reasonable display when the number of observations is not large. In Figure 3.12 we probably have reached the upper limit of the number of values that can be effectively shown without offsetting the plotting symbols in the horizontal direction to avoid overlap. When the number of values is large, or even moderate, the histogram is the better display to use. This is illustrated in Figure 3.14; the histogram shows redshifts of quasars from a catalog compiled by Adelaide Hewitt and Geoffrey Burbidge, two astronomers at the Kitt Peak National Observatory in Tucson, Arizona [59].

It should be remembered that a histogram reduces the information in the data. A measured value, such as redshift, is itself usually an interval of values because there is limited accuracy in measuring devices and because data are often rounded. When a histogram is made, the interval width of the histogram is generally greater than the data inaccuracy interval, so accuracy is lost. As we decrease the interval width of a histogram, accuracy increases but the appearance becomes more ragged until finally we have what amounts to a point graph. In most applications it makes sense to choose the interval width on the basis of what seems like a tolerable loss in the accuracy of the data; no general rules are possible because the tolerable loss depends on the subject matter and the goal of the analysis. (One exception to this statement is the very small fraction of cases in which the purpose of the histogram is to estimate a probability density rather than to simply show the data [44, 114]; this usage will not be treated here.)

Point graphs and histograms certainly do a good job of showing us individual distributions of data sets, but they generally do not provide *comparisons* of distributions that are as incisive as methods that will be described later in this section. From Figures 3.12 and 3.13 there is a suggestion that the VV times are less than the NV times — that is, that the increased prior information given to the VV group reduced viewing

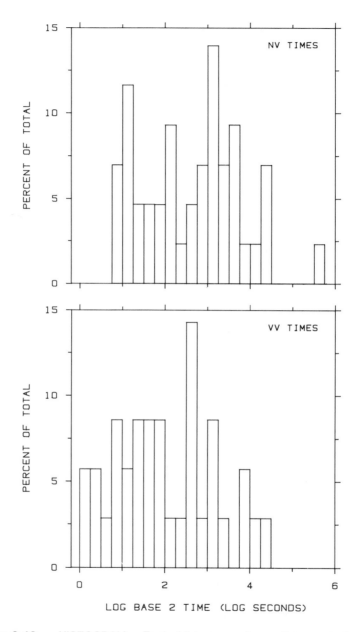

Figure 3.13   HISTOGRAM.   Each histogram shows the percentage of values in intervals of equal length.   The histogram does a good job of displaying each data set, but is usually not as effective for comparing distributions as other methods.

times — but the two graphs give us little quantitative information about the magnitude of the difference.

Percentile Graphs

Figure 3.15 shows *percentile graphs* of the two distributions of stereogram times. A *p*th *percentile* of a distribution is a number, q, such that approximately p percent of the values of the distribution are less

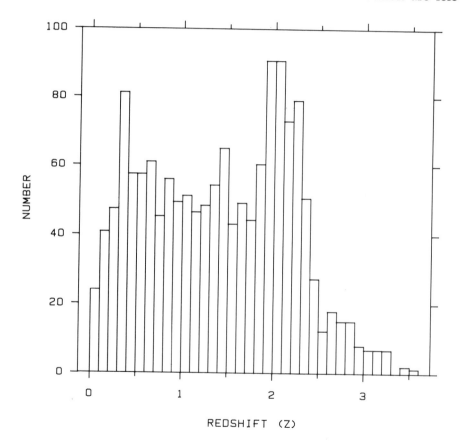

Figure 3.14   HISTOGRAM. In most applications it makes sense to choose the interval width on the basis of what seems like a tolerable loss in accuracy of the data. In this example the width is 0.1 units.

than or equal to q; p is the *p-value* of q. Suppose x_1 is the smallest observation in a data set, x_2 is the next to smallest, and so forth up to x_n, which is the largest observation. For example, if the data are

$$5 \quad 1 \quad 9 \quad 3 \quad 14 \quad 9 \quad 7$$

then

$$x_1 = 1 \quad x_2 = 3 \quad x_3 = 5 \quad x_4 = 7 \quad x_5 = 9 \quad x_6 = 9 \quad x_7 = 14 \ .$$

We will take x_i to be the p_ith percentile of the data where

$$p_i = 100 \ \frac{i-0.5}{n} \ .$$

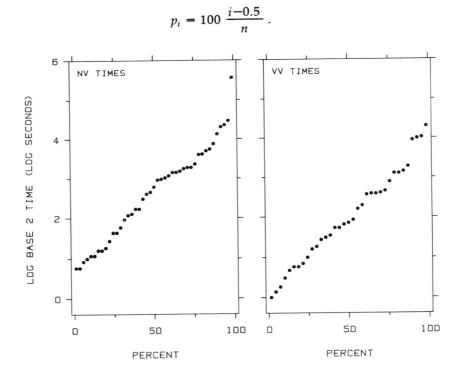

Figure 3.15   PERCENTILE GRAPH. On each panel, the data are graphed against their *p*-values. The *p*-value for an observation is very nearly the percentage of the data that is less than or equal to the observation; the observation is said to be the *p*th percentile.

For the above set of seven values

$$p_1 = 100(1 - 0.5) / 7 = 7.1$$

$$p_2 = 100(2 - 0.5) / 7 = 21.4$$

and so forth to

$$p_7 = 100(7 - 0.5) / 7 = 92.9 .$$

On the percentile graph each x_i is graphed against its p-value, p_i.

Subtracting 0.5 in the formula for the p-value of x_i is a convention in statistical science [21] and arises from the desire to make the definition of the percentile of a set of data as consistent as possible with the concept of the percentile of a theoretical probability distribution, such as the normal. One piece of heuristic reasoning that might satisfy some is the following: Suppose x_i is the result of rounding. When we count how many observations are less than or equal to x_i, we count only 1/2 for x_i itself, because there is a 50-50 chance that the actual value of the observation is less than or equal to x_i, the recorded value. But for percentile graphs the subtraction of 0.5 is a trivial issue that has little affect on the visual appearance of the display.

Percentile graphs are often more effective for comparing data distributions than point graphs or histograms because the p_i are shown, which means corresponding percentiles can be compared. For example, in Figure 3.15 we can easily see that the 50th percentile, or the *median*, of the NV times is slightly less than 3 $\log_2$ seconds; this median value can be compared with that of the VV times, which is about 2 $\log_2$ seconds. Comparing percentiles is usually the most informative way to compare two distributions; we will return to this point later.

Box Graphs

It is sometimes enough, in order to convey the salient features of the distribution of a set of data, to show just a summary of the data. One such summary, shown in Figure 3.16, is the Tukey *box graph* [125]. The five horizontal lines on each box graph portray five percentiles whose p-values, from bottom to top, are 10, 25, 50, 75, and 90. All values in the data set above the 90th percentile and below the 10th percentile are graphed, as on a point graph.

We need a rule to compute the percentiles that appear on the box graph. So far, we know only that x_i is the p_ith percentile. It is not always the case that the p_i will happen to include the numbers needed for the box graph. For the example introduced earlier, the x_i and p_i are

i	x_i	p_i
1	1	7.1
2	3	21.4
3	5	35.7
4	7	50
5	9	64.3
6	9	78.6
7	14	92.9

In this example, one of the x_i happened to be the 50th percentile, however, none of the other box graph percentiles appear. We can get other percentiles by linearly interpolating the x_i and p_i values.

Here is a simple way to do the linear interpolation. Let p be the p-value of the percentile. We want a value of v such that

$$100 \frac{v-0.5}{n} = p .$$

Solving for v we get

$$v = \frac{np}{100} + 0.5 .$$

If v turns out to be an integer then x_v is the pth percentile. However, v will often not be an integer. Let k be the integer part of v and let f be the fractional part; for example, if $v = 10.375$ then $k = 10$ and $f = 0.375$. The pth percentile using linear interpolation is

$$(1-f)x_k + fx_{k+1} .$$

Let us apply this to the computation of the 25th percentile for the above set of seven values.

$$v = \frac{7 \cdot 25}{100} + 0.5$$

$$= 2.25 .$$

The 25th percentile is

$$0.75 \, x_2 + 0.25 \, x_3$$

$$= 0.75 \cdot 3 + 0.25 \cdot 5$$

$$= 3.5 \, .$$

The interpolation rule always leads to a simple result for the 50th percentile; if n is odd, it is the middle observation, $x_{(n+1)/2}$ and if n is even, it is the average of the two middle observations, $x_{n/2}$ and $x_{n/2+1}$.

Box graphs have many strengths. One is that the chosen percentiles can be compared effectively. For example, in Figure 3.17 we can see easily that the 50th percentiles of the NV times and VV times differ by

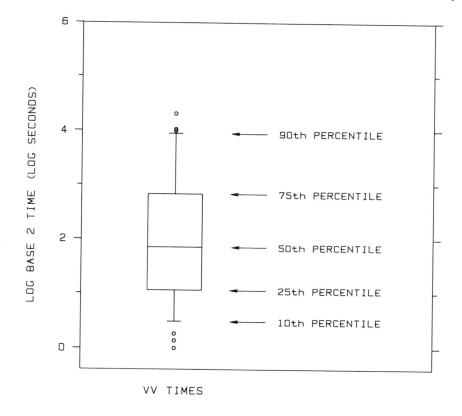

Figure 3.16   TUKEY BOX GRAPH. A box graph shows selected percentiles of the data, as illustrated in this figure. All values beyond the 10th and 90th percentiles are graphed individually as on a point graph.

roughly one $\log_2$ second, or a factor of 2. A second strength is that by graphing the large and small values, unusual values are not swept under the rug as they often are when the summary of the distribution consists of a sample mean and a sample standard deviation. (This point will be discussed further in Section 3.7.) Finally, box graphs can be used even when the number of distributions is not small.

In Figure 3.18 ten distributions are compared by box graphs. The data on the vertical axis are the payoffs from 254 runnings of the daily New Jersey Pick-It Lottery from May 22, 1975 to March 16, 1976 [102], just after the lottery began. In this game a player picks a three-digit number from 000 to 999. It costs 50¢ to bet on one number. Players who selected the winning number share the prize, which is half of the

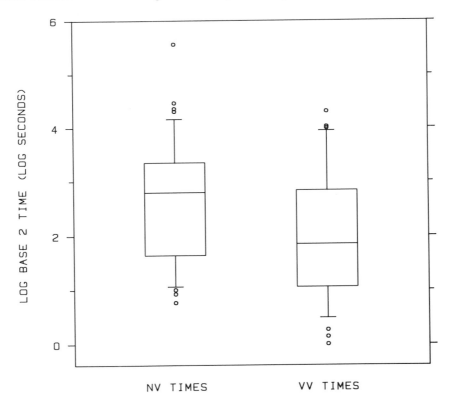

Figure 3.17   BOX GRAPH. Box graphs are an excellent way to compare distributions because they allow us to compare corresponding percentiles. In this example we see the 50th percentile of the NV times is greater than that for the VV times by about one $\log_2$ second, or a factor of 2.

money bet on that day. Since the drawing of the winning number is random, so that all numbers are equally likely, the best strategy is to pick a number that few other people are likely to pick.

The payoffs in Figure 3.18 have been divided into ten groups according to the winning number. The first group, labeled "0", is winning numbers from 000 to 099; the second group is 100 to 199; the third group is 200 to 299; and so forth. Thus the ten box graphs give a comparison of the ten distributions of payoffs.

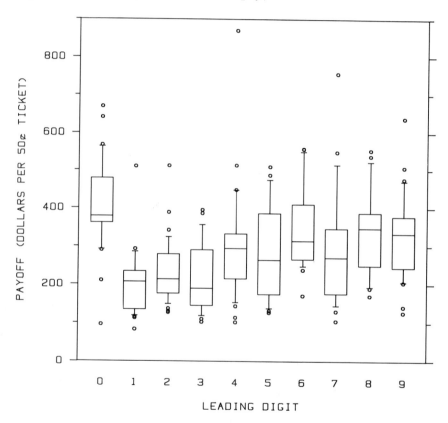

Figure 3.18 BOX GRAPH. The vertical scale is payoff of the New Jersey lottery, or numbers game, in which a player picks a three-digit number from 000 to 999. Winners share half of the pot. Each box graph shows the distribution of payoffs for all numbers with a particular leading digit. A leading digit of zero has the highest payoffs because fewer people tend to pick them. As the leading digit increases from one to nine the payoffs increase in a zigzag fashion, showing odd first digits are preferred to even.

Figure 3.18 has a clear message: the payoffs for numbers starting with zero tend to be high, which means bettors avoid them. One exception to this behavior is a zero-starting number with a payoff around $100, which is nearly the lowest value of all payoffs; in this case the winning number was 000, and it is not surprising that it was a popular one. There is an interesting trend in the remaining nine groups of numbers. The payoffs tend to increase in going from the smaller to the larger numbers, but in a zigzag fashion, suggesting that odd first digits are preferred to even.

If bettors' choices were uniformly distributed over all the numbers, the expected payoff would be $250 (not $500 since the state takes half of the money). However, the graph suggests that by the right choice of a number with a leading 0 we might be able to push the expected payoff above $500, the break-even point. Unfortunately, this is no longer true. Richard Becker and John Chambers showed that as time went along New Jersey Pick-It players caught on, the distribution of chosen numbers became more nearly uniform, and the maximum payoffs declined and rarely exceeded $500 [9].

The details of the box graph given in Figure 3.16 are not meant to create dogma. Variations are often sensible. Figure 3.16 is already a variation of the original method, which is called a *box plot* by its inventor, John Tukey [125]. In a particular application it might make sense to choose other percentiles or to eliminate the graphing of the individual large and small values or to draw the box graphs horizontally rather than vertically. Also, procedures other than linear interpolation can be used to compute percentiles. One simple rule is to select the x_i whose p_i comes closest to the p-value of the desired percentile. In the above example the 25th percentile would be 3 using this procedure, since its p-value, 21.4, is closest to 25. If n is not small, say n is greater than 50, linear interpolation and this procedure will usually give similar results.

Percentile Graphs with Summaries

The percentile graph and the box graph can be combined as in Figure 3.19 to form a *percentile graph with summary*. The horizontal reference lines show the five percentiles of the box graph; this allows us to compare these five percentiles with more visual efficiency than if the reference lines were not there.

Percentile Comparison Graphs

The *percentile comparison graph* was invented in 1966 by Martin Wilk and Ram Gnanadesikan [135]. It is not widely known in science and technology, but its use deserves to spread because of its enormous power for comparing two data distributions.

When distributions are compared, the goal is usually to rank the categories according to how much each has of the variable being measured; for the stereogram times we want to know which group took more time, and for the lottery data we are interested in finding the leading digits that give the highest payoffs.

The most effective way to investigate which of two distributions has more is to compare the corresponding percentiles. This was the insightful observation of Wilk and Gnanadesikan and their invention

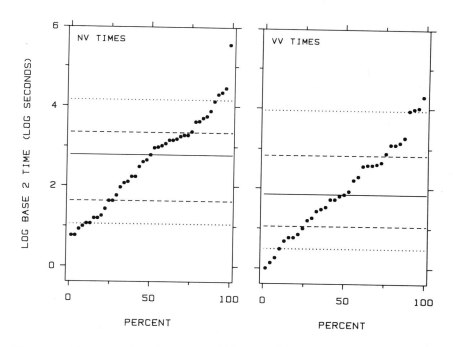

Figure 3.19   PERCENTILE GRAPH WITH SUMMARY. The five percentiles of the box graph are shown on a percentile graph by horizontal lines.

could not be more simple or elegant — graph the percentiles of one distribution against the corresponding percentiles of the other distribution. For example, we might graph the 50th percentile of the first data set against the 50th of the second data set, the 75th percentile of the first against the 75th percentile of the second, and so forth.

The top panel of Figure 3.20 is a percentile comparison graph; the two data sets are the scores of males and the scores of females on the verbal SAT test in 1983 [111]. There were 464,733 people in the males' data set and 497,809 in the females' data set. The highest possible score on the test is 800 and the lowest is 200. The following are the p-values of the percentiles of the distributions that are shown on the graph: 1   2   3   4   5   10   20   30   40   50   60   70   80   90   95   96   97   98   99. The point in the lower left corner of the data region is the 1st percentile for the males against the 1st percentile for the females, and the point in the upper right corner of the data region is the 99th percentile for the males against the 99th percentile for the females. The bottom panel of Figure 3.20 uses the Tukey sum-difference graph, discussed in Section 3.1, to give a clearer picture of the differences of the percentiles.

How do we make the percentile comparison graph? Suppose, first, that there is a moderate number of observations in the smaller of the two data sets, say no more than 50. Let $x_1,...,x_n$ be the first data set, ordered from smallest to largest, and let $y_1,...,y_m$ be the second set of data, also ordered.

Suppose $m = n$. Then y_i and x_i are both $100(i-0.5)/n$ percentiles of their respective data sets, so we would make the percentile comparison graph by graphing y_i against x_i. Thus in the $m = n$ case the graph is quite simple — we just graph the ordered values for one group against the ordered values of the other group.

Suppose $m < n$. Then y_i is the $100(i-0.5)/m$ percentile of the y data, so on the percentile comparison graph we graph y_i against the $100(i-0.5)/m$ percentile of the x data, which typically must be computed by interpolation. Thus in the case of an unequal number of observations in the two data sets, there are as many points on the graph as there are values in the smaller of the two data sets.

Figure 3.21 illustrates the unequal case; the display is a percentile comparison graph of the stereogram data: the 43 NV times and 35 VV times. There are 35 points on the graph. For example, the 9th VV time is $y_9 = 1.0$ $\log_2$ seconds; this is a percentile with p-value 24.3, and it is graphed against the 24.3 percentile of the NV times, which was computed by interpolating the 10th and 11th NV times, y_{10} and y_{11}; the interpolated value is 0.06 $y_{10} + 0.94$ $y_{11} = 1.62$ $\log_2$ seconds.

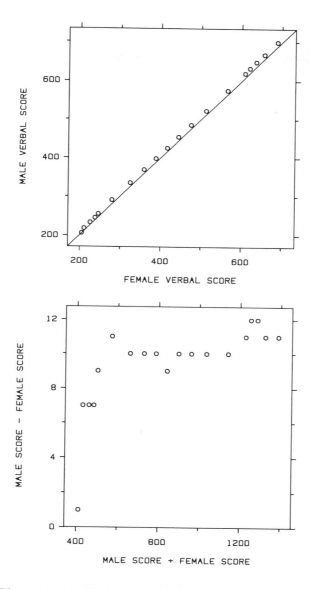

Figure 3.20   PERCENTILE   COMPARISON   GRAPH.   The   percentile
comparison graph, illustrated in the top panel, is a simple but powerful tool
for   comparing   two   distributions.   Percentiles   from   one   distribution   are
graphed against corresponding percentiles from the other distribution. The
data in this figure are scores of males and females on the verbal SAT test.
The percentiles compared are 1, 2 ,..., 5; 10, 20 ,..., 90; and 95, 96 ,..., 99.
The bottom panel is a Tukey sum-difference graph of the values in the top
panel.   The   graph   shows   that   throughout   most   of   the   range   of   the
distribution, scores of males are about 10 points higher.

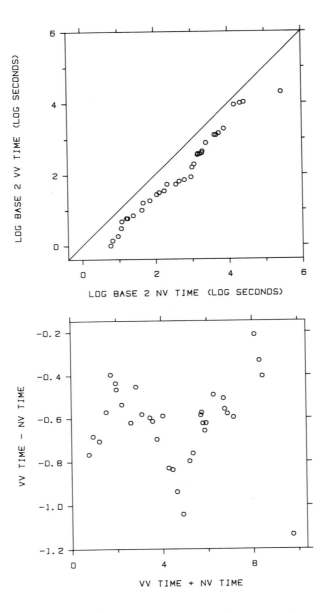

Figure 3.21 PERCENTILE COMPARISON GRAPH. In the top panel percentiles of the VV times are graphed against corresponding percentiles of the NV times. The bottom panel is a Tukey sum-difference graph. Throughout the entire range of the distribution the NV times are greater than the VV times; the average increase is about 0.6 $\log_2$ seconds, which is a factor of 1.5.

Suppose the smaller of the two data sets has a large number of values. For example, for the SAT data the smaller group, the males, has 464,899 values. We do not need, of course, to graph 464,899 points, because far fewer points can characterize the differences between the two distributions. In such a case a liberal helping of percentiles, with p-values ranging from close to 0 to close to 100, can be graphed against one another. In many cases, as few as 15 to 25 percentiles can adequately compare the two distributions. This procedure was used for the percentile comparison graph of the SAT scores in Figure 3.20.

The question of which of two distributions has more and by how much is a simple one whose answer can be complicated. The percentile comparison graph, by giving us a detailed comparison of the two distributions, can show whether the answer is simple or complicated, and if complicated, just what the complication is. This will be illustrated by several examples.

Figure 3.20 shows that the way in which the scores of males and females differ is relatively simple. Throughout most of the range of the distribution the males' percentiles are about 10 points higher than the females' percentiles, but at the very bottom end the difference tapers off. Thus a reasonable summary of the pattern of the points is a line parallel to the line $y = x$ with an equation $y = x + 10$. The comparison of the two distributions can be summarized by the simple statement, the males' scores are about 10 points higher throughout most of the range of the distributions.

Figure 3.22 is a percentile comparison graph of made-up test scores. The pattern is a line through the origin with equation $y = 0.8x$. Now it is not true that the corresponding percentiles differ by a constant amount as they did for the verbal SAT scores; now the high percentiles differ by more than the low ones. But because the general pattern is a line through the origin with slope 0.8, the percentage decrease of the males' scores is a fixed amount. That is, because the males' scores, y, are approximately related to the females' scores, x, by $y = 0.8x$, we have $(y-x)/x = -0.2$, which means the males' scores are approximately 20% lower throughout the range of the distribution.

If we were to take the logarithms of the values in Figure 3.22 the multiplicative pattern would be transformed into an additive pattern like Figure 3.20. In Figure 3.21, logarithms performed such a multiplicative-to-additive transformation for the stereogram times. The general pattern of the points in Figure 3.21 is a line, $y = x + k$, where k is about 0.6 $\log_2$ seconds. Had we graphed the points without taking logarithms the general pattern would have been a line through the origin with slope $2^{0.6} = 1.5$.

Figure 3.23 compares two other sets of hypothetical scores. The pattern of the data is a line with a slope less than 1; the line $y = x$ intersects this pattern at the 50th percentiles of the distributions. The 50th percentiles of the two groups are equal, but the distributions differ in a major way: the high scores for the females are higher than the high scores for the males, and the low scores for the males are higher than the low scores for the females. The two distributions are centered at the same place but the females' scores are more spread out.

Figure 3.24 also compares hypothetical scores. Throughout most of the range of the distribution, males and females are the same, but at the

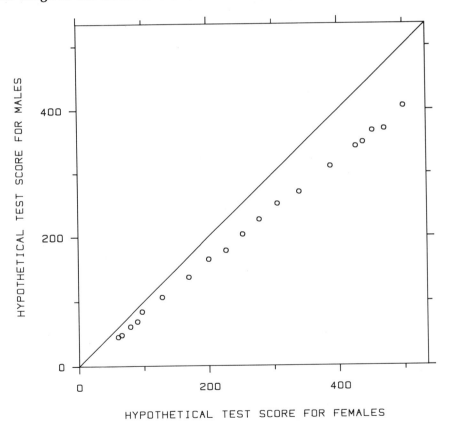

HYPOTHETICAL TEST SCORE FOR FEMALES

Figure 3.22   PERCENTILE COMPARISON GRAPH. The data are hypothetical test scores. Since the points lie close to a line through the origin with slope 0.8, scores of males are about 20% lower throughout most of the range of the distribution.

very top end the females have higher scores. That is, the exceptionally high scores for the females are better than the exceptionally high scores for the males.

Figure 3.25 is back to real data: 1983 mathematics SAT scores for males and females [111]. The top panel compares the same percentiles that are compared for the verbal scores in Figure 3.20; the bottom panel is a Tukey sum-difference graph. From the 99th to the 50th percentile most of the percentiles for the males are 55 to 60 points higher than those for the females. But from the 50th percentile to the lowest percentiles the differences decrease from about 55 points to about 10

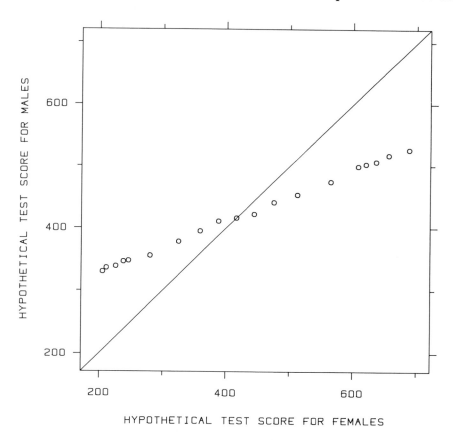

Figure 3.23 PERCENTILE COMPARISON GRAPH. The points lie close to a line that has slope less than one, and the 50th percentiles lie on the line *y* = *x*. Thus the 50th percentiles, or middles, of the two distributions are the same but the female scores are more spread out.

points. The way in which the scores of males and females differ is considerably more complicated than the simple linear patterns in some of the previous percentile comparison graphs.

Means are often used to characterize how two distributions differ, but this often misses important information or worse yet, misleads. The mean scores for the math test are 445 for the females and 493 for the males, a difference of 48. Using just the means misses the important fact that high scorers, middle scorers, and low scorers differ by different amounts. Data distributions can be complicated, and when they are, the percentile comparison graph can reveal the complication to us.

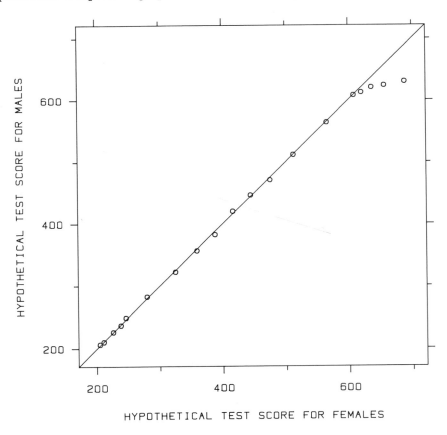

Figure 3.24   PERCENTILE COMPARISON GRAPH. Throughout most of the range of the distribution, male and female scores are nearly the same, but for the very highest percentiles, female scores are higher.

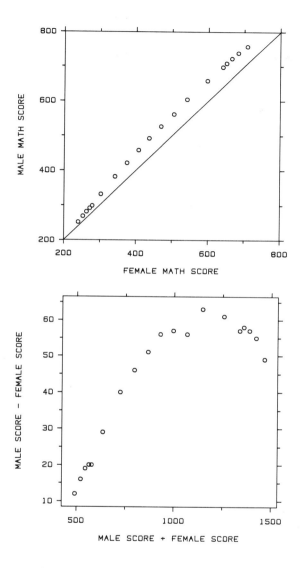

Figure 3.25   PERCENTILE COMPARISON GRAPH. The top panel is a percentile comparison graph of scores of males and females on the math SAT test. The same percentiles graphed in Figure 3.20 are graphed here. The bottom panel is a Tukey sum-difference graph of the values in the top panel. The graph shows that for the top half of the distributions, scores of males are typically 55 to 60 points higher, and that for the bottom half the difference ranges from 10 to 55 in going from the lowest percentiles to the 50th. The average scores, 445 for the females and 493 for the males, do not convey nearly as much information about how the two distributions differ.

3.3 ONE QUANTITATIVE VARIABLE WITH LABELS: DOT CHARTS

Ordinary Dot Charts

We often need to display measurements of a quantitative variable in which each value has a label associated with it. Figure 3.26 shows an example. The data are from a survey on the amount of use of graphs in 57 scientific publications [27]. For each journal, 50 articles from the period 1980-1981 were sampled. The variable graphed in Figure 3.26 is the fraction of space of the 50 articles devoted to graphs (not including legends) and the labels are the journal names. Figure 3.26 is a *dot chart*, a graphical method that was invented [28] in response to the standard ways of displaying labeled data — bar charts, divided bar charts, and pie charts — which usually convey quantitative information less well to the viewer than dot charts. (This is demonstrated in Section 4 of Chapter 4.)

When there are many values in the data set, as in Figure 3.26, the light dotted lines on the dot chart enable us to visually connect a graphed point with its label. When the number of values is small, as in Figure 3.27, the dotted lines can be omitted, since the visual connection can be performed without them.

The data in Figure 3.27 are the ratios of extragalactic to galactic energy in seven frequency bands [93], where energy is measured per unit volume. The frequencies in the seven bands increase in going from the top of the graph to the bottom. In five of the seven bands the galaxies have much higher intensities than the space between galaxies. One of these five bands is visible light; this should come as no surprise since on a clear night on the earth we can see galactic matter in the form of stars (or light reflected from a star by our moon) and only blackness in between. For microwaves and x-rays there is much more energy coming from outside the galaxies. The extragalactic microwave radiation, discovered by Nobel prize winners Arno Penzias and Robert Wilson of AT&T Bell Laboratories in 1965 [107], has an explanation: it is the remnant of the big bang that gave our universe its start. But the extragalactic x-ray radiation remains a mystery whose solution might also tell us something fundamental about the structure of the universe.

When they appear, the dotted lines on the dot chart are made light to keep them from being visually imposing and obscuring the large dots that portray the data. When we visually summarize the distribution of the data, the data dots stand out and the graph is a percentile graph,

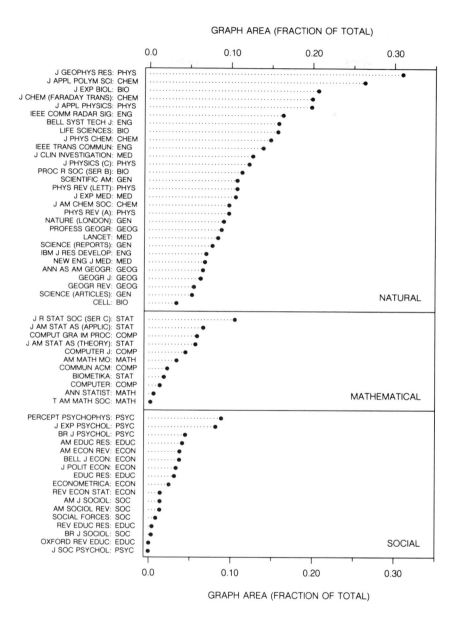

GRAPH AREA (FRACTION OF TOTAL)

Figure 3.26   DOT CHART. A dot chart shows the fraction of space devoted to graphs for 57 scientific journals. The dot chart is a graphical method for data where each numerical value has a label. The dotted lines, which enable us to connect each value with its label, end at the data dots because the baseline is zero.

provided the data are ordered from smallest to largest. When we want to emphasize this distribution, a *p*-value scale can be put on the right vertical scale line as in Figure 3.28.

The data in Figure 3.28 are the per capita state taxes (sales, income, and fees for state services) in the 50 states of the U.S. during the fiscal year 1980 [137, p. 116]. The graph shows that state taxes vary by a factor of about 3. New Hampshire, the state where so many presidential candidates have gotten their start, or their finish, is clearly a state ready to listen to candidates who advocate lower taxes.

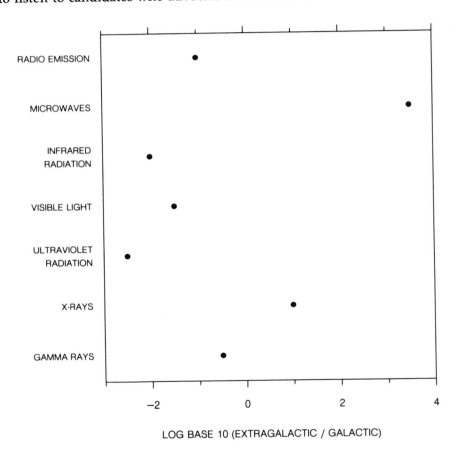

LOG BASE 10 (EXTRAGALACTIC / GALACTIC)

Figure 3.27   DOT CHART. The dotted lines are omitted because the labels and the numerical values can be visually connected without them.

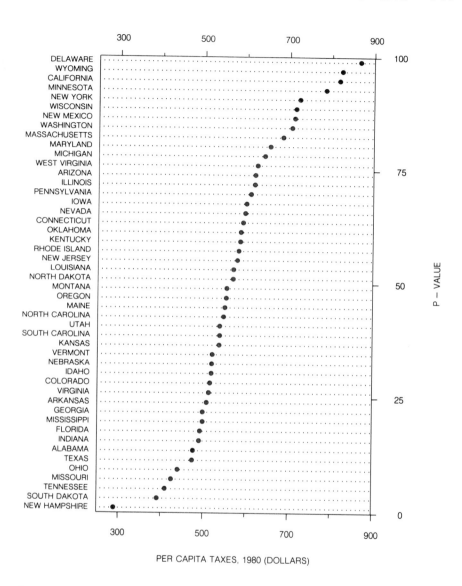

Figure 3.28 DOT CHART. When the data are ordered from smallest to largest, the dot chart provides a percentile graph; the *p*-values are shown by the right vertical scale line. The dotted lines go all of the way across the graph. The baseline is a number near 275, and if the dotted lines ended at the data dots, line length would encode taxes minus a number near 275 that has no significant meaning.

When there is a zero on the scale of a dot chart, or some other meaningful baseline value from which the dotted lines emanate, then the dotted lines can end at the data dots, as in Figure 3.26. The dotted lines should go across the graph when the baseline value has no particular meaning, as in Figure 3.28. Here is the reason. When the dotted lines stop at the data dots, there are two aspects of the graphical symbols that encode the quantitative information — the lengths of the dotted lines and the relative positions of the data dots along the common scale. The lengths of the dotted lines encode the magnitudes of the deviations from the baseline. In Figure 3.26 the baseline is zero, so line length encodes the fractional graph areas, which is perfectly reasonable. However, if the baseline value has no important meaning, the deviations have no meaning. Suppose that in Figure 3.28 the dotted lines ended at the data dots. Then line length would encode taxes minus a number around 275. Since this number has no significant meaning in this application, line length would be encoding meaningless values; changing line length would be wasted energy and might even have the potential to mislead. By making the dotted lines go across the graph in Figure 3.28, the portions between the left vertical scale line and the data dots are visually de-emphasized.

The dotted lines also should go across the graph when there is a scale break, as in Figure 3.29, which graphs speeds of animals [136]. If we stopped the dotted lines at the data dots in this figure, those that were broken by the scale break would not have any meaning, even though the baseline is meaningful.

Two different methods can be used to put scale breaks on dot charts. One, shown in Figure 3.29, is to use a vertical full scale break. A second method, shown in Figure 3.30, can be used when better resolution is needed on one or both sections of the scale; for example, the resolution of the scale for the slowest four animals is considerably better in Figure 3.30 than in Figure 3.29.

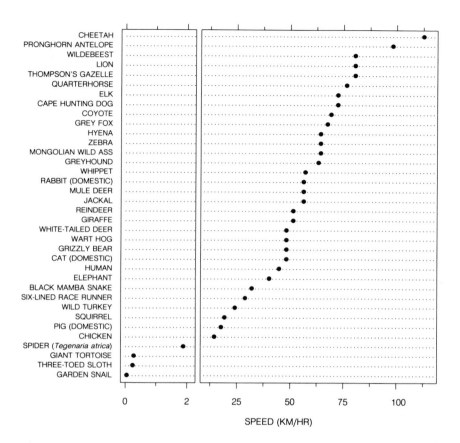

Figure 3.29   DOT CHART. A vertical full scale break is used on this dot chart. The dotted lines go all of the way across the graph since if they ended at the data dots, the lengths of those crossing the break would be meaningless.

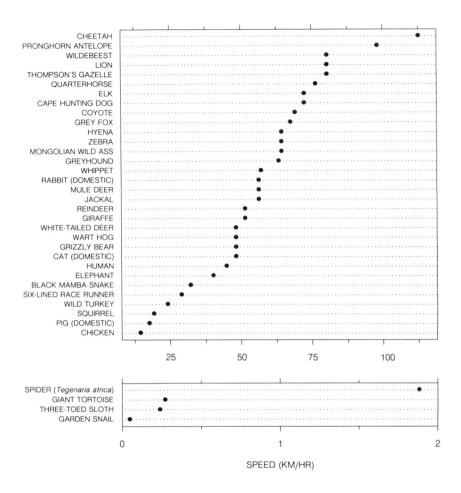

Figure 3.30 DOT CHART. This method can be used to break the scale of a dot chart when better resolution is needed on one or both panels formed by a vertical full scale break.

Two-Way, Grouped, and Multi-Valued Dot Charts

Figure 3.31 is a *two-way dot chart,* a method for showing labeled data that form a *two-way classification.* In this case the two-way data are the percentages of U.S. immigrants from six groups of nationalities during four time periods [76]. (The percentages add to 100% for each time period.) An observation is classified by the time period and the nationality group. Each column of the graph shows the values for one time period and each row shows one nationality. The graph portrays clearly the data's main event: The proportions for Europeans and Canadians have decreased through time and those for Asians and Latin Americans have increased.

Another way to show two-way data is by a *grouped dot chart.* In Figure 3.32 the immigration data are grouped by nationality group and in Figure 3.33 they are grouped by time period. The first grouped dot chart emphasizes the changes through time and the second emphasizes the mixture of nationality groups for each time period.

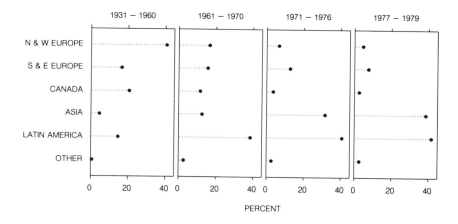

Figure 3.31   TWO-WAY DOT CHART. The two-way dot chart can be used to show data classified by two factors. In this example the data are the percentages of immigrants in six nationality categories for four time periods.

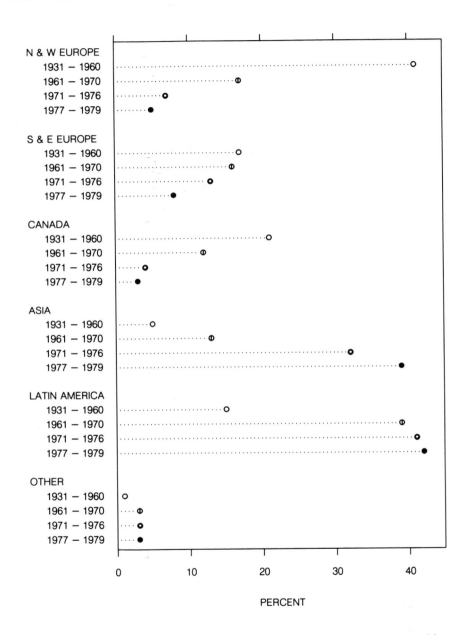

Figure 3.32   GROUPED DOT CHART. The immigration data are grouped by nationality. This emphasizes the time trend in the data for each nationality group.

A final way to show two-way data, provided one of the two groupings has a small number of categories, is the *multi-valued dot chart* in Figure 3.34. The data are the immigration percentages for just the first and last time periods.

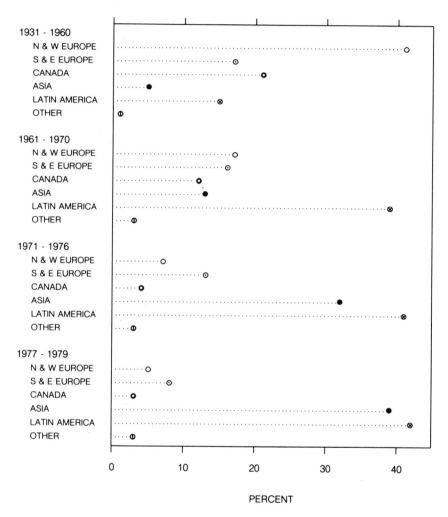

Figure 3.33   GROUPED DOT CHART. The immigration data are grouped by time. This emphasizes the mixture of nationality groups for each time period.

3.4 TWO QUANTITATIVE VARIABLES

Many scientific investigations are aimed at discovering how two quantitative variables are related. An example is measurements of caloric intake and blood sugar levels for a group of people, where the purpose is to discover how the two variables are related. In a two-variable study we often want to find out how one, the *dependent variable*, depends on the other, the *independent variable*. For example, we might want to know how blood sugar depends on caloric intake. This section is about graphing two quantitative variables.

Overlap: Logarithms, Residuals, Moving, Sunflowers, Jittering, and Circles

In Section 2 of Chapter 2 it was pointed out that a recurring problem of graphing two variables is overlapping plotting symbols, which is caused by graph locations of different values being identical or very close. When overlap occurs, different plotting symbols can obscure

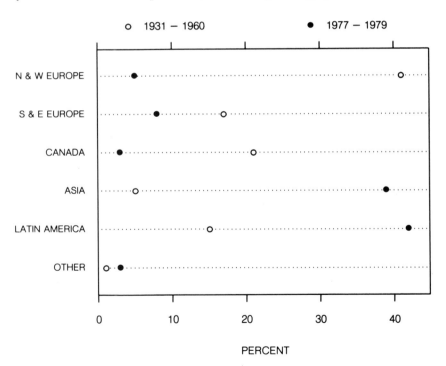

Figure 3.34   MULTI-VALUED DOT CHART. The dot chart is multi-valued because there is more than one value on each line.

one another and we can lose an appreciation of the values of the data. Methods that help avoid a loss of visual distinguishability will now be described.

When both scales of a two-variable graph have poor resolution, severe overlap can occur. This is illustrated in Figure 3.35, which shows brain weights and body weights of 27 animal species [113, p. 39]. The values of each variable are skewed to the right, that is, most of the data are squashed together near the origin and a few values stretch out toward the high end of the scale. In Section 1 of this chapter and in Section 4 of Chapter 2 we have seen that taking logarithms and graphing residuals are two methods that can improve resolution; for this

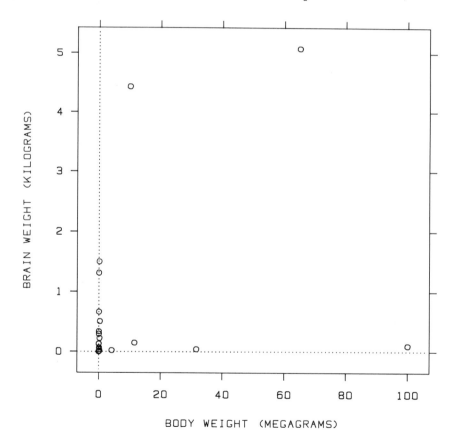

Figure 3.35   OVERLAP. Overlapping plotting symbols must be visually distinguishable. If the resolution along both scales of a two-variable graph is poor because the measurements are skewed, overlap can cause problems, as on this graph.

reason these two methods can reduce or eliminate overlap. For Figure 3.35, logarithms solve the problem; in Figure 3.36 logarithms are graphed and now there is no overlap.

The top panel of Figure 3.37 shows data on magnetic moments and beta decays of mirror nuclei [19]. Theory suggests that the variable on the vertical scale is linearly related to the variable on the horizontal scale, and the data support the theory since the points lie close to the line on the graph, which was fitted using least squares on all but three of the points. Plotting symbols on the graph overlap because the data are squashed together along the line. Graphing residuals in the bottom panel of 3.37 improves the resolution and nearly eliminates the overlap.

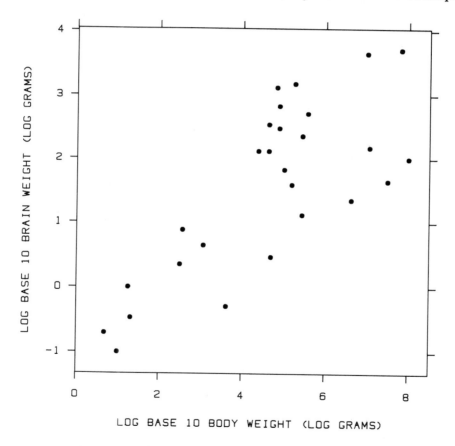

Figure 3.36 LOGARITHMS. The logarithms of the data in Figure 3.35 are graphed and now there is no overlap. Taking logs will often alleviate the overlap caused by skewed positive data.

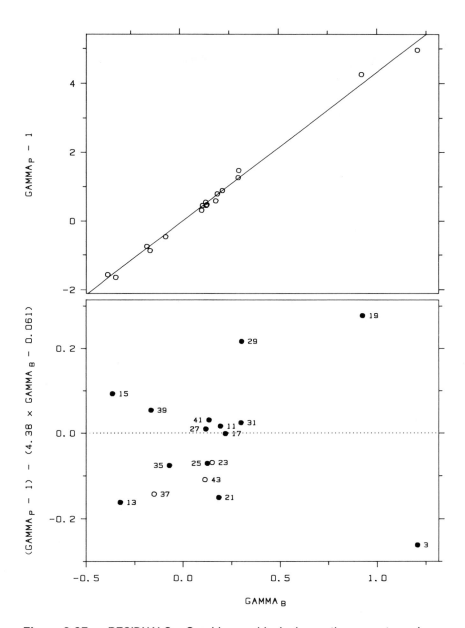

Figure 3.37   RESIDUALS. Graphing residuals is another way to reduce overlap. The data in the top panel are squashed together along the line. Graphing residuals in the bottom panel improves the resolution and nearly eliminates the overlap.

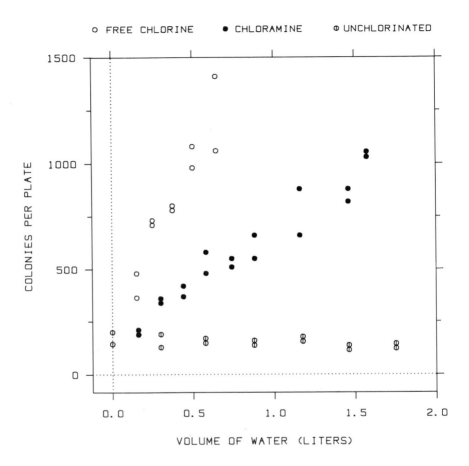

Figure 3.38   MOVING. If the number of overlapping plotting symbols is small, the graph locations of the points can be altered slightly to reduce the overlap. On this graph, symbols that just touch one another have been moved vertically.

Information now can be added to the graph; the numbers by the points are mass numbers and points graphed with unfilled circles are those omitted in the least squares fit. The two panels of Figure 3.37 show far more about the data than the top panel alone.

Another method for fighting overlap that works well if the number of overlapping symbols is small, is to move slightly the graph locations of certain points. This has been done in Figure 3.38; the data are from an experiment on the production of mutagens in drinking water [23]. Any symbol that touches another has had its actual location altered slightly. It is, of course, important to mention this movement if the graph is used to communicate quantitative information to others.

Sunflowers are a graphical method that can relieve exact and partial overlap [34]. They are illustrated with geological data in Figure 3.39 [25] and with data on graphical perception in Figure 3.40 [35]. A dot by itself means one point. A dot with line segments (petals) means more than one point; the number of petals indicates the number of points. The method is helpful when there is exact overlap or when many points are crowded into a small region. For the data in Figure 3.40 there is exact overlap; for Figure 3.39 the overlap is not exact, but points are very close to one another. When there are a large number of points on the graph there is a need for a sunflower algorithm: partition the data region into squares, count the number of points in each square, use sunflowers to show the counts, and position them in the centers of the squares.

The data in Figure 3.40 are from a perceptual experiment that will be discussed in detail in Section 3 of Chapter 4 [35]. Subjects judged the distances of four points — A, B, C, and D — from a line and recorded the percents that the B, C, and D distances were of the A distance. The true percents for B, C, and D were 52.5%, 47.5%, and 57.5% respectively. Figure 3.40 graphs the judged percents for D against the percents for B for 126 subjects. The graph was made to see if the judgments are correlated, an important issue whose answer affected the way the data were analyzed. The graph shows clearly that there is a large amount of

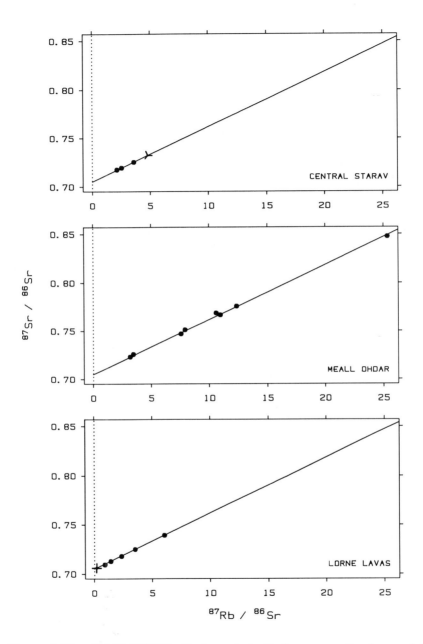

Figure 3.39 SUNFLOWERS. Each symbol with lines emanating from a dot is a sunflower. The number of petals (lines) is the number of data points at or near the center of the sunflower; sunflowers can be used to solve the overlap problem.

correlation. There is substantial overlap of the graph locations because answers tended to be multiples of 5. Figure 3.41 shows a scatterplot of the judgments with the overlap problem ignored, and only 51 points appear; not showing the multiplicity is misleading.

Another solution for exact overlap of graph locations is *jittering*: adding a small amount of random noise to the data before graphing [21]. This is illustrated in Figure 3.42 for the perception data. Jittering is a simpler remedy than sunflowers, but does not help, as sunflowers can, when resolution is degraded by a large number of partially overlapping symbols.

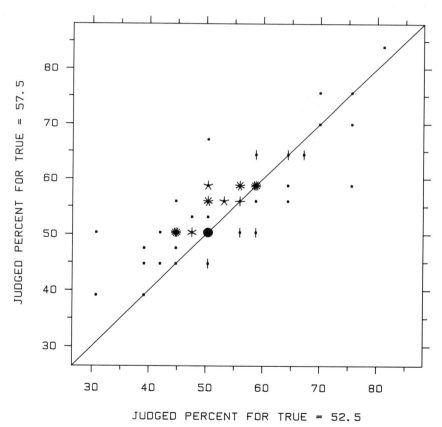

Figure 3.40   SUNFLOWERS. The sunflowers in this example alleviate exact overlap in the data.

If there is only partial overlap and no exact overlap, using an unfilled circle as the plotting symbol can improve the distinguishability of individual points [34]. This is illustrated in Figure 3.43. Circles can tolerate substantial partial overlap and still maintain their individuality. (Examples outside the graph domain are the symbol of the Olympics and the three-ring sign for Ballantine beer.) The reason is that distinct circles intersect in regions that are visually very different from circles. Squares, rectangles, and triangles do not share this property and degrade more rapidly.

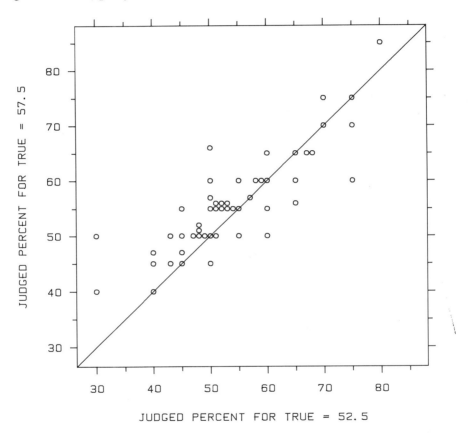

Figure 3.41   OVERLAP. This graph shows the result of graphing the data in Figure 3.40 and ignoring the overlap. Not indicating the multiplicity is misleading.

Box Graphs for Summarizing Distributions of Repeat Measurements of a Dependent Variable

Suppose the data consist of many repeat measurements of a dependent variable, y, for each of several different levels of an independent variable, x. One way to graph such data is illustrated in Figure 3.44. Each box graph portrays 25 values of the dependent variable for each of 11 distinct values of the independent variable; the center of the box graph is positioned horizontally at the value of the independent variable. In a sense we are back to the setting of

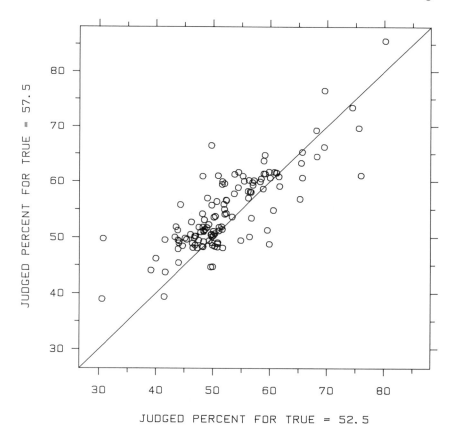

JUDGED PERCENT FOR TRUE = 52.5

Figure 3.42   JITTERING. Another way to fight exact overlap is to add a small amount of random noise to the data. Now all of the data from Figure 3.41 can be seen.

Section 3.2 on graphing distributions, since the goal is to see how the distribution of the measurements of the dependent variable changes as the independent variable changes.

The data in Figure 3.44 are from an interesting experiment in bin packing [11]: k numbers, called weights, are randomly picked from the interval zero to u, where u is a positive number less than or equal to one; for the data in Figure 3.44, u was 0.8. There are bins of size one and the object is to pack the weights into those bins; no overflowing is allowed, and we can use as many bins as necessary, but the goal is to use as few as possible. Unfortunately, to do this in an optimal manner is an NP-complete problem, which means that for anything but very small values of k the computation time is enormous. Fortunately, there are heuristic algorithms which, while not optimal, do an extremely good

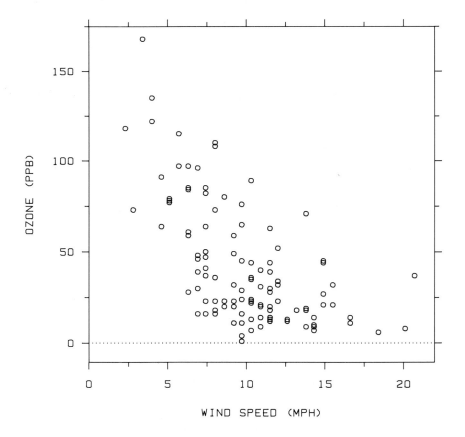

Figure 3.43   CIRCLES. Unfilled circles are good plotting symbols since they tend to maintain their individuality when there is partial overlap.

job of packing. Mathematicians and computer scientists had studied the worst-case behavior of bin packing [37] but there came a point where many appreciated that average behavior was an important issue as well; algorithms can be studied profitably by probing them with inputs, sometimes randomly generated, and using graphs and statistical methods to study the results [11].

In Figure 3.44 the horizontal scale shows the number of weights, k, on a log base 10 scale. k varies from 125 to 128,000 by steps of a factor 2; that is, the first number is 125, the second is 250, and so forth up to $125 \times 2^{10} = 128,000$. There were 25 runs of the bin packing procedure for each value of k; for each run, k weights were chosen randomly from the interval 0 to 0.8 and a packing carried out. The

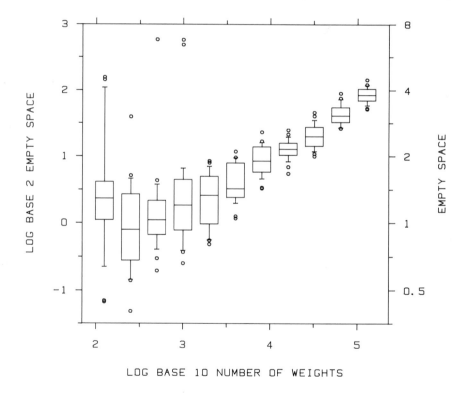

LOG BASE 10 NUMBER OF WEIGHTS

Figure 3.44   BOX GRAPHS FOR REPEAT MEASUREMENTS OF A DEPENDENT VARIABLE. The purpose of the graph is to see how the dependent variable, the variable on the vertical axis, depends on the independent variable, the variable on the horizontal axis. For each value of the independent variable there are 25 measurements of the dependent variable; the distribution of these 25 values is summarized by a box graph.

algorithm used to do the packing was *first fit decreasing*: The weights are ordered from largest to smallest and are packed in that order. For each weight the first bin is tried; if it has room, the weight is inserted and if not the second bin is tried; if the second bin has room, the weight is inserted and if not, the third bin is tried; the algorithm proceeds in this way until a bin with room, possibly a completely empty one, is found. The vertical scale in Figure 3.44 is the logarithm base 2 of the amount of empty space in the bins that have at least one weight. Since the bin size is one, this amount of empty space is equal to the number of bins used minus the sum of the weights. In this example, empty space is the dependent variable and number of weights is the independent variable.

What does Figure 3.44 show us about bin packing? One thing is that the first-fit-decreasing algorithm is very efficient. The amount of empty space is never greater than 8 in these runs. For runs of size 128,000 the performance is superlative; the median empty space is about 4 even though the sum of the weights in this case averages $128,000 \times 0.8/2 = 51,200$. The figure also shows that median log empty space grows nonlinearly with log number of weights, although the pattern becomes linear for large numbers of weights. This latter result is predicted by a theorem about the asymptotic behavior of empty space [12]. Figure 3.44 also shows that for the smaller numbers of weights there are outliers: values that are large compared to the majority of the values.

Strip Summaries Using Box Graphs

Box graphs can be used even when there are no repeat measurements of the dependent variable by grouping the data according to the values of the independent variable. This grouping is illustrated in Figure 3.45. The data have been divided into five groups by vertical strips with as nearly an equal number of observations in each strip as possible. In Figure 3.46 box graphs summarize the distributions of the y values for the five strips. Each box graph is centered, horizontally, at the median of the x values for its strip.

The data in this example, which were also graphed in Section 2 of Chapter 2, are from an experiment on 144 hamsters in which their lifetimes and the fractions of their lifetimes they spent hibernating were measured [89]. The objective of the experiment was to see how lifetime depends on hibernation. Figure 3.46 shows that as fraction of lifetime spent hibernating increases, the distribution of lifetime increases.

Smoothing: Lowess

One hypothesis suggested by Figure 3.46 is that hamster DNA parcels out a fixed amount of nonhibernation hours; a hamster gets only so much awake time, and if it hibernates longer, it lives longer by the same amount, but otherwise there is no effect on lifetime. Suppose ℓ = lifetime and p = fraction of lifetime spent hibernating. If this hypothesis is true then $(1-p)\ell$, the amount of time spent not hibernating does not depend on $p\ell$, the amount of time spent hibernating.

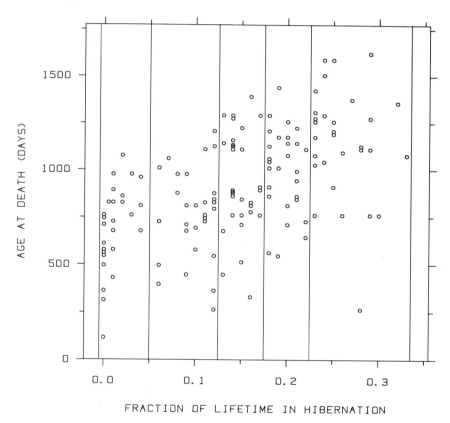

Figure 3.45   DEPENDENT-INDEPENDENT VARIABLE DATA. Age at death is graphed against fraction of lifetime spent hibernating for 144 hamsters. The data have been divided into five strips with nearly equal numbers of points, in preparation for the graph in Figure 3.46.

Figure 3.47 is a graph of time spent not hibernating against time spent hibernating. It shows that, overall, the hypothesis is false; increased hibernation time results in increased nonhibernation time. But how would we describe the dependence? Is there a linear or nonlinear dependence? With a graph of just the (x_i, y_i) values it is hard to answer these questions.

We could study the dependence by strip summaries with box graphs, but Figure 3.48 shows another method: a smooth curve put through the points. For each point, (x_i, y_i), on the graph there is a

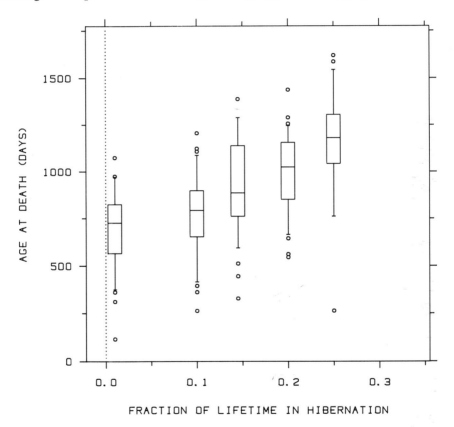

Figure 3.46   STRIP SUMMARIES USING BOX GRAPHS. The distribution of the *y* values of the points in each of the five vertical strips of Figure 3.45 is shown by a box graph. Each box graph is centered, along the horizontal scale, at the median of the *x* values of the points in the strip.

smoothed value, $(x_i, \hat{y}_i)$. $\hat{y}_i$ is the *fitted value* at x_i. The curve is graphed by connecting successive smoothed values, moving from left to right, by lines. The purpose of the curve is to summarize the *middle* of the distribution of y for each value of x. Thus the curve is performing the same task as the medians of the box graphs in strip summaries; if we took a narrow vertical strip, the curve should describe the middle of the distribution of the y values in the strip. Statistical scientists call this a *regression curve*, a misnomer since there is nothing regressive about it at all. The method used to compute the smoothed values will be discussed later.

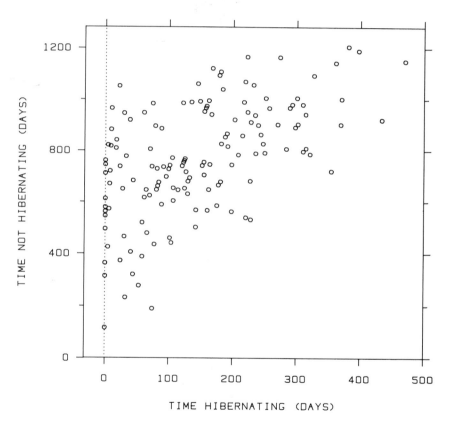

Figure 3.47   DEPENDENT-INDEPENDENT VARIABLE DATA. The total time spent not hibernating is graphed against the time spent hibernating for the 144 hamsters. There appears to be a dependence of y on x but it is difficult to assess the nature of the dependence from the graph.

The smooth curve shows that there is some truth to the hypothesis stated earlier. While there is, overall, an increase in nonhibernation lifetime as hibernation increases, the response is in fact constant until the amount of hibernation is above 100 days. From 100 days and above, the effect is nearly linear and the slope is about 1, so each minute spent hibernating beyond 100 days produces on the average about one extra minute of nonhibernation lifetime. We have been assuming that there is a causal mechanism, but this is reasonable in view of current biological information [89].

The curve in Figure 3.48 was produced by a data smoothing procedure called *robust locally weighted regression* [26]; the name of the procedure is often shortened to *lowess* (locally-weighted scatterplot

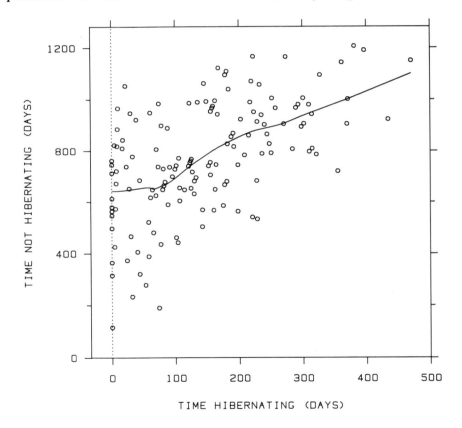

Figure 3.48 LOWESS. The smooth curve, which was computed by a procedure called lowess, summarizes how *y* depends on *x*. For each point, (x_i, y_i), on the graph, lowess produces a smoothed value, $(x_i, \hat{y}_i)$. The curve is graphed by connecting successive smoothed values, moving from left to right, by straight lines.

smoother). The user must choose a smoothness parameter f, which is a number between 0 and 1. As f increases, the smooth curve becomes smoother. In Figure 3.48 the value of f is 0.5 and in Figure 3.49 it is 0.25. Lowess is very computing intensive, but there is a fast, efficient computer program that carries it out [110].

Choosing f requires some judgment for each application. In most applications an f that works well is usually between 0.5 and 0.8. The goal is to try to choose f to be as large as possible to get as much smoothness as possible without distorting the underlying pattern in the data.

Residuals, useful in so many situations, can help in choosing f. This will be illustrated with an example. Figure 3.50 is a graph of the air pollutant ozone against wind speed for 111 days in New York City

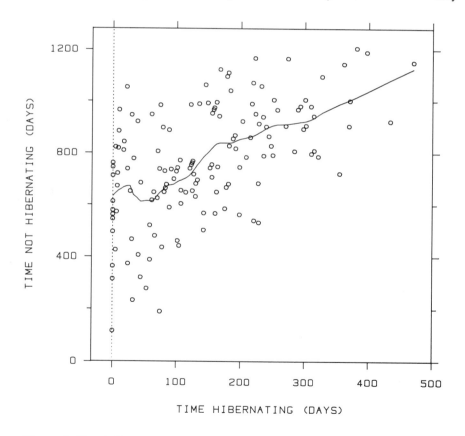

Figure 3.49   LOWESS. The smoothness of the lowess curve depends on a smoothness parameter, f, which varies between 0 and 1. As f increases the curve becomes smoother. In Figure 3.48, $f = 0.5$ and in this figure, $f = 0.25$.

from May 1 to September 30 of 1973. From this graph we can see that the general pattern is for ozone to decrease as wind speed increases because of the increased ventilation of air pollution that higher wind speeds bring. However, it is difficult to see more precise aspects of the pattern, for example, whether there is a linear or nonlinear decrease.

The top panel of Figure 3.51, which has a lowess curve with $f = 0.8$, suggests the decrease is nonlinear. How do we know the lowess curve is not distorting the pattern? Since we cannot discern easily the pattern when a lowess curve is absent we cannot expect to assess easily how well lowess is doing. The solution is to graph $y_i - \hat{y}_i$ against x_i, add a lowess smoothing to this graph of residuals, and see if there is an effect. This is illustrated in the bottom panel of Figure 3.51.

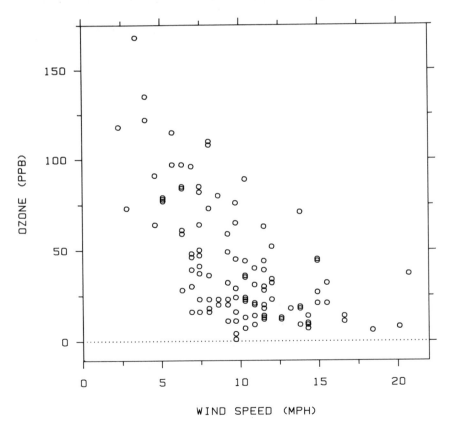

Figure 3.50   DEPENDENT-INDEPENDENT VARIABLE DATA. The data are daily measurements of ozone and wind speed for 111 days. It is difficult to see the nature of the dependence of ozone on wind speed.

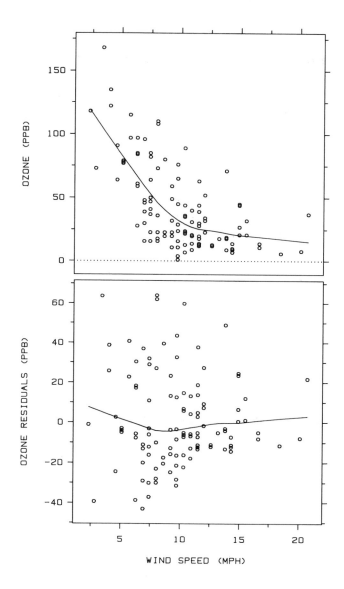

Figure 3.51   CHECKING LOWESS. On the top panel the graph from
Figure 3.50 now has a lowess curve with $f = 0.8$. It is difficult to assess
visually whether lowess is correctly depicting the dependence. On the
bottom panel the residuals, $y_i - \hat{y}_i$, are graphed against x_i, and a lowess
curve is superposed; the curve suggests there is a small dependence of the
residuals on x_i, which means f is too large in the smoothing of the top
panel.

The lowess curve suggests that there is some dependence of the residuals on x_i. This should not happen; the curve should be nearly a horizontal line since the residuals should be variation in y_i not explainable by x_i. The problem is that the lowess smoothing in the top panel has missed part of the pattern because f is too large, and this missed part has gone into the residuals.

In Figure 3.52, f has been reduced to 0.5. The curve on the graph of the residuals is now reasonably close to a horizontal line, so the amount of smoothing for the curve in the top panel is not too great.

This method of graphing and smoothing residuals is a one-sided test: it can show us when f is too large but sets off no alarm when f is too small. One way to keep f from being too small is to increase it to the point where the residual graph just begins to show a pattern, and then use a slightly smaller value of f.

Lowess is quite detailed and mathematical, and a full discussion of how it works would sidetrack us too much. In the remainder of this section a brief description will be given; the details can be found in the source [26] or in [21]. Suppose the x_i are ordered from smallest to largest so that x_1 is the smallest and x_n is the largest. For each pair of values, (x_i, y_i), lowess produces a fitted value, $\hat{y}_i$. Figure 3.53 shows how the fitted value is computed at one x_i. Look at the upper left panel. The data, which are made up, are shown by the unfilled circles; the value of x_i at which the fitted value is to be computed is x_6, which is marked by the vertical dotted line. The value of f is 0.5 in this example; it is multiplied by 20, the number of observations, which gives the number 10. We now pick from among the x_i the 10th closest x_i to x_6, which is x_1. (x_6 itself is included in this count.) A vertical strip, depicted by the solid vertical lines, is defined by putting the left boundary of the strip at x_1 and the right boundary on the other side of x_6 at the same distance from x_6 as x_1.

Look at the lower left panel. A weight function, $w(x)$, is defined. The points, (x_i, y_i) for $i = 1$ to n, are assigned weights $w(x_i)$. Notice that (x_6, y_6) has the largest weight; moving away from x_6 the weight function decreases and becomes zero at the boundaries of the strip.

Look at the upper right panel. A line is fitted to the points of the graph using *weighted* least squares with weight $w(x_i)$ at (x_i, y_i). This means that (x_6, y_6) plays the largest role in determining the line and the role played by other points decreases as their x values increase in distance from x_6. Points on and outside the strip boundary play no role at all. The fitted value, $\hat{y}_6$, is the y-value of the line at $x = x_6$. The point $(x_6, \hat{y}_6)$ is depicted by the filled circle.

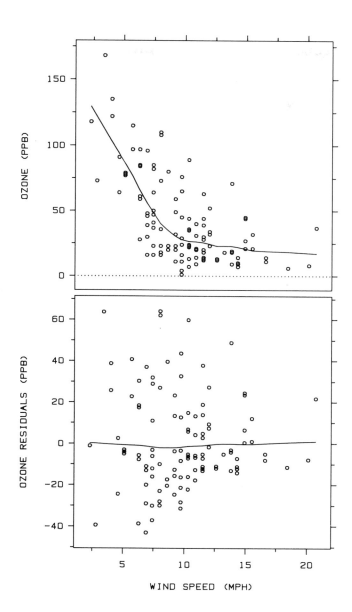

Figure 3.52   CHECKING LOWESS. On the top panel the value of *f* for lowess has been reduced to 0.5 since Figure 3.51 suggests *f* = 0.8 is too large. The bottom panel shows no dependence of the residuals on x_i, which suggests the lowess curve with *f* = 0.5 is not distorting the pattern of the dependence of ozone on wind speed.

Look at the lower right panel. The result of the previous operations is the one lowess smoothed value, $(x_6, \hat{y}_6)$, shown by the filled circle. The same operations are carried out for each point, (x_i, y_i), on the graph.

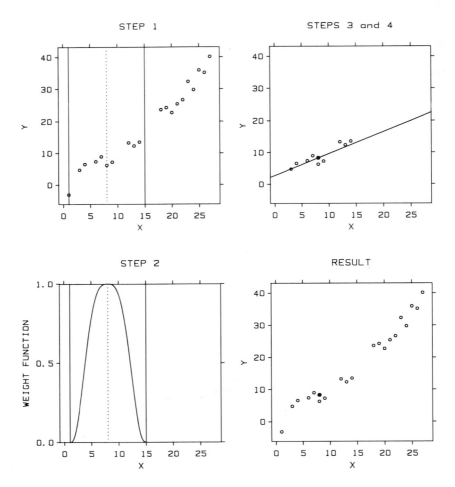

Figure 3.53   HOW LOWESS WORKS. The graphs show how the fitted value at x_6 is computed. (Top Left) f, which is 0.5, is multiplied by 20, the number of points, which gives 10. A vertical strip is defined around x_6 so that the boundary is at the 10th nearest neighbor. (Bottom Left) Weights are defined for the points using the weight function. (Top right) A line is fitted using weighted least squares. The value of the line at x_6 is the lowess fitted value, $\hat{y}_6$. (Bottom right) The result is one value of lowess, shown by the filled circle. The computation is repeated for each point on the graph.

Figure 3.54 shows the sequence of operations for the rightmost point, (x_{20}, y_{20}). The right boundary of the strip does not appear in the two left panels because it is beyond the right extreme of the horizontal scale line.

There is another piece to the lowess algorithm. What has been described is the locally weighted regression part of robust locally weighted regression. There is also a *robustness* part. Suppose the data contain one or more *outliers*; an outlier is a point, (x_i, y_i), with an

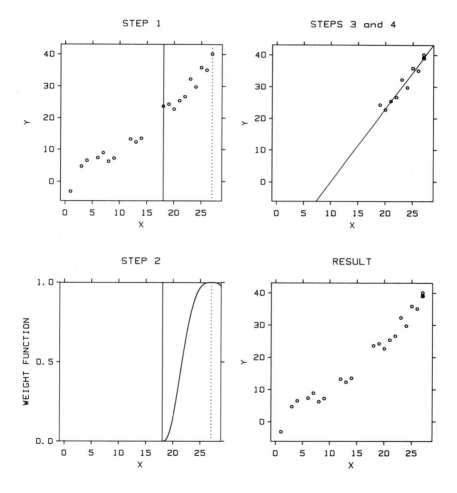

Figure 3.54 HOW LOWESS WORKS. The computation of the lowess fitted value at x_{20} is illustrated.

unusually large or small value of y_i compared with other points in a vertical strip around x_i. The upper panel of Figure 3.55 shows an example. The unfilled circles are the data and one point, (x_{11}, y_{11}), has a y value that is much larger than the y values of points whose x values are close to x_{11}. Carrying out lowess as described above yields the filled circles; the outlier has distorted the fitted values in the neighborhood of x_{11} so that the general pattern of the data is no longer described.

Lowess has a robustness feature in which, after a first smoothing as described above, outliers are identified and downweighted in a second smoothing. This identification, downweighting, and resmoothing can be done any number of times, although two times is almost always sufficient. The result of the full lowess algorithm, including the robustness part, is shown in the lower panel of Figure 3.55. Now the smoothed values describe the behavior of the majority of the data.

Time Series: Connected, Symbol, Connected Symbol, and Vertical Line Graphs

A *time series* is a set of measurements of a variable through time. Figure 3.56 shows an example. The data are yearly values, from 1868 to 1967, of the aa index [96], which measures the magnitude of fluctuations in the earth's magnetic field. The index is the average of measurements of geomagnetic fluctuations at observatories in Australia and England that are roughly antipodal: at opposite ends of an earth diameter. Figure 3.56 shows there has been an increase in the overall level of the aa index from 1900 to 1967. The solar wind causes fluctuations in the earth's magnetic field, so the increase in the index suggests that the solar wind has increased during this century [49]. Figure 3.56 also shows the aa index has a cycle of about 11 years. This is the same as the sunspot cycle; increased sunspots are associated with increased solar activity and therefore an increased solar wind, but interestingly, the sunspots do not show an increase in their overall level, as the aa index does.

A time series is a special case of the broader dependent-independent variable category. Time is the independent variable. One important property of most time series is that for each time point of the data there is only a single value of the dependent variable; there are no repeat measurements. Furthermore, most time series are measured at equally-spaced or nearly equally-spaced points in time. These special properties invite special graphical methods which, as will be illustrated at the end of this section, are relevant for any situation with a single-valued dependent variable and an equally-spaced independent variable.

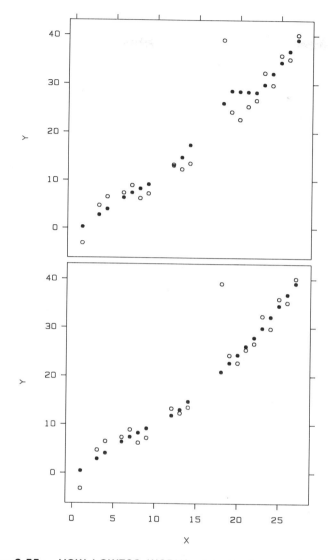

Figure 3.55 HOW LOWESS WORKS. Lowess has a robustness feature that prevents outliers from distorting the smoothed values. (Top panel) The open circles are the points of the graph; there is one outlier between $x = 15$ and $x = 20$. The smoothed values for lowess without the robustness feature, which are shown by the filled circles, have been distorted in the neighborhood of the outlier. (Bottom panel) The filled circles are from lowess with the robustness feature; now the smoothed values follow the general pattern of the data.

There are many ways to graph a time series. Figure 3.56 is a *connected symbol graph* since symbols together with lines connecting successive points in time are used. Figure 3.57 is a *symbol graph* because just the symbols are used, and Figure 3.58 is a *connected graph* because just the lines are used. Figure 3.59 is called a *vertical line graph* for the obvious reason.

Each of these four methods of graphing a time series has its data sets for which it provides the best portrayal. For the aa data the best one is the connected symbol graph. The symbol graph does not give a

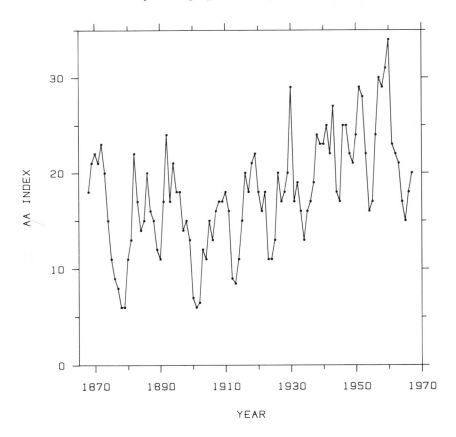

Figure 3.56 CONNECTED SYMBOL GRAPH. The time series shown on the graph is the yearly average of the aa index: measurements of the magnitudes of fluctuations in the earth's magnetic field. A connected symbol graph, which allows us to see the individual data points and the ordering through time, reveals an 11-year cycle and a trend from 1900 to 1967.

clear portrayal of the cyclic behavior, because we cannot perceive the order of the series over short time periods of several years, which makes seeing the 11-year cycle difficult. In the words of spectrum analysis, we cannot appreciate the high and middle frequency behavior of the series on the symbol graph.

On the connected graph in Figure 3.58 the individual data points are not unambiguously portrayed. For example, it is clear that there is an unusual peak in the observations around 1930, but it is hard to decide if the peak is a single outlier for one year or is supported by a rise and fall of a few values. On the connected symbol graph, and the other graphs, it is clear that the peak consists of one value.

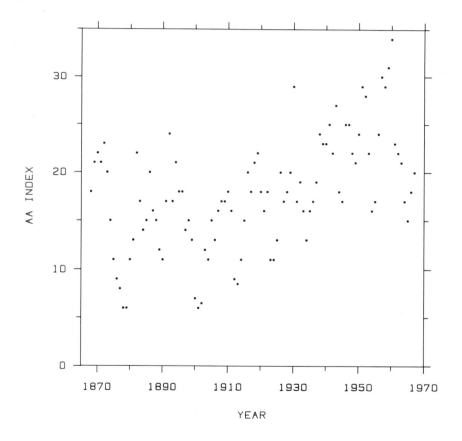

Figure 3.57   SYMBOL GRAPH. A symbol graph of the aa data does not reveal the 11-year cycle.

On the vertical line graph in Figure 3.59 there is an unfortunate asymmetry: The peaks of the 11-year cycle stand out more clearly than the troughs. There is also a disconcerting visual phenomenon: Our visual system cannot simultaneously perceive the peaks and the troughs. This is what psychophysicists call a figure-ground effect [55, pp. 10-11]; for example, there is a famous black and white drawing where if you focus on the black, you see profiles of two faces looking at one another and if you focus on the white, you see a vase, but both cannot be simultaneously perceived [55, p. 11].

There is, however, a place for vertical line, connected, and symbol graphs. A symbol graph of a time series is appropriate if what we want

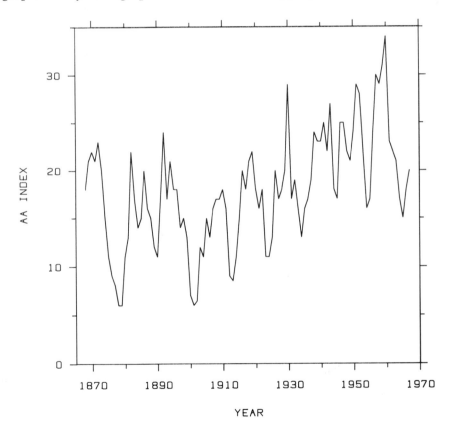

Figure 3.58   CONNECTED GRAPH. The connected graph does not reveal the positions of the aa measurements. It is not possible to determine if the peak around 1930 consists of one or many values.

to convey is the long-term trend, that is, the low frequency behavior. In such a case it is not necessary to perceive the exact time order over short time intervals. Figure 3.60 is an example. The data are the daily ozone measurements we have seen before. One very low ozone value, an outlier on the log scale, has been omitted in Figure 3.60. In this example the day-to-day movement of ozone is less interesting than the trend, so the symbol graph is used. A lowess curve with $f = 0.5$ is superposed to help us see the trend.

A connected graph is appropriate when the time series is smooth, so that perceiving individual values is not important. A vertical line graph is appropriate when it is important to see individual values, when we need to see short-term fluctuations, and when the time series has a large

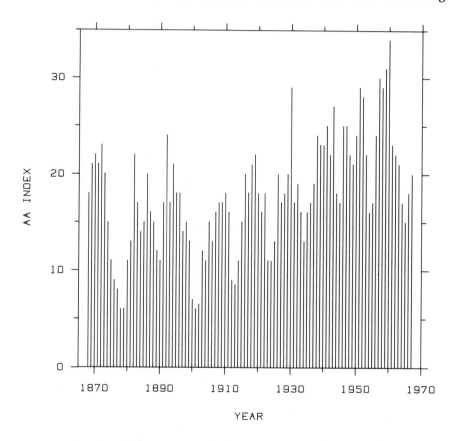

Figure 3.59   VERTICAL LINE GRAPH. On this graph the peaks stand out more clearly than the troughs.

number of values; the use of vertical lines allows us to pack the series tightly along the horizontal axis. The vertical line graph, however, usually works best when the vertical lines emanate from a horizontal line through the center of the data and when there are no long-term trends in the data.

Figure 3.61 is the graph of CO_2 and its components that was discussed in detail in Section 2 of Chapter 1. A connected graph is used for the two top panels because the data are smooth and seeing

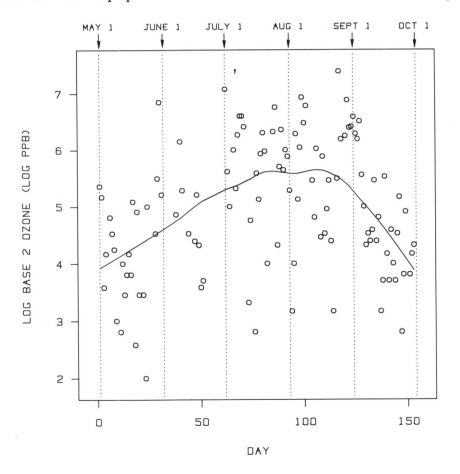

Figure 3.60   SYMBOL GRAPH. A symbol graph is appropriate for a time series when the goal is to show the long-term trend in the series, but not high frequency behavior. On this symbol graph a lowess curve is superposed to help assess the trend.

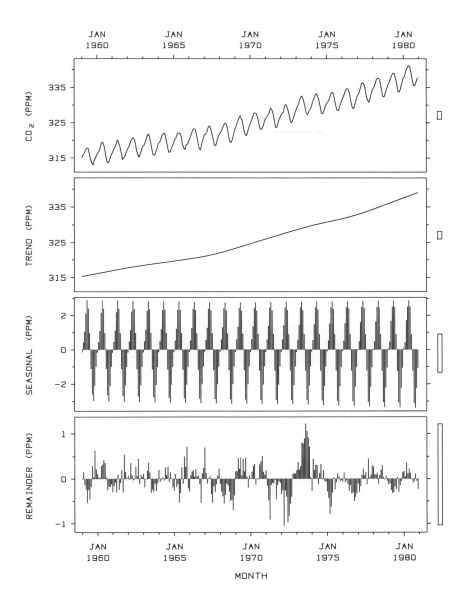

Figure 3.61   CONNECTED AND VERTICAL LINE GRAPHS. The graph shows the monthly average CO_2 concentrations from Mauna Loa and the three components. Connected graphs are used in the top two panels since it is not important to see individual values. Vertical line graphs are used in the bottom two panels since it is important to see individual values and to assess behavior over short periods of time and since each series has many values.

individual values was not judged important. A vertical line graph, emanating from zero, is used for the two bottom panels because it is important in this application to see the individual monthly values and to assess behavior over short time periods and because the time series is long.

Time Series: Seasonal Subseries Graphs

Figure 3.62 shows a *seasonal subseries graph,* a graphical method that was invented in 1980 to study the behavior of a seasonal time series or the seasonal component of a seasonal time series [36]. The data in Figure 3.62 are the seasonal component of the CO_2 series in Figure 3.61. In this example it is important to study how the individual monthly subseries are changing through time; for example, we want to analyze the behavior of the January values through time. We cannot make a graphical assessment from Figure 3.61 since it is not possible to focus on the values for a particular month; the graphical method in Figure 3.62 makes it possible.

In the seasonal subseries graph, the January values of the seasonal component are graphed for successive years, then the February values are graphed, and so forth. For each monthly subseries the mean of the values is portrayed by a horizontal line. The individual values of the subseries are portrayed by the vertical lines emanating from the horizontal line. In Figure 3.62 the January subseries is the first group of values on the left, the February subseries is the next group of values, and so forth. The graph allows an assessment of the overall pattern of the seasonal, as portrayed by the horizontal mean lines, and also of the behavior of each monthly subseries. Since all of the monthly subseries are on the same graph we can readily see whether the change in any subseries is large or small compared with the overall pattern of the seasonal component.

Figure 3.62 shows interesting features. The first is the overall seasonal pattern, with a May maximum and an October minimum. This pattern has long been recognized and is due to the earth's vegetation (See the discussion in Section 2 of Chapter 1.) The second feature is the patterns in the individual monthly subseries. Subseries near the yearly maximum tend to be increasing; the biggest year-to-year increases occur during the months March and April. Subseries near the yearly minimum tend to be decreasing; the biggest year-to-year decreases occur during the months September and October. The net effect, of course, is that the seasonal oscillations are increasing.

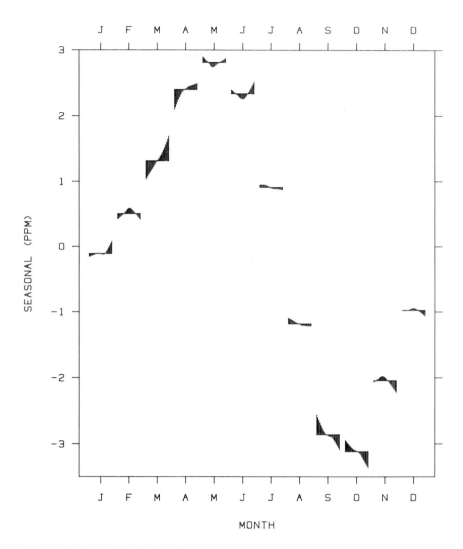

Figure 3.62   SEASONAL SUBSERIES GRAPH. The seasonal component from Figure 3.61 is graphed. First the January values are graphed for successive years, then the February values, and so forth. For each monthly subseries the mean of the values is portrayed by the horizontal line. The values of each monthly subseries are portrayed by the ends of the vertical lines. Now we can see the average seasonal change and the behavior of the individual monthly subseries. Monthly subseries near the yearly maximum tend to be increasing and those near the minimum tend to be decreasing.

An Equally-Spaced Independent Variable with a Single-Valued Dependent Variable

When two-variable data have a single-valued dependent variable and equally-spaced values of the independent variable, the methods of graphing a time series that were just discussed can be considered. Figure 3.63 shows one example. The dependent variable is an estimate of the spectrum of the aa index, and the independent variable is frequency, measured in cycles per year. There are 101 estimates of the spectrum at 101 frequencies spaced 0.005 cycles/year apart. Since the spectrum estimate is a smooth function of frequency, a connected graph was used.

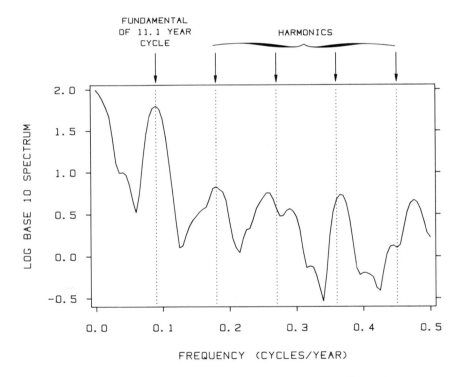

Figure 3.63   SINGLE-VALUED DEPENDENT VARIABLE WITH EQUALLY-SPACED INDEPENDENT VARIABLE. Data with a single-valued dependent variable and an equally spaced independent variable can be graphed using connected, symbol, connected symbol, and vertical line graphs. In this example the dependent variable is an estimate of the spectrum of the aa index and the independent variable is frequency. A connected graph is used to show the data.

The rise in the spectrum near zero frequency is just the trend observed earlier in the graph of the series against time. Heading toward higher frequencies, the first peak, whose frequency is marked with a vertical reference line, provides an estimate of the average fundamental frequency of the cycles in the aa index; the estimated frequency is 0.09 cycles/year, which has a period of 11.1 years. The first four harmonics (multiples) of this fundamental are also marked by reference lines. It seems likely that the peaks in the spectrum near the first three harmonics are also a result of the 11.1 year cycle.

The spectrum in this example was estimated by the following procedure: subtract the mean; multiply by a full cosine taper [15, ch. 5]; compute the squared modulus of the Fourier transform; smooth with a boxcar window with five raw spectrum values per estimate.

Step Function Graphs

A *step function graph* is appropriate when the dependent variable is constant over intervals of the independent variable. Figure 3.64 is a step-function graph that shows the weight of the Hershey Bar over a time period of about 20 years. In his essay, "Phyletic Size Decrease in

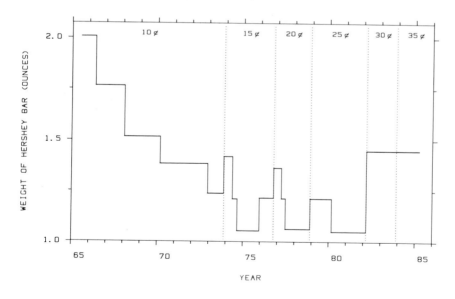

Figure 3.64   STEP FUNCTION GRAPH. The weight of the Hershey Bar is graphed against time. A step function graph is appropriate when the dependent variable is constant over intervals of the independent variable.

Hershey Bars," Stephen Jay Gould showed that the history from 1965 generally has been one of a decline in size of a bar with a fixed price, followed by a sudden rise in both price and size, and then followed by a gradual decline in size [54, pp. 313-319]. This is illustrated in Figure 3.64, which includes some additional data not available to Gould at the time.

With the additional data, we can now see something else quite striking in Figure 3.64. It appears that one ounce is a reflecting barrier below which bar weight will not drop. Maybe the barrier is psychological. Hershey executives might see one ounce as the last line of defense, and fear that were bar weight to drop below it, there would be nothing to stop its ultimate extinction. But what will happen when the United States converts to the metric system? One ounce is 28.35 grams. The human mind puts special emphasis on simple numbers, and a new psychological barrier of 25 grams may take over.

Figure 3.64 seems to beg for a new graph using just the same data as the old one, but graphed in a new way. The idea, which arises from the field of economics, is that what really counts is the cost (price) per unit of weight. In other words, how much does one bite of a Hershey Bar cost? Figure 3.65 shows the cost per ounce through time, again using a step function graph, which reveals the real law of nature: the

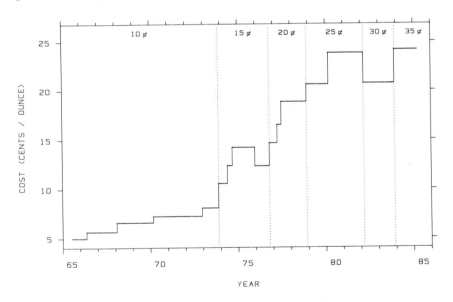

Figure 3.65   STEP FUNCTION GRAPH. The cost per ounce of the Hershey Bar is graphed against time. There are only two points in time when cost per ounce decreased.

inexorable rise in price per mouthful through time. The changing size is just a way of helping to obey the law, and we can see a critical fact not apparent in the first step function graph — every *price increase*, except the change from the 25¢ bar to the 30¢, was in fact an increase in cost per ounce. During the time period of this data there were only two points in time when cost per ounce decreased — once, when the price rose to 30¢, and once, in 1975, when the weight increased but the price stayed constant.

3.5 TWO OR MORE CATEGORIES OF MEASUREMENTS OF TWO QUANTITATIVE VARIABLES: SUPERPOSITION AND JUXTAPOSITION

This section is about graphical methods for two or more categories, or groups, of measurements of two quantitative variables. We saw in Section 2 of Chapter 2 that graphing different data sets can be a challenge. If we *superpose* them in the same data region, we must be sure that the graphical elements portraying each of the data sets can be visually discriminated from the graphical elements showing the other data sets. If we graph them on *juxtaposed* data regions we want to be able to compare the different data sets as readily as possible. This section discusses graphical methods for achieving these goals.

Superposed Plotting Symbols

Figure 3.66 has four superposed data sets. The measurements are from the survey of graphs in scientific publications discussed in Section 3.3 [27]. For a large number of scientific journals, measurements were made of the fraction of space each journal devoted to graphs (not including legends) and the fraction of space each journal devoted to graph legends. Figure 3.66 is a graph of log (legend area/graph area) against log (graph area) for 46 journals. The ratio of legend area to graph area is a rough measure of the amount of legend explanation given to graphs. The letters encode four journal categories:

Biological — biology, medicine

Physical — physics, chemistry, engineering, geography

Mathematical — mathematics, statistics, computer science

Social — psychology, economics, sociology, education.

One advantage of the letters is that it is easy to remember the groups, and looking back and forth between the graph and the key is not necessary. But a serious disadvantage of the letters is that they do not provide high visual discrimination with one another; it is hard, compared with other encoding schemes, to perceive the points for a particular group as a whole, mentally filtering out the points of other groups.

Figures 3.67 and 3.68 present two other methods for encoding the four categories. To make the ensuing discussion about visual discrimination more meaningful, look at each of Figures 3.66 to 3.68 and try to see the points of each category as a unit as if the other points were not there.

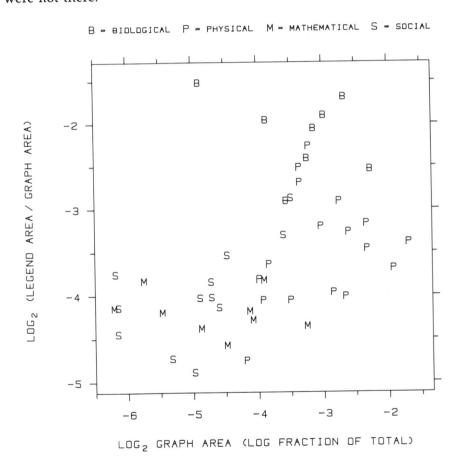

Figure 3.66   SUPERPOSED SYMBOLS. Four categories of measurements of two variables are graphed. The letters encoding the four categories do not provide high visual discrimination of the four sets of points.

The encoding scheme in Figure 3.67, commonly used in science and technology, is different geometric shapes; the visual discrimination appears somewhat greater than for the letters in Figure 3.66. It is harder to remember the category associated with a shape than with a letter, but this is a minor point. In Figure 3.68, four types of circle fill are used to encode the categories. Theoretical and experimental evidence from the field of visual perception suggests that different methods of fill should provide high visual discrimination [34]. In fact, Figure 3.68 appears to provide better discrimination than the other two figures.

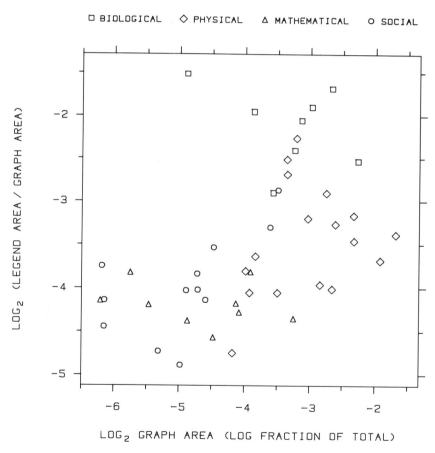

Figure 3.67   SUPERPOSED SYMBOLS. The data of Figure 3.66 are graphed with the categories encoded by differently shaped plotting symbols. This provides somewhat greater visual discrimination than using the letters.

Figure 3.68 shows two interesting phenomena: social science journals and mathematical science journals tend to use graphs less than the other two categories, and the biological science journals tend to have more in the figure legends. The second phenomenon is probably due to the tendency in biological journals to put experimental procedures in figure legends.

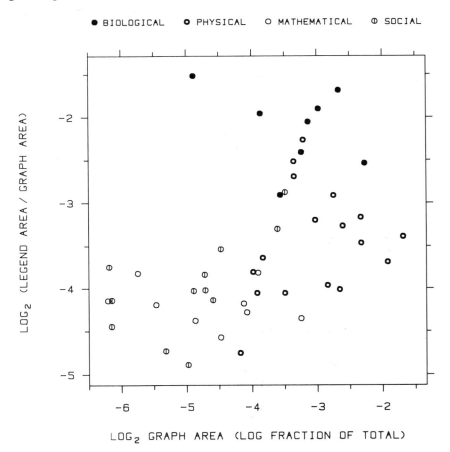

Figure 3.68 SUPERPOSED SYMBOLS. The data of Figure 3.66 are graphed with the categories encoded by circles with different methods of fill. This provides the highest visual discrimination of the methods shown in Figures 3.66 to 3.68.

The encoding scheme in Figure 3.68 works well if there is not much overlap of the plotting symbols. When there is overlap, the solid portions of the symbols can form uninterpretable blobs. In such a case we must attempt to use symbols that provide as much visual discrimination as possible, subject to the constraint that the symbols tolerate overlap. The constraint seems to restrict us to symbols consisting of curves and lines, with no solid parts, and with a minimum of ink. One encoding scheme that does reasonably well is shown in Figure 3.69.

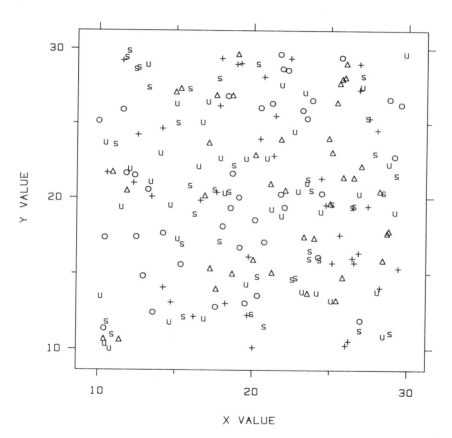

Figure 3.69   SUPERPOSED SYMBOLS. The plotting symbols used on this graph provide fair visual discrimination and can tolerate overlap.

Figure 3.70 shows two sets of plotting symbols, one in each row. The top set is to be used when there is little overlap, and the bottom set is to be used when overlap causes problems with the top set. For each set, the suggestion is to use the first two symbols on the left if there are two categories, the first three symbols on the left if there are three categories, and so forth.

Superposed Curves in Black and White

Sometimes superposed data sets come in the form of superposed curves, as in Figure 3.71. The data will be described shortly. Often, we can make each curve solid and still have the requisite visual discrimination. If at the intersection of two curves, the slopes of the curves are very different, our eyes have no trouble visually tracking each curve. For example, in Figure 3.71, *5 gt airburst* and *3 gt* are easy to follow at their crossing between 100 and 150 days. But if two curves come together with similar slopes, they can lose their identity; *5 gt* and *5 gt airburst* almost do this at their intersection just after 100 days.

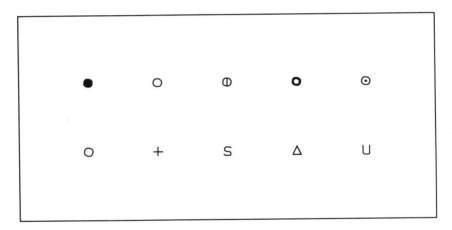

Figure 3.70   PLOTTING SYMBOLS. The top set can be used when there is little overlap, and the bottom can be used when overlap causes problems with the top set. The first two symbols on the left are to be used when there are two categories, the first three symbols are to be used when there are three categories, and so forth.

If solid curves lose their identity we can switch to different curve types, as in Figure 3.72. The goal, as it was for symbols, is to choose curves that have high visual discrimination. We want to see each curve effortlessly and as a whole and not have to visually trace it out as we do a secondary road on an automobile map. Figure 3.73 is a palette of curve types that shows the variety possible from dots and dashes.

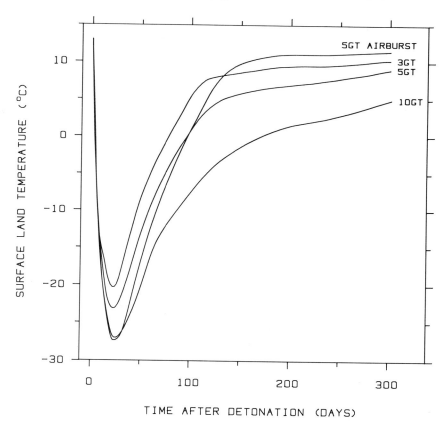

Figure 3.71 SUPERPOSED CURVES. Superposed curves need to be visually discriminated. In this case the behavior of the data is simple enough that each curve is visually distinct.

Juxtaposition

Sometimes the only solution for visual discrimination of different data sets is to give up superposition and use juxtaposition of two or more panels. This is illustrated in Figure 3.74.

Figure 3.74 shows model predictions of temperature in the Northern Hemisphere following different types of nuclear exchanges [127]. The temperatures following major exchanges drop precipitously due to soot from conflagrations of cities and forests and due to dust from soil and vaporization of earth and rock. The soot and dust substantially reduce radiation from the sun which, in turn, causes the temperature to drop.

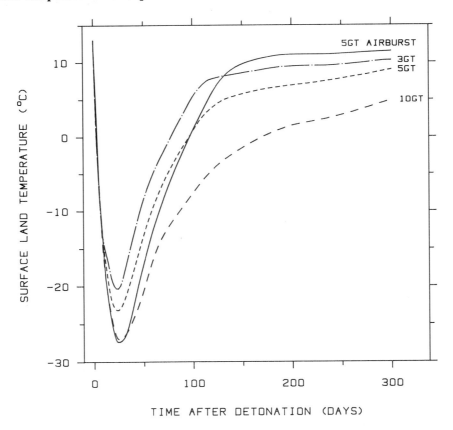

Figure 3.72   SUPERPOSED CURVES.   Visual   discrimination   can   be increased by different curve types.

The temperatures are computed from physical models that describe the creation of particles, the production of radiation, convection, and a script for the nuclear war. The panels in Figure 3.74 are different exchange scenarios, which are explained in Table 3.1. The total world nuclear arsenal of strategic weapons is 17 gigatons (gt), which is roughly equal to 10^6 Hiroshima bombs.

Table 3.1 NUCLEAR EXCHANGE SCENARIOS.

Code	Description
10 gt	10 gt exchange.
5 gt	5 gt exchange.
5 gt air	5 gt airburst in which all weapons are detonated above ground.
5 gt dust	5 gt exchange with only the effects of dust included, but not fires.
3 gt	3 gt exchange.
3 gt silo	3 gt exchange aimed only at missile silos.
1 gt	1 gt exchange.
0.1 gt city	0.1 gt exchange aimed only at major cities.

Figure 3.73 CURVE TYPES. Dots, dashes, and combinations provide a variety of patterns for graphing curves.

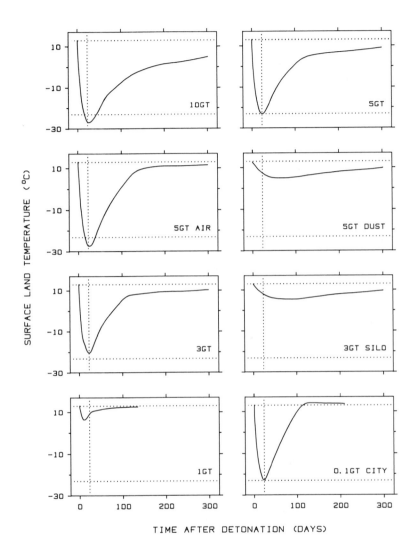

Figure 3.74   JUXTAPOSITION. Each curve shows averaged Northern Hemisphere temperature following a nuclear war. The scenarios of the war are different for different panels. On this graph the different data sets are juxtaposed. Comparisons of the curves are enhanced by the strategically placed reference lines: the upper horizontal reference line on each panel shows the current average ambient Northern Hemisphere temperature, the lower horizontal reference line shows the minimum temperature for the *5 gt* exchange, and the vertical reference line shows the time of the *5 gt* temperature minimum.

Juxtaposition is needed for this temperature data. Superposition results in the tangle of Figure 3.75. We could attempt to improve the graph by using different curve types, but no black and white method appears to reduce the clutter substantially. Actually, it is not necessary to settle for one extreme or the other; we might have attempted four juxtaposed panels, each with two curves superposed.

When it works, superposition is better than juxtaposition because it allows a more incisive comparison of the values of the different data sets. For example, in Figure 3.75 we can see very clearly that the

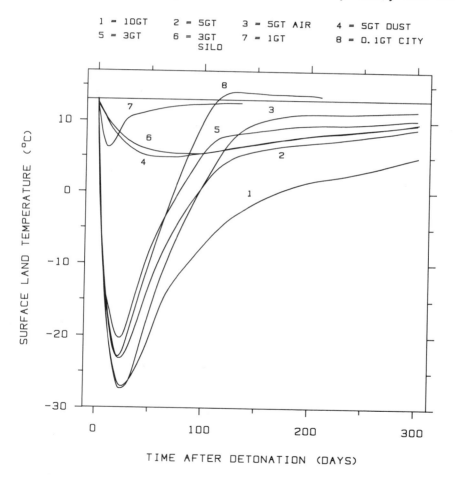

Figure 3.75 SUPERPOSITION. The curves of Figure 3.74 cannot be easily visually discriminated when they are superposed.

minimum for each scenario occurs at about the same time and we can effectively compare the values of the minima; the problem in this example is that it is not easy to see which curve goes with which scenario.

In giving up superposition for juxtaposition we decrease our ability to compare the values of different data sets in order to increase our ability to discriminate the data sets. However, we can employ a method that greatly improves our ability to compare the values on different juxtaposed panels — *strategically place the same lines or curves on all panels to serve as visual references.* For example, in Figure 3.74 the lower horizontal reference line on all panels is the value of the *5 gt* minimum; this line allows us to compare the temperature minima more effectively. The top horizontal reference line is the Northern Hemisphere average ambient temperature; this line helps us to judge the progress each curve makes in getting back to normal conditions. The vertical reference line shows the time of the *5 gt* minimum; this line provides a more effective comparison of the times of the minima.

Figure 3.74 does a good job of showing the temperature profiles. The major exchanges result in a rapid drop to around $-25\,°C$ and then a slow recovery lasting many months. The *0.1 gt city* attack has such a strong effect because of the tremendous concentration of combustible materials in urban areas.

Visual references on juxtaposed panels can take many different forms: lines, curves, or plotting symbols. We will now give two more examples to show how varied the nature of the visual reference can be.

Figure 3.76 is a graph of brain weights and body weights for four categories of species [40]. Juxtaposition is necessary because superposition results in so much overlap that visual resolution of the four groups is impossible whatever (black and white) method is tried. The same three lines are drawn on each panel. The top line shows the major axis of the primate point cloud, the middle line shows the major axes of the bird and nonprimate mammal point clouds, and the lower line is for the fish. These three lines help us to compare the relative positions of the four point clouds. All three lines have slope 2/3, because brain weights tend to be related to body weights to the 2/3 power; the reason for this relationship is discussed in Section 3 of Chapter 1.

In Figure 3.77 the four lines have the same slopes but the intercepts are different. The data are the logarithms of the winning times for four track events at the Olympics from 1900 to 1984 [22, 138, p. 833]. The lines were fit to the data using least squares; the slope was held fixed but the intercept was allowed to vary from one data set to the next.

Because the number of units per cm is the same on the four vertical scales, the lines on the four panels have the same angle with the horizontal. In this example the lines help us to see that the decrease in the log running times has been nearly linear and that the slopes for the four data sets are the same. This means that the overall percent decrease since 1900 has been about the same for the four races.

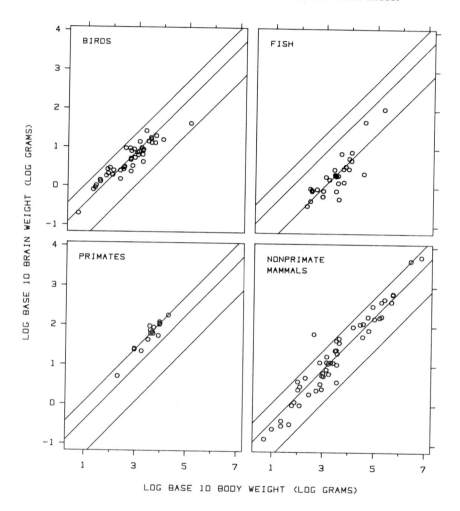

Figure 3.76 JUXTAPOSITION. Log brain weights are graphed against log body weights for four categories of species. The same three reference lines are drawn on the four panels. Each line has slope 2/3; the top line describes the primates, the middle line describes the birds and nonprimate mammals, and the bottom line describes the fish. These strategically placed lines enhance our ability to compare data on different panels.

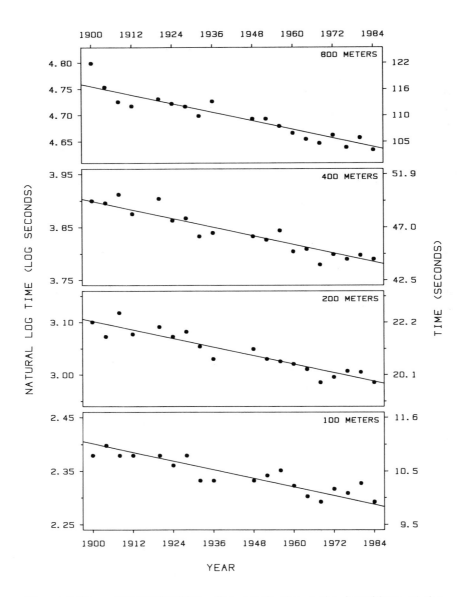

Figure 3.77   JUXTAPOSITION. The graph shows the logarithms of the winning times at the Olympics in four races. The vertical scales on the four panels have the same number of log seconds per cm. The four lines on the panels have the same slope, determined by a least squares fit. Since logarithms are graphed and since the points nearly follow lines with the same slope, we can conclude that the percent decrease in the running times is roughly constant through time and the constant is the same for all four races.

Figure 3.78 shows curves used as references. The data are from an experiment on graphical perception [33] that will be discussed in Section 3 of Chapter 4. A group of 51 subjects judged 40 pairs of values on bar charts and the same 40 pairs on pie charts; each judgment consisted of studying the two values and visually judging what percent the smaller was of the larger. The left panel of Figure 3.78 shows the 40 average judgment errors (averaged across subjects) graphed against the true percents for the 40 pie chart judgments. The right panel shows the same variables for the bar chart judgments. Lowess curves, described in Section 3.4, were fit to each of the two data sets; both curves are graphed on each panel and serve as visual references to help us compare the average errors for the two types of charts.

Color

If color is available we do not as frequently need to give up superposition and use juxtaposition. Our visual system does a marvelous job of discriminating different colors. In Figures 3.79 and 3.80 superposition in black and white is used for two sets of data that we have seen earlier in the chapter. We cannot effectively discriminate the different data sets. Color is used in Plates 1 and 2, which follow page 212, and discrimination is considerably enhanced.

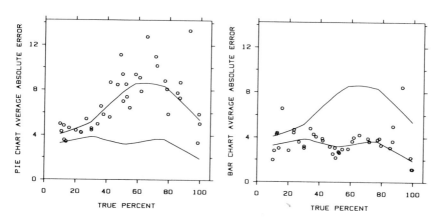

Figure 3.78   JUXTAPOSITION. The graph compares pie chart and bar chart judgment errors of 51 subjects. Two curves show how the bar chart errors and the pie chart errors depend on the true percent being judged. Graphing the two curves on both panels helps us to compare the two sets of data.

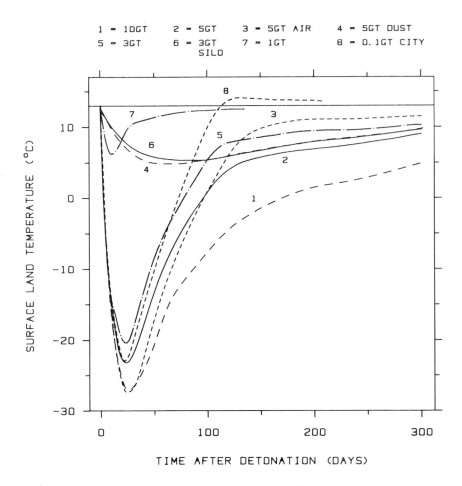

Figure 3.79   COLOR. Color is a good method for providing visual discrimination. The eight curves are not as easy to discriminate as they are in the color encoding in Plate 1, which follows page 212.

Many people will find the colors in Plates 1 and 2 unesthetic, garish, and clashing. This was done on purpose to maximize the visual discrimination. Pleasing colors that blend well tend not to provide as good visual discrimination.

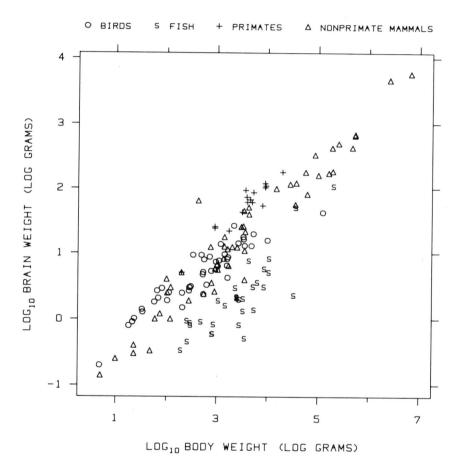

Figure 3.80 COLOR. The four categories of data cannot be easily discriminated. Discrimination is greatly enhanced by color encoding in Plate 2.

3.6 THREE OR MORE QUANTITATIVE VARIABLES

Science and technology would be far simpler if data, like the people of Edwin A. Abbott's *Flatland* [1], always stayed in two dimensions. Unfortunately, data can live in three, four, five or any number of dimensions. Consider, for example, measurements of temperature, humidity, barometric pressure, percentage cloud cover, solar radiation intensity, and wind speed at a particular location at noon on 100 different days. The data on these six variables consist of 100 points in a six-dimensional space. How are we to graph them to understand the complex relationships? How are we to peer into this six-dimensional space and see the configuration of points?

Graphs are two-dimensional. If there are only two variables — for example, just temperature and humidity in our meteorological data set — then the data space is two-dimensional, and a Cartesian graph of one variable against the other shows the configuration of points. As soon as data move to even three variables and three dimensions we must be content with attempting to infer the multidimensional structure by a two-dimensional medium. In this section, some methods for doing this are described.

Framed-Rectangle Graphs

Figure 3.81 is a *framed-rectangle graph* [33], which can be used to show how one variable depends on two others. The data are the per capita debts in dollars of the 48 continental states of the U.S. in 1980 [137, p. 116]. Each value is portrayed by a solid rectangle inside a frame that has tick marks halfway up the vertical sides. The frames are the same size, which helps us judge the relative magnitudes of the values by providing a common visual reference. For geographical data, such as those in Figure 3.81, the framed-rectangle graph conveys the values far more efficiently and accurately to the human viewer than the very common statistical map [97, pp. 282-288] in which the data are encoded by shading the geographical units, which in this example are the states. Issues of graphical perception such as this are the topic of Chapter 4.

The data in Figure 3.81 are three-dimensional; geographical location needs two dimensions and debt is the third. Furthermore, we are in the dependent-independent variable case because the goal is to see how debt depends on geographical location.

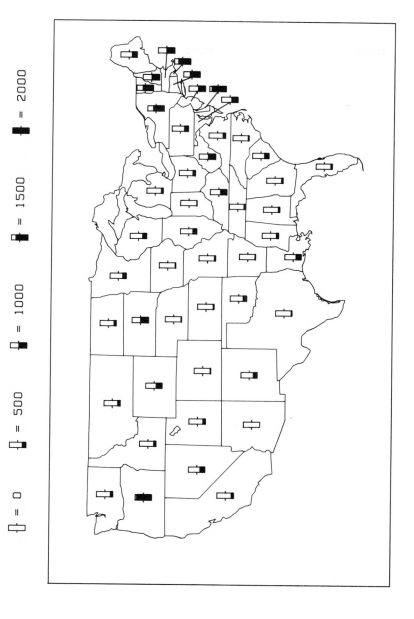

Figure 3.81 FRAMED-RECTANGLE GRAPH. The data are the per capita debts in dollars of the 48 continental states of the United States in 1980. The frames of the framed rectangles help us to judge the values of the data by providing a common visual reference.

The framed-rectangle graph can be useful in any situation where we want to see how measured values of one variable, z, depend on values of two others, x and y. However, since the framed rectangles cannot withstand overlap, the method is helpful only when the number of observations is small or moderate and when there is not too much crowding of the (x,y) values in any one region of the plane.

Figure 3.81 shows that the middle Atlantic states and New England are the regions of the country where the states are least afraid to go into debt. States in the South and in the West tend to be more restrained in their indebtedness, although Oregon, with its near $2000 per capita debt, leads the country and is a striking anomaly.

Scatterplot Matrices

An award should be given for the invention of the *scatterplot matrix*, but the inventor (or inventors) is unknown — an anonymous donor to the world's collection of graphical methods. Early drafts of *Graphical Methods for Data Analysis* [21] contain the first written discussion of the idea, but it was in use before that. The inventor may not have fully appreciated the significance of the method or may have thought the idea too trivial to bring it forward, but its simple, elegant solution to a difficult problem is one of the best graphical ideas around.

Suppose the multidimensional data consist of k variables, so that the data points lie in a k-dimensional space. One way to study the data is to graph each pair of variables; since there are $k(k-1)/2$ pairs, such an approach is practical only if k is not too large. But just making the $k(k-1)/2$ graphs of each variable against each other, without any coordination, often results in a confusing collection of graphs that are hard to integrate, both visually and cognitively.

The important idea of the scatterplot matrix is to arrange the graphs in a matrix with shared scales. An example is shown in Figure 3.82. There are four variables: wind speed, temperature, solar radiation, and concentrations of the air pollutant, ozone. The data, from a study of the dependence of ozone on meteorological conditions [18], are measurements of the four variables on 111 days from May to September of 1973 at sites in the New York City metropolitan region. There is one measurement of each variable on each day; so the data consist of 111 points in a four-dimensional space. (The details of the measurements are the following: solar radiation is the amount from 0800 to 1200 in the frequency band 4000-7700Å; wind speed is the average of values at 0700 and 1000; temperature is the daily maximum; and ozone is the average of values from 0800 to 1200.)

Each panel of the matrix is a scatterplot of one variable against another. For the three graphs in the second row of Figure 3.82, the vertical scale is ozone, and the three horizontal scales are solar radiation, temperature, and wind speed. So the graph in position (2,1) in the matrix — that is, the second row and first column — is a scatterplot of ozone against solar radiation; position (2,3) is a scatterplot of ozone against temperature; position (2,4) is a scatterplot of ozone against wind speed.

The upper right triangle of the scatterplot matrix has all of the $k(k-1)/2$ pairs of graphs, and so does the lower right triangle; thus

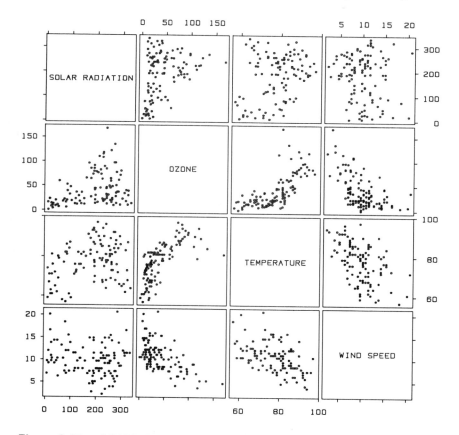

Figure 3.82   SCATTERPLOT MATRIX. The data are measurements of solar radiation, ozone, temperature, and wind speed on 111 days. Thus the measurements are 111 points in a four-dimensional space. The graphical method in this figure is a scatterplot matrix: all pairwise scatterplots of the variables are aligned into a matrix with shared scales.

altogether there are $k(k-1)$ panels and each pair of variables is graphed twice. For example, in Figure 3.82 the (1,3) panel is a graph of solar radiation on the vertical scale against temperature on the horizontal scale, and the (3,1) panel has the same variables but with the scales reversed.

The most important feature of the scatterplot matrix is that we can visually scan a row, or a column, and see one variable graphed against all others with the three scales for the one variable lined up along the horizontal, or the vertical. This is the reason, despite the redundancy, for including both the upper and lower triangles in the matrix. Suppose that in Figure 3.82 only the lower left triangle were present. To see temperature against everything else we would have to scan the first two graphs in the temperature row and then turn the corner to see wind speed against temperature; the three temperature scales would not be lined up, which would make visual assessment more difficult.

Space and resolution quickly become a problem with the scatterplot matrix; the method of construction in Figure 3.82 reduces the problem somewhat. The labels of the variables are inside the main-diagonal boxes so that the graph can expand as much as possible. The tick mark labels for the horizontal scales, as well as for the vertical scales, alternate sides so that labels for successive scales do not interfere with one another. And the panels have been squeezed tightly together, allowing just enough space to provide visual separation.

The scatterplot matrix in Figure 3.82 reveals much about the ozone and meteorological data. Ozone is a secondary air pollutant; it is not emitted directly into the atmosphere but rather is a product of chemical reactions that require solar radiation and emissions of nitric oxide and hydrocarbons from smoke stacks and automobiles. For ozone to get to very high levels, stagnant air conditions are also required.

It is no surprise then to see a relationship between solar radiation and ozone in panel (2,1), but the nature of the relationship is enlightening. There is an upper envelope in the form of an inverted "V". For low values of solar radiation, high values of ozone never occur. The major reason is that the photochemical reactions that produce ozone need a minimum amount of solar radiation. The (2,1) panel also shows that when solar radiation is between 200 and 300 Langleys, ozone can be either high or low. If we scan across the ozone row to panels (2,3) and (2,4) it becomes clear that the high ozone days are those with high temperatures and low wind speeds — stagnant days. Overall, there is a strong association between wind speed and ozone and between temperature and ozone. Both wind speed and temperature are measures of stagnancy; as wind speed decreases or as temperature

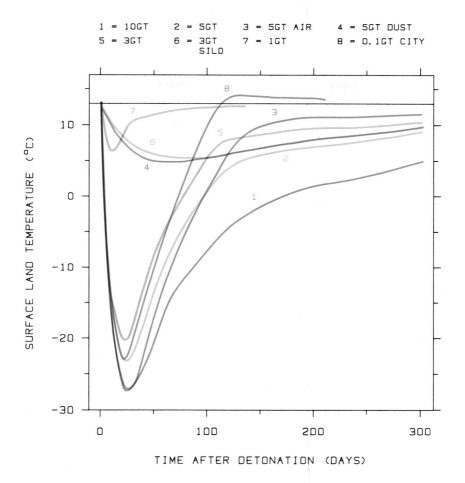

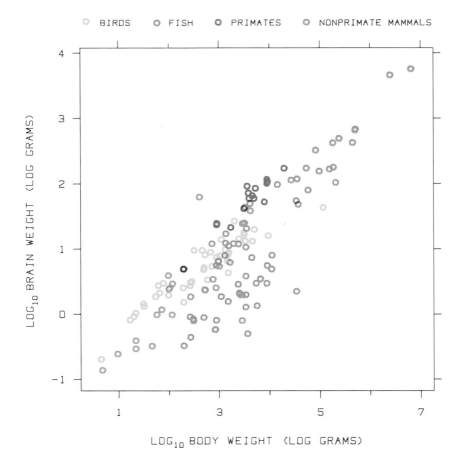

Plate 2.   Color provides good discrimination of the different data sets. Compare with Figure 3.80.

increases, conditions become more stagnant and ozone rises. But the (3,4) panel shows that wind speed and temperature are related and thus are measuring stagnancy, to some extent, in the same way.

Panel (2,1) shows that for the very highest levels of solar radiation, ozone does not get high. Panels (3,1) and (4,1) show why. For the very highest levels of solar radiation, wind speed tends not to be low and temperature tends not to be high. In fact, there is a type of feedback mechanism at work here. The very highest levels of solar radiation at ground level can occur only on the brisk days with no air pollution, because when the pollution is present, the sun's rays are attenuated by particles in the air that form as part of the photochemistry.

Clearly, the scatterplot matrix has revealed much to us about the ozone and meteorological data.

A View of the Future: High-Interaction Graphical Methods

The computer graphics revolution has brought us into a new arena for graphing data. This does not mean simply that the ideas, methods, and principles of this book can be implemented in powerful, yet easy-to-use software systems, although that is surely true. It means more. Modern computer graphics has given us a new type of methodology: *high-interaction methods*. A person sitting in front of a computer screen now can have a high degree of interaction with a graph, changing it, even in a continuous way in real time, by using a physical device such as a light pen, a mouse, a graphics tablet, or even a finger. This capability gives us more than just a fast, convenient way to iterate to a single graph, just the way we want it. The changing of the graphical image on the screen can itself give information and be a graphical method, and we can see in just a few seconds what amounts to dozens of static graphs. There are many ways to change the graphical image on the screen, and they are all graphical methods.

Brushing a scatterplot matrix is a high-interaction graphical method that was invented in 1984 for analyzing multidimensional data [10]. Only a small part of the system will be described here; the reader should appreciate that it is no small challenge to describe a high-interaction computer graphical method, with dynamic elements that change in real time, on the static pages of a book.

Brushing a scatterplot matrix, as the name suggests, is based on the scatterplot matrix. This is illustrated in Figure 3.83 where three variables are graphed. The data are from an industrial experiment [43, p. 155] in which three measurements were made on each of thirty rubber specimens; the measurements are hardness, tensile strength, and

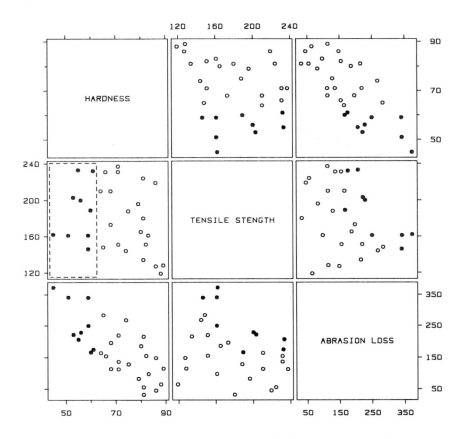

Figure 3.83   BRUSHING A SCATTERPLOT MATRIX: A HIGH-INTERACTION
GRAPHICAL METHOD.   High-interaction computer graphics is ushering in a
new era in graphical methods for data analysis.   This display appears on the
screen of a graphics terminal.   The brush is the dashed rectangle on the
(2, 1) panel.   Points selected by the brush are highlighted on all panels.   The
brush is moved by the user moving a mouse; as the brush moves, different
points are selected and the highlighting changes instantaneously.   In this
figure points with low values of hardness are selected.   The (3, 2) panel
shows that for hardness held fixed to low values, abrasion loss depends
nonlinearly on tensile strength.

abrasion loss, which is the amount of rubber rubbed off by an abrasive material. The goal of the experiment was to determine how abrasion loss depends on tensile strength and hardness, and in the original analysis, abrasion loss was modeled as a linear function of hardness and tensile strength [43, ch. 7]. In a later analysis, using some involved graphical statistical methods [21], it was discovered that abrasion loss depends nonlinearly on tensile strength, although it does depend linearly on hardness. Brushing a scatterplot matrix, however, gives us a very simple way of seeing the nonlinearity.

The principal high-interaction object in brushing is the *brush*: a rectangle on the screen, which is shown by dashed lines on the (2, 1) panel of Figure 3.83. The user moves the brush around the screen by moving a mouse, a physical device connected to the display terminal. The mouse is also used to change the size and shape of the brush.

Figure 3.84 shows one hardware configuration on which the brushing idea has been implemented. The young man in the front is holding a three-button mouse; the user moves the mouse on the table, which causes the brush to move on the screen. The high-interaction graphics code runs on the terminal, a Teletype 5620, but the preliminary data structuring is done on a supermicro, an AT&T 3B2 computer, which is underneath the display terminal.

Figure 3.83 shows the result of brushing when the *highlight* operation has been selected by a pop-up menu. The data in this example consist of 30 points in a three-dimensional space. Each panel in the figure is a projection of the points onto a plane. When the brush encloses graphed values on one panel it is in a sense selecting a subset of the points in three dimensions; the graphed values of these points are highlighted on all panels by graphing them using filled circles. As the brush is moved, different values are enclosed and the highlighting changes instantaneously. For example, in Figure 3.85 the brush has moved to the right on the (2,3) panel and different points are highlighted.

Let us now consider what this highlighting has shown us about the rubber data. In Figure 3.83 the brush was positioned so that points with low values of hardness are highlighted. Look at panel (3,2). The highlighted points are a graph of abrasion loss against tensile strength for low values of hardness; in other words, we see the dependence of

Figure 3.84   MOUSE, TERMINAL, AND COMPUTER. The young man in the front is holding the mouse, the device used to control the size and shape of the brush and to move it around the screen. The high-interaction graphics code runs on the terminal, a Teletype 5620, but the preliminary data structuring is done on a supermicro, an AT&T 3B2 computer, which is underneath the display terminal.

abrasion loss on tensile strength with hardness held fixed, or nearly so. The highlighted points show that for hardness held to low values there is a nonlinear dependence of abrasion loss on tensile strength.

In Figure 3.85 middle values of hardness are selected. On the (3,2) panel the highlighted points show that for hardness held to middle levels the dependence of abrasion loss on tensile strength is again nonlinear and the pattern — a drop followed by a leveling out of the effect — is similar to that with hardness held to low values. The pattern emerges, although a little less crisply, in Figure 3.86, where hardness is held to high values.

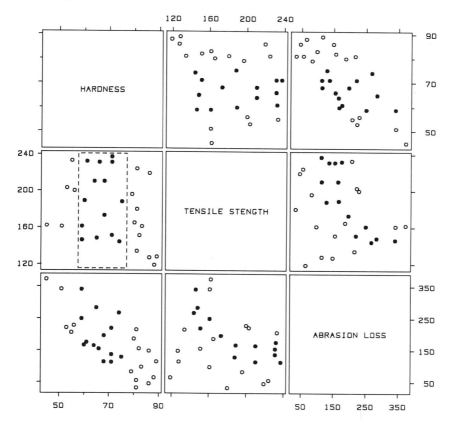

Figure 3.85 BRUSHING. Middle values of hardness have been selected. The highlighted values on the (3, 2) panel show that for hardness held fixed to middle levels, the dependence of abrasion loss on tensile strength is nonlinear.

The brushing has let us see easily the nonlinearity in these data. High-interaction graphical methods are now a reality. Graphical methods for data analysis have entered a new era.

3.7 STATISTICAL VARIATION

Measurements vary. Even when all controllable variables are kept constant, measurements vary because of uncontrollable variables or measurement error. One of the important functions of graphs in science and technology is to show the variation.

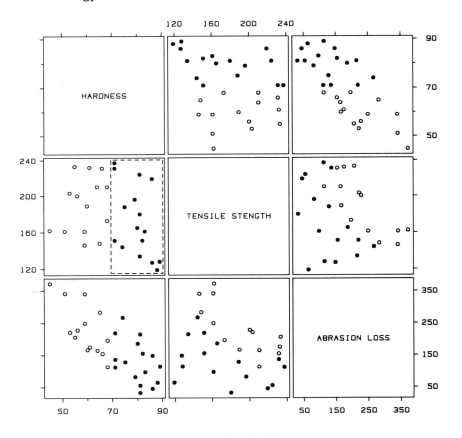

Figure 3.86 BRUSHING. High values of hardness have been selected. The highlighted values on the (3, 2) panel also suggest the nonlinearity.

Empirical Distribution of the Data

There are two very different domains of showing variation. One is to show the actual variation in the measurements, that is, to show the values of the data. This is the empirical distribution of the data that was discussed in Section 3.2. Figure 3.87 is an example from Section 3.4 — the bin-packing data. For each value of the x variable, the empirical distribution of the 25 values of the y variable is shown by a box graph.

When the goal is to convey just the empirical distribution of the data and not to make *formal* statistical inferences about a population distribution from which the data might have come, we can use the graphical methods for showing data distributions that were discussed in Section 3.2. The box graphs in Figure 3.87 are an example.

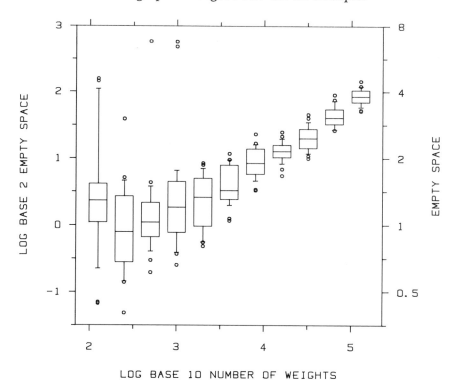

Figure 3.87   SHOWING EMPIRICAL VARIATION. For each value of log number of weights there are 25 measurements of log empty space whose distribution is summarized by a box graph.

Another method for showing the variation in the data, one that is very common in science and technology, is to use a plotting symbol and error bars to portray the *sample mean* and the *sample standard deviation*. Suppose the values of the data are $x_1,...,x_n$ then the sample mean is

$$\bar{x} = \frac{1}{n} \sum_{i=1}^{n} x_i$$

and the sample standard deviation is

$$s = \left[\frac{1}{n-1} \sum_{i=1}^{n} (x_i - \bar{x})^2 \right]^{\frac{1}{2}} .$$

Figure 3.88 uses a filled circle and error bars to show the mean plus and minus one sample standard deviation for each of the 11 data sets of the bin packing example. This graph does a poor job of conveying the variation in the data. The means show the centers of the distributions, but the standard deviations give us no sense of the upper and lower limits of the sample and camouflage the outliers: the unusually high values of empty space that occur for low numbers of weights. The box graphs in Figure 3.87 do a far better job of conveying the empirical variation of the data.

This result — the mean and sample standard deviation doing a poor job of conveying the distribution of the data — is frequently the case, because without any other information about the data, the sample standard deviation tells us little about where the data lie. This is further illustrated in Figure 3.89. The top panel shows four sets of made-up data. The four sets have the same sample size, the same sample mean, and the same sample standard deviation, but the behavior of the four empirical distributions is radically different. The means and sample standard deviations in the bottom panel do not capture the variation of the four data sets.

There is an exception to this poor performance of the sample standard deviation. If the empirical distribution of the data is well approximated by a normal probability distribution then we know approximately what percentage of the data lies between the mean plus and minus a constant times s. For example, approximately 68% lies between $\bar{x} \pm s$, approximately 50% lies between $\bar{x} \pm 0.67 s$, and approximately 95% lies between $\bar{x} \pm 1.96 s$. However, empirical distributions are often not well approximated by the normal. The normal distribution is symmetric, but real data are often skewed to the right. The normal distribution does not have wild observations, but real data often do.

One approach to showing the empirical variation in the data might be to check how well the empirical distribution is approximated by a normal, and then use the mean and sample standard deviation to summarize the distribution if the approximation is a good one. For example, one method for checking normality is a normal probability plot [21]. If the goal were to make inferences about the population distribution then checking normality is a vital matter and well worth the effort, as will be discussed shortly. But going through the trouble of checking normality, when the *only* goal is to show the empirical variation in the data, is often needless effort. The direct, easy, and rapid approach to showing the empirical variation in the data is to show the

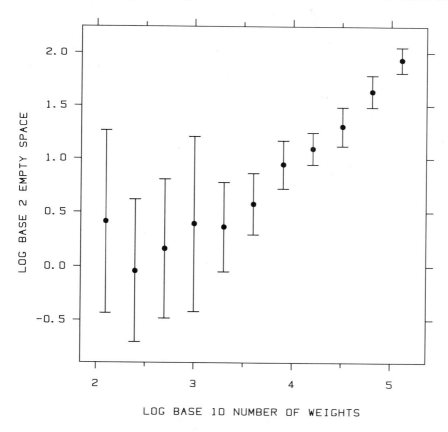

Figure 3.88   MEANS AND SAMPLE STANDARD DEVIATIONS. Showing just means and sample standard deviations is often a poor way to convey the variation in the data. This example shows means and sample standard deviations for the 11 sets of data graphed in Figure 3.87. The outliers in the data are not conveyed.

data. This means using graphical methods such as box graphs and percentile graphs to show the empirical distribution of the data. Thus, after this long discussion we have been led to the following circular advice: If the goal is to show the data, then show the data.

Sample-to-Sample Variation of a Statistic

The second domain of variation is the *sample-to-sample variation of a statistic*. Let us consider a simple but common sampling situation. Suppose we have a random sample of measurements, x_i for $i = 1$ to n, from a population distribution. Suppose we are interested in making inferences about the mean, μ, of the population distribution. The population mean can be estimated by the sample mean, $\bar{x}$, of the data.

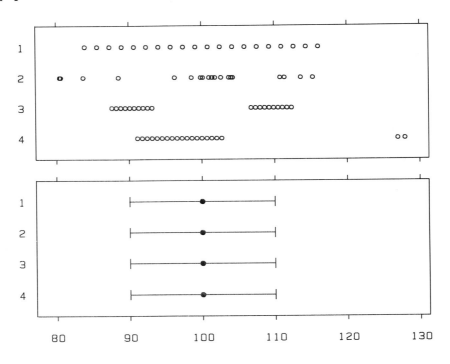

Figure 3.89   FAILURE OF MEANS AND SAMPLE STANDARD DEVIATIONS. Means and sample standard deviations cannot characterize the wide variety of distributions that data can have. Four sets of data are graphed in the top panel and their means and sample standard deviations are graphed in the bottom panel. The four distributions have the same numbers of observations, the same means, and the same sample standard deviations, but the distributions are very different.

The sample mean is a *statistic,* a numerical value based on the sample, and if we took a new sample of size n, $\bar{x}$ would be different; the variation in $\bar{x}$ from one sample of size n to the next is the sample-to-sample variation in $\bar{x}$.

$\bar{x}$ also has a population distribution and the sample-to-sample variation in $\bar{x}$ is characterized by it. Suppose σ is the standard deviation of the population distribution of the data, then the standard deviation of the population distribution of $\bar{x}$ is $\sigma/\sqrt{n}$. As n gets large this standard deviation gets small, the population distribution of $\bar{x}$ closes in on μ, and $\bar{x}$ varies less and less from sample to sample. The standard deviation of the mean, like μ, is unknown but it can be estimated; since s, the sample standard deviation, is an estimate of σ, $\sigma/\sqrt{n}$ can be estimated by $s/\sqrt{n}$, which is often called the *standard error of the mean,* although *estimated standard deviation of the sample mean* is a more complete name.

One-Standard-Error Bars

The current convention in science and technology for portraying sample-to-sample variation of a statistic is to graph error bars to portray plus and minus one standard error of the statistic, just the way the sample standard deviation is used to summarize the empirical variation of the data.

Figure 3.90 shows statistics from experiments on graphical perception that will be discussed in more detail in the next chapter. Subjects in the three experiments made graphical judgments that can be grouped into seven types. The types for each experiment are described by the labels in Figure 3.90. For each judgment type in each experiment a statistic was computed that measures the absolute error; the statistic is averaged across all subjects and across all judgments of that type made in the experiment. The filled circles in Figure 3.90 graph the statistics. The subjects in each experiment are thought of as a random sample from the population of subjects who can understand graphs. If we took new samples of subjects, the statistics shown in Figure 3.90 would vary. The error bars in Figure 3.90 show plus and minus one standard error of the statistics. (The statistics in this example are not means; the standard errors are computed from a formula that is more complicated than that for the standard error of the mean [35], however, we do not need to be concerned with the formula here.)

Now the critical point is the following: A standard error of a statistic has value only insofar as it conveys information about *confidence intervals.* The standard error by itself conveys little. It is confidence intervals that convey the sample-to-sample variation of a statistic.

In some cases confidence intervals are formed by taking plus and minus a multiple of the standard error. For example, suppose the x_i are a sample from a normal population distribution, suppose the statistic is $\bar{x}$, and suppose our purpose is to estimate the mean, μ, of the population

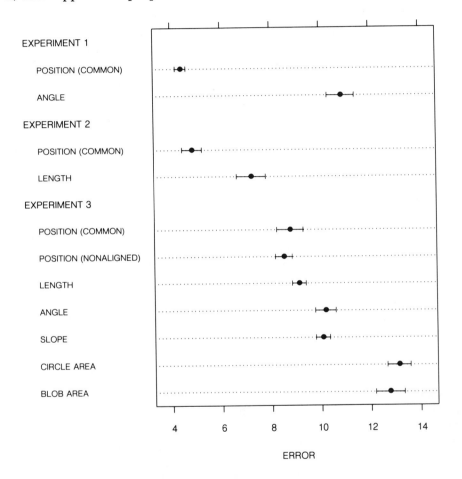

Figure 3.90   ONE-STANDARD-ERROR BARS TO SHOW SAMPLE-TO-SAMPLE VARIATION. The filled circles show statistics from experiments on graphical perception. Each error bar, conforming to the convention in science and technology, shows plus and minus one standard error. The interval formed by the error bars is a 68% confidence interval, which is not a particularly interesting interval. One standard error bars are probably a naive translation of the convention for numerical reporting of sample-to-sample variation.

distribution. Let $t_d(\alpha)$ be a number such that the probability between $-t_d(\alpha)$ and $t_d(\alpha)$ for a t-distribution with d degrees of freedom is α. Then the interval

$$\bar{x} - t_{n-1}(\alpha)s/\sqrt{n} \quad \text{to} \quad \bar{x} + t_{n-1}(\alpha)s/\sqrt{n}$$

is a $100\alpha\%$ confidence interval for the mean. In other words, μ is in the above interval for $100\alpha\%$ of the samples of size n drawn from the population distribution. This confidence interval is just the sample mean plus and minus a constant times the standard error of the mean. If n is about 60 or above, the t distribution is very nearly a normal distribution. This means

$$t_{n-1}(0.5) \approx 0.67 \qquad t_{n-1}(0.68) \approx 1 \qquad t_{n-1}(0.95) \approx 1.96 \ ,$$

so in this case $\bar{x} \pm s/\sqrt{n}$ is approximately a 68% confidence interval, $\bar{x} \pm 0.67 \, s/\sqrt{n}$ is approximately a 50% interval, and $\bar{x} \pm 1.96 \, s/\sqrt{n}$ is approximately a 95% interval.

There are other sampling situations, however, where confidence intervals are *not* based on standard errors. For example, if the x_i are from an exponential distribution, then confidence intervals for the population mean are based on the sample mean, but they do not involve the standard error of the mean [86, p. 103].

How did it happen that the solidly entrenched convention in science and technology is to show one standard error on graphs? In some cases plus and minus one standard error has no useful, easy interpretation. True, in many cases plus and minus one standard error is a 68% confidence interval; Figure 3.90 is one example. Is a 68% confidence interval interesting? Are confidence intervals thought about at all when error bars are put on graphs?

It seems likely that the one-standard-error bar of graphical communication in science and technology is a result of the convention for numerical communication. If we want to communicate sample-to-sample variation numerically in cases where confidence intervals are based on standard errors, then it is reasonable to communicate the standard error and let the reader do some arithmetic, either mentally or otherwise, to get confidence intervals. A reasonable conjecture is that this numerical convention was simply brought to graphs. But the difficulty with this translation is that we are visually locked into what is shown by the error bars; it is hard to multiply the bars visually by some constant to get a desired visual confidence interval on the graph. Another difficulty, of course, is that confidence intervals are not always based on standard errors.

Two-Tiered Error Bars

Figure 3.91 uses *two-tiered error bars* to convey sample-to-sample variation. For each statistic the ends of the inner error bars, which are marked by the short vertical lines, are a 50% confidence interval; the ends of the outer error bars a 95% confidence interval. When confidence intervals are quoted numerically in scientific writings the level is almost always a high one such as 90%, 95%, or 99%; the outer

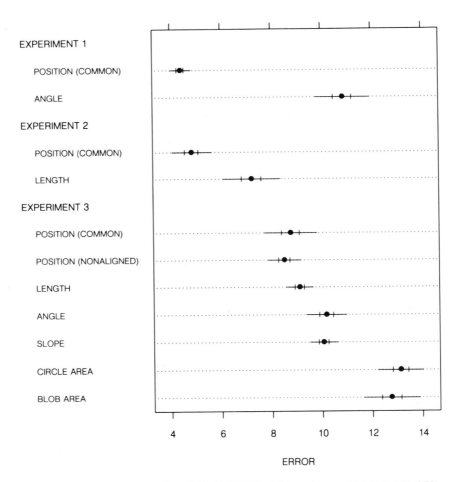

Figure 3.91   TWO-TIERED ERROR BARS. The outer error bars are 95% confidence intervals and the inner error bars are 50% confidence intervals. The goal in this method is to show confidence intervals and not standard errors, although for some statistics, confidence intervals happen to be formed from multiples of standard errors.

interval in the two-tiered system simply reflects this practice. The inner interval of 50% gives a middle range for the sample-to-sample variation of the statistic that is analogous to the box of a box graph.

Two-tiered error bars are suggested as a replacement for one-standard-error bars. The most important aspect is that the goal is to show confidence intervals and not standard errors. Even when confidence intervals are based on standard errors, the two-tiered error bars are more sensible since they convey more cogent confidence interval information. The details of the two-tiered system are not meant to create dogma, but rather to encourage thought about what is shown. Variations should occur; for example, if an interval of very high confidence is desired, the ends of the outer bars could represent a 99.9% interval.

4

GRAPHICAL PERCEPTION

When a graph is constructed, quantitative and categorical information is *encoded* by symbols, geometry, and color. *Graphical perception* is the *visual decoding* of this encoded information. Graphical perception is the vital link, the raison d'être, of the graph. No matter how intelligent the choice of information, no matter how ingenious the encoding of the information, and no matter how technologically impressive the production, a graph is a failure if the visual decoding fails. To have a scientific basis for graphing data, graphical perception must be understood. Informed decisions about how to encode data must be based on knowledge of the visual decoding process.

The chapter sets out a *paradigm* of graphical perception. "Paradigm" is used here in the sense of Thomas S. Kuhn [84] — a model or pattern that organizes knowledge about a subject, explains phenomena, and serves as a basis for what measurements to take. The paradigm arises, as many do, from meshing two disciplines: statistical graphics and visual perception. It has been built from intuition about graphical issues that has developed in the field of statistical graphics [21, ch. 8], from theory and experimental results from the field of visual perception [8], and from experiments in graphical perception [33, 35]. There are three basic elements of the current paradigm:

(1) A specification of *elementary graphical-perception tasks,* which are the tasks we perform in visually decoding quantitative information from graphs, and an ordering of the tasks based on how accurately we perform them.

(2)   A statement on the role of *distance* in graphical perception.

(3)   A statement on the role of *detection* in graphical perception.

The paradigm leads to principles of data display. These principles are utilized to alter and enhance many conventional methods for graphing data and to invent new methods; the result is a more accurate and efficient visual decoding of quantitative information. In fact, aspects of the paradigm have been involved in earlier chapters to make and improve graphs.

Section 4.1 discusses the mental-visual tasks that are performed when a graph is studied. Section 4.2 describes the three basic elements of the paradigm: elementary graphical-perception tasks, distance, and detection. Section 4.3 uses the theory of visual perception and experiments in graphical perception to develop the paradigm; this section is the most technical and on a first reading many will want to skip to the summary and discussion at the end of the section. In Section 4.4 principles that arise from the paradigm are applied to graphical data display to improve many conventional ways of displaying data and to develop new methods.

4.1   COGNITIVE TASKS AND PERCEPTUAL TASKS

When we study a graph, there are a variety of mental-visual tasks that are performed to extract the quantitative information. Figure 4.1 will be used to discuss them. The figure shows the United States divorce rate — measured in divorces per 1000 married women 15 to 44 years old — for 16 three-year periods beginning in 1930-1932 and ending in 1975-1977 [129, p. 82]. The value on the horizontal scale for a graphed point is the middle year of the interval; for example, the first divorce rate, which is for the years 1930 to 1932, is graphed at 1931.

Once the variables being graphed are understood, we can extract quantitative information from Figure 4.1 at a very elementary mental-visual level. We derive this information by scanning the plotting symbols, the connecting lines, and the scale lines, and without consciously looking at the tick mark labels. For example, we can judge the relative positions of the points along the horizontal scale to get information about the rates; this allows us to see that the rates for the later years are considerably higher than those for the earlier years, that there is a peak in the middle of the data, and that the rate at the peak is roughly midway between the rates at the beginning and end of the data record. We can also judge the slopes of the lines connecting the plotting symbols; this allows us to see, for example, that the last four rates increase more rapidly than the first four rates.

These visual judgments of quantitative information that were just described can be made effortlessly and almost instantaneously. We perform them by judging geometrical aspects of the graphical elements such as position and size. They involve what Julesz calls *pre-attentive vision* [72], but here, because of the context, they will be referred to as *graphical-perception tasks*.

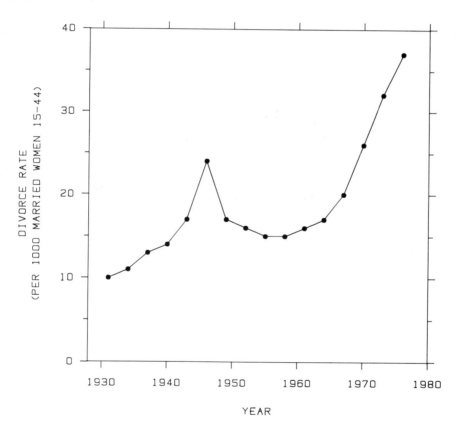

Figure 4.1   COGNITION AND PERCEPTION. When we study a graph, the quantitative information is visually decoded by elementary graphical-perception tasks, such as judging position along a common scale and judging slope, and by cognitive tasks, such as reading values off the scale and doing rapid mental calculation.

We also can extract quantitative information from Figure 4.1 at a different mental-visual level. We can scan horizontally or vertically and read off values of the points using the scale lines and tick mark labels, and do rapid mental calculation and perform quantitative reasoning in a conscious way. For example, we can see that the peak in the middle of the data occurs in the second half of the 1940s, just after the midpoint of the decade (and, of course, just after the end of World War II). We can see that the divorce rate for the 1931 period is close to 10 and that the divorce rate for the 1976 period is slightly above 35, and conclude that the rate increased by a factor of about 3.5 from 1931 to 1976. These *graphical-cognition tasks* can be performed easily but require more conscious thought than the more basic perceptual tasks.

It is the graphical-perception tasks with which the paradigm of this chapter deals, but a few comments will be made about cognition.

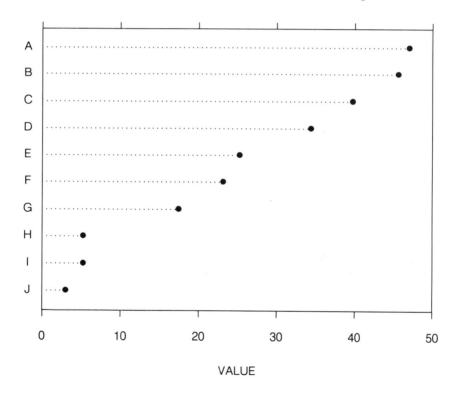

Figure 4.2   POSITION ALONG A COMMON SCALE. The data on this graph can be decoded visually by making judgments of positions along the common horizontal scale.

4.2 THE ELEMENTS OF THE PARADIGM

Elementary Graphical-Perception Tasks

Table 4.1 shows ten *elementary graphical-perception tasks* that we perform to decode information from graphs. They apply to *quantitative* information such as viscosity, gross national product, time, bits of information, and divorce rate and not to *categorical* information such as blood type, country of birth, and type of metal. We will now illustrate the tasks with several examples, all using made-up data.

To visually compare the values of the data in Figure 4.2 we can make judgments of positions along a common scale, in this case the horizontal scale. In Figure 4.3 the graph has three panels and the horizontal scale lines for the three are the same. To compare values that are on the same panel we can judge positions along a common scale, but

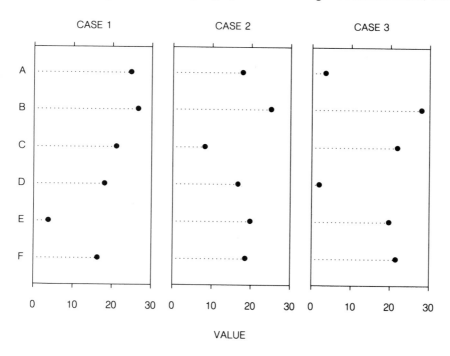

Figure 4.3   POSITION ALONG IDENTICAL, NONALIGNED SCALES. Values on different panels of this graph can be compared by making judgments of positions along identical, nonaligned scales.

to compare values on separate panels we must make judgments of positions on identical, but nonaligned scales.

The vertical scale in Figure 4.4 shows statistics and two-tiered error bars portraying 50% and 95% confidence intervals for the statistics. To compare the values of the statistics and the ends of the intervals we can make judgments of positions along the vertical scale. The lengths of the confidence intervals of one level of confidence, for example the 95% intervals, are measures of the precisions of the statistics; a longer interval means less precision. To decode the precisions visually we can make length judgments.

In Figure 4.5 the relative values of the *y* measurements can be extracted by judgments of positions along the vertical scale, and the *x*

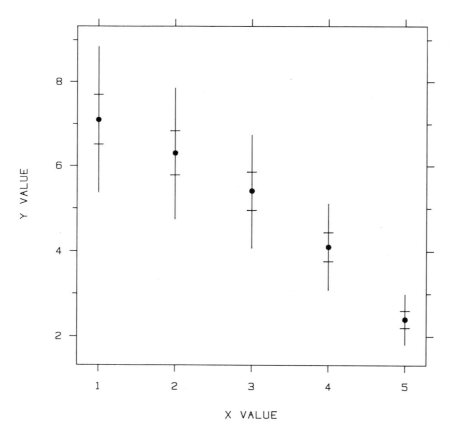

Figure 4.4   LENGTH. The lengths of the 95% confidence intervals, or of the 50% intervals, serve as measures of precision of the graphed statistics. To compare the magnitudes of either set of precision measures, we can make length judgments.

Table 4.1   ELEMENTARY GRAPHICAL-PERCEPTION TASKS.   The list below shows ten elementary graphical-perception tasks: basic perceptual judgments that we perform to visually decode quantitative information encoded on graphs.

 1. Angle
 2. Area
 3. Color hue
 4. Color saturation
 5. Density (Amount of black)
 6. Length (Distance)
 7. Position along a common scale
 8. Position along identical, nonaligned scales
 9. Slope
10. Volume

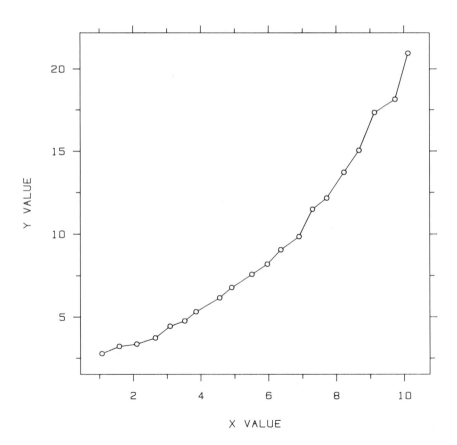

Figure 4.5   SLOPE. The local rate of change of *y* as a function of *x* can be decoded by judging the slopes of the lines connecting successive points.

measurements can be extracted by judgments along the horizontal scale. But we also can judge the local rate of change of y as a function of x by judging the relative values of the slopes of the connecting lines; the overall visual impression is an increasing trend in the local rate of change as x increases.

Figure 4.6 is a *pie-chart*. To extract the percentages visually we can make angle comparisons. Figure 4.7 is a graph that shows three variables: x, y, and z. The first two, x and y, are shown in the usual way by positions along the two scales, and z is portrayed by the areas of the circles. Thus to visually decode the values of z we must make area judgments.

Figure 4.8 is a scatterplot of two variables. One aspect of the data that we can judge from the graph is the relative number of points per unit area in different regions of the plane. To extract this information we must judge the visual density of the points; for example, the density of the point cloud appears to be greater in the middle than in the extremes in the upper right and lower left.

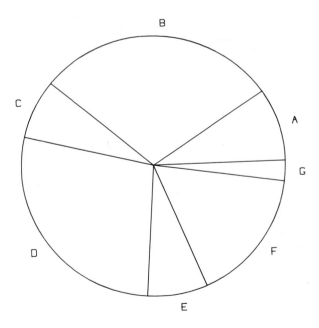

Figure 4.6   ANGLE. The values encoded by this pie chart can be decoded by angle judgments.

The remaining three elementary tasks in Table 4.1 — volume, color saturation, and color hue — are not widely required for visually decoding quantitative information from graphs in science and technology. An example that would require volume judgments is portraying the sizes of the planets by perspective drawings of spheres whose volumes are proportional to the planet volumes. Color hue refers to the spectral quality of a color; blue, red, green and yellow are all different hues. We have seen in Section 5 of Chapter 3 that hue can be used successfully to encode the values of a categorical variable.

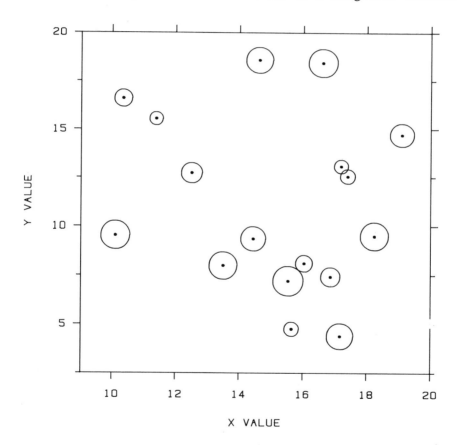

Figure 4.7   AREA. This graph shows three variables. Two are portrayed by the centers of the circles and a third is portrayed by the circle areas. The values of the third can be decoded by area judgments.

Various schemes also exist for using hue to encode a quantitative variable [14]. Color saturation refers to the intensity of a color; for example, saturation decreases as we go from a deep red to a pink and finally to a grey. Measurements of a quantitative variable can be graphed by defining a quantitative scale of saturation and then encoding by saturations whose values are proportional to the values of the data [14].

Distance

The elementary graphical-perception tasks are only one factor that we must consider in addressing graphical perception. Another factor is

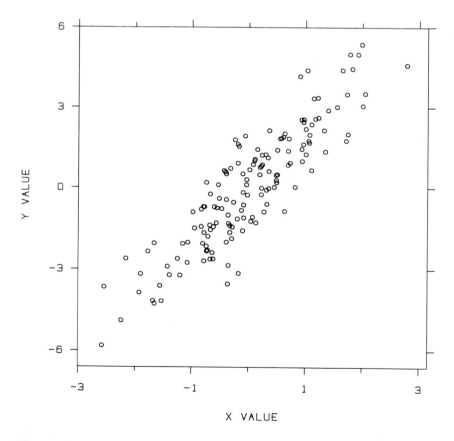

Figure 4.8   DENSITY. The relative number of points per unit area in different regions of the graph can be decoded by density judgments.

distance. In Figure 4.9 we can extract the values of the data by making judgments of position along the horizontal scale. However, along an axis perpendicular to the horizontal scale, point B is closer to point A than point I, and point E is equidistant from A and I. The ways in which we judge these values is affected by the distances among them. The role of distance will be investigated in Section 4.3 and illustrated with examples in Section 4.4.

Detection

Detection is in a sense the most fundamental perceptual issue. If an aspect of a graphical element encodes a datum, then we must first be able to detect the aspect before we can perform any elementary graphical-perception tasks. In Figure 4.10, 25 points are graphed, but because of overlap we cannot visually distinguish all of the points; there

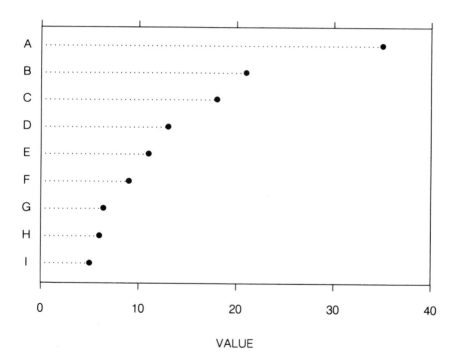

Figure 4.9 DISTANCE. Distance is an important factor in graphical perception. Our visual comparison of the value of A and the value of B will differ from our visual comparison of the value of E and the value of I since A and B are closer in the vertical direction than E and I.

are many elementary graphical-perception tasks that we cannot perform at all because we cannot detect the requisite aspects of the graphical elements. This issue of detection in this example is so obvious that it is conceptually trivial, although it is not at all trivial to deal with the problem in practice as we have seen in Section 4 of Chapter 3; but there are much more subtle issues of detection with which we will deal in Section 4.4.

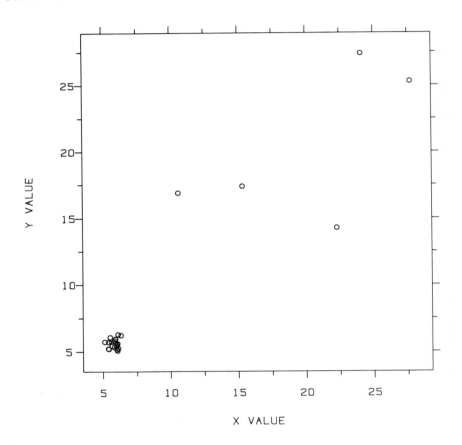

Figure 4.10   DETECTION. Detection is an important factor in graphical perception. We must first detect graphical elements before we can perform elementary graphical-perception tasks. This graph shows one trivial example. The values of many of the points in the cluster in the lower left cannot be judged by any elementary graphical-perception task since many individual points cannot be detected.

4.3 THEORY AND EXPERIMENTATION

This section uses theory and experimental results of visual perception and uses experiments in graphical perception to investigate the paradigm described in the previous section. The material here is the most technical and detailed of the chapter; those who want to move directly to the application of the paradigm to data display can skip to the summary and discussion at the end of this section.

Weber's Law

Weber's Law, formulated by the 19th century psychophysicist E. H. Weber, is one of the fundamental and most-discussed laws of human perception [134, pp. 481-588]. Suppose x is the magnitude of a physical attribute; to be specific let it be the length of a line segment. Let $w_p(x)$ be a positive number such that a line of length $x + w_p(x)$ is detected with probability p to be longer than the line of length x. Weber's Law states that for fixed p,

$$w_p(x) = k_p x \quad ,$$

where k_p does not depend on x. The law appears to describe reality extremely well for many perceptual judgments including position, length, and area [7].

One implication of Weber's Law is that we need a fixed percentage increase in line length to achieve detection. For example, it is easy to detect a difference between two lines of lengths 2 cm and 2.5 cm, because the percentage increase of the second over the first is 25%; however, it is much harder to detect a difference between two lines that are 50 cm and 50.5 cm, even though the difference is also 0.5 cm, because the percentage increase is only 1%.

Weber's Law suggests that judgments of positions along nonaligned, identical scales are more accurate than length judgments. When we make a pure length comparison, we have only the two physical quantities to help make the judgment. When we compare two positions along identical but nonaligned scales we have many visual cues, and therefore many length judgments that can help us judge the encoded numbers; because of Weber's Law, some lengths will be easier to compare than others. Figure 4.11 provides an example. In the top panel there are two solid rectangles with unequal vertical lengths. It is not easy for our visual systems to detect a difference; all that can be used is judgments of the two lengths. In the bottom panel, the two solid rectangles are embedded in two frames that have equal heights and that have ticks halfway up the sides of the frames; these graphical elements

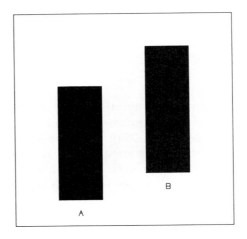

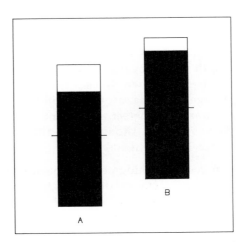

Figure 4.11   BARS, FRAMED RECTANGLES, AND WEBER'S LAW. The bars in the top panel are of unequal vertical length, but it is difficult to judge which is longer. In the bottom panel the bars are embedded in frames that form a scale, and now it is clear that B is longer. This is explained by Weber's Law, which says that discrimination of magnitudes depends on the percent difference of the magnitudes.

are the framed rectangles of the framed-rectangle graph that was discussed in Section 6 of Chapter 3. Now we can visually compare the two encoded quantities by the following: (1) comparing the vertical lengths of the solid rectangles; (2) comparing the distances of the tops of the solid rectangles from the ticks; (3) comparing the distances of the tops of the solid rectangles from the tops of the frames. The judgments in (3) let us see clearly that quantity B is bigger than quantity A; all three pairs of lengths differ by the same number of centimeters, but the percentage difference of the lengths in (3) is the greatest, and by Weber's Law it is this difference that we can detect most easily.

Stevens' Law

Suppose we display objects and ask a person to judge the magnitudes of some attribute of the objects; for example we might show circles and ask the person to judge the areas. *Stevens' Law*, formulated and extensively investigated by S. S. Stevens [119], says that the person's perceived scale is

$$p(x) = cx^\beta ,$$

where x is the magnitude of the attribute. The perceived scale is the actual scale to a power, so Stevens' Law is often called Stevens' Power Law.

Stevens' Law is an excellent descriptor of perceived scales for a wide variety of attributes, including length, area, and volume. Many experiments have been run to estimate β [7]. Average values of β across subjects in a particular experiment depend, of course, on the attribute, but also on the nature of the experiment. For length judgments an average β is usually in the range 0.9 to 1.1; for area, most are in the range 0.6 to 0.9; for volume, most are in the range 0.5 to 0.8 [7, p. 64].

Since β is usually nearly one for length judgments, the perceived scale is nearly proportional to the actual scale, so that there is little bias in length judgments. For area judgments there is usually bias. Consider a situation where $\beta = 0.7$, a value reported by S. S. Stevens [119, p. 15]. Suppose areas of 2, 4, and 8 are judged. The perceived ratio of the first to the second is $(2/4)^{0.7} = 0.62$, which is greater than the actual ratio of 0.5; the perceived ratio of the third to the second is $(8/4)^{0.7} = 1.62$, which is less than the actual ratio of 2. This means there is a conservativism in which small areas appear bigger than they actually are and large areas appear smaller. The situation is even worse for volume judgments because the values of β are even less than for area.

Let x_j for $j = 1$ to n be repeated judgments of the magnitude of a physical attribute, let a be the true value being judged, and let $\bar{x}$ be the mean of the judgments,

$$\bar{x} = \frac{1}{n} \sum_{j=1}^{n} x_j .$$

One numerical measure of the judgment errors is the average *mean-square-error*,

$$mse = \frac{1}{n} \sum_{j=1}^{n} (x_j - a)^2 .$$

Now

$$mse = \frac{1}{n} \sum_{j=1}^{n} (x_j - a + \bar{x} - \bar{x})^2$$

$$= \frac{1}{n} \sum_{j=1}^{n} [(x_j - \bar{x})^2 + 2(x_j - \bar{x})(\bar{x} - a) + (\bar{x} - a)^2]$$

$$= (\bar{x} - a)^2 + \frac{1}{n} \sum_{j=1}^{n} (x_j - \bar{x})^2$$

$$= b + v ,$$

where

$$b = (\bar{x} - a)^2$$

and

$$v = \frac{1}{n} \sum_{j=1}^{n} (x_j - \bar{x})^2 .$$

The value b is a measure of the *bias* in the judgments and the value v is the *variance* of the judgments. Both contribute to the mean-square-error.

As the bias of judgments increases, the mean-square-error increases if the variance is constant. Stevens' Law has shown that length judgments are unbiased, that area judgments are biased, and that volume judgments are even more biased. This suggests that we can expect length judgments to be the most accurate of the three, area judgments to be next, and volume judgments to be the least accurate, provided the variances of the three tasks do not differ in a way that alters the ordering.

Angle Judgments

Like area and volume judgments, angle judgments are subject to bias. Scientists studying visual perception as far back as the 19th century established that acute angles are underestimated and obtuse angles are overestimated [67]. More recent experiments have shown another type of angle-judgment bias: angles whose bisectors are horizontal tend to be seen as larger than those whose bisectors are vertical [90]. In view of these biases in angle judgments, we might expect angle judgments to be less accurate than position and length judgments.

The Angle Contamination of Slope Judgments

The left panel of Figure 4.12 has two line segments with slopes a/c and b/c. The ratio of the slope of line segment BC to the slope of line segment AB is $r = b/a$. Let r' be the corresponding slope ratio in the right panel. The visual impression from Figure 4.12 is that $r > r'$. This is not the case; r is equal to r'.

The angles of line segments contaminate our judgment of slopes, which causes bias. In the left panel of Figure 4.12 the angles of the line segments with the horizontal are α and β. The difference of these angles is greater than the difference of the corresponding angles in the right panel; this makes the line segments in the right panel appear to have slopes that are closer than those in the left panel. David Marr [94, p. 27] and Kent A. Stevens [118] have demonstrated that when people judge the slants and tilts of surfaces of three-dimensional objects it is angles that are judged. After spending millennia judging angles, it is not surprising that our visual system has a predilection for judging angles of line segments on graphs.

A little mathematics shows why, if we are geared to angle judgments, there is a problem in judging slopes. Consider a line segment such as AB in the left panel of Figure 4.12. The slope of the line segment is tan(α). Suppose the angle of the line segment is changed by a small amount, ϵ. Then the new slope is tan(α+ϵ). The change in the slope is

$$\tan(\alpha + \epsilon) - \tan(\alpha)$$

and for ϵ small this change is approximately $\epsilon s(\alpha)$ where

$$s(\alpha) = \tan'(\alpha) = \frac{1}{\cos^2(\alpha)}.$$

The function $s(\alpha)$ is a sensitivity function that tells us about the change in slope when we change α by a small amount. As α approaches $\pi/2$ radians, $s(\alpha)$ goes to infinity. Thus, when α is near $\pi/2$ a very small change in the angle of the segment results in a prodigious change in the slope. This means, of course, that the judgments of slopes of line segments whose angles are close to $\pi/2$ will have poor accuracy.

Since the slope goes to infinity as α goes to $\pi/2$, we might argue that it is not surprising that the accuracy of slope judgments becomes

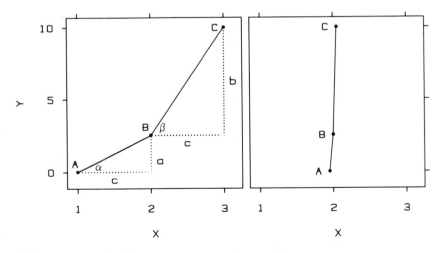

Figure 4.12   ANGLE CONTAMINATION OF SCOPE JUDGMENTS. In the left panel, the ratio of the slope of line segment BC to the slope of AB appears larger than in the right panel. Actually, the slope ratio is the same in both panels. The reason for the incorrect graphical perception is that in the right panel the angles of the segments with the horizontal are more nearly equal than in the left panel.

poor because we can expect that the *absolute* error of magnitude judgments will increase as the magnitude increases. It might be that the *relative* error of slope judgments — that is, the error divided by the true slope — is stable. For example, in Figure 4.12 it was the *ratio* of the slopes in which we were interested and not the difference. If we change the angle α by ϵ, the relative change in the slope is

$$\frac{\tan(\alpha+\epsilon) - \tan(\alpha)}{\tan(\alpha)}$$

and for ϵ small this value is approximately $\epsilon t(\alpha)$ where

$$t(\alpha) = \frac{\tan'(\alpha)}{\tan(\alpha)} = \frac{2}{\sin(2\alpha)} .$$

But $t(\alpha)$ also goes to infinity as α goes to $\pi/2$, so the relative accuracy of slope judgments also degrades. The relative accuracy also degrades as α tends to 0, but it is to be expected that the relative accuracy of the judgment of very small magnitudes be low.

Suppose a person is asked to judge the ratio, b/a, of the slopes in the left panel of Figure 4.12. Suppose the ratio, β/α, of the angles, were judged instead, then the bias in the judgment would be

$$\frac{\beta}{\alpha} - \frac{b}{a} = \frac{\arctan\left(\dfrac{b}{c}\right)}{\arctan\left(\dfrac{a}{c}\right)} - \frac{b}{a} .$$

Later, we will compare this theoretical bias, based on an assumption of contamination by angles, with the actual bias that occurred in one of the experiments in graphical perception that will now be described.

Experiments in Graphical Perception

Until now, the discussion in this section has been based on the theory of visual perception and some armchair reasoning. The theory and reasoning are helpful, but can take us just so far. The critical information about the paradigm comes from direct experimentation. We will now discuss three experiments that probed the accuracies of elementary graphical-perception tasks and the role of distance [33, 35].

In one of the three experiments, which we will call *experiment three* [35] since it was the last to be run, subjects studied the seven types of displays of graphical objects shown in Figure 4.13.   Table 4.2 describes the judgment that the subjects made for each of the seven types of display and the elementary graphical-perception task that was involved. The *blobs* in the seventh display are irregular regions whose boundaries are specified by trigonometric polynomials. The displays used in the experiment were larger than is shown in Figure 4.13; in the experiment each display filled an 8.5" x 11" page.

On each display in Figure 4.13 the graphical object to the left is a standard; subjects were told to judge what percent the attribute of each of the other objects was of the standard. For example, for the angle display, subjects were asked to judge what percent each of the three angles was of the standard. Subjects were told that in all cases the attributes of the three objects to the right were less than the attribute for the standard, so the true percents being judged were between 0 and 100. There were ten occurrences of each type of display in Figure 4.13; thus subjects made 210 = 7×3×10 judgments — three judgments per display, seven types of displays, and ten displays of each type. The number of subjects that participated in the experiment was 127.

Table 4.2   SUBJECT JUDGMENTS IN EXPERIMENT THREE. The table shows the judgment that the subjects made for each of the seven types of displays in Figure 4.13 and the elementary graphical-perception task involved in the judgment.

Panel Number in Figure 4.13	What Subjects Judged	Elementary Graphical-Perception Task
1	Vertical distances of dots above the common bottom baseline	Position along a common scale
2	Vertical distances of dots above the bottom baselines	Position along identical, nonaligned scales
3	Lengths of the lines	Length
4	Slopes of the lines	Slope
5	Sizes of the angles	Angle
6	Areas of the circles	Area
7	Areas of the blobs	Area

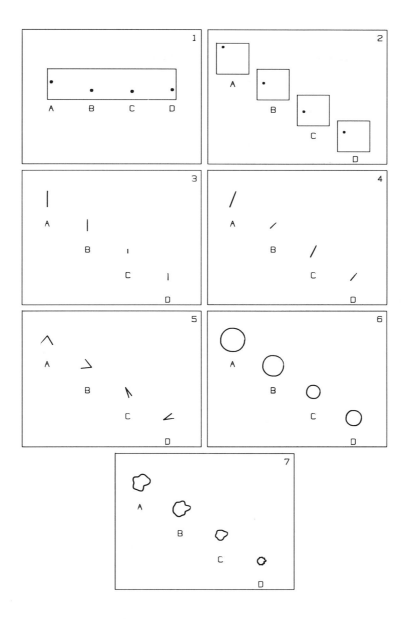

Figure 4.13   DISPLAYS FROM EXPERIMENT THREE.   Subjects   in experiment three were shown the seven types of displays in this figure.   In each case subjects judged what percents the attributes of the three graphical objects to the right were of the attribute of the standard, the object to the left.

The error of each judgment of each subject was computed where

$$\text{error} = |\text{judged percent} - \text{true percent}|.$$

There are three factors in the experiment upon which these errors depend — the size of the standard, the true percent being judged, and the distance of the judged object from the standard. A statistical model was fit to the data that related the errors to the three factors; standard statistical procedures were used to estimate unknown parameters in the model, to verify that the model did indeed provide a reasonable fit to the data, and to adjust the area judgment errors for a gentle upward drift that occurred during the experiment.

The bottom section of Figure 4.14 shows measures of error for each type of judgment in experiment three; the error measures are for one particular standard size and for one particular distance from the standard. The two-tiered error bars show 50% and 95% confidence intervals.

As we saw from the displays in Figure 4.13, the judged objects were three different distances from the standard; we found no significant difference between the two positions closest to the standard, so we merged the effects for these two, but the increased distance of the third position did cause a significant increase in the errors. The accuracy measures in Figure 4.14 are for the close, merged positions. This choice, and the choice of the standard size, matched the aspects of accuracy measures computed from the other two experiments [33]; the accuracy measures for the two other experiments are also shown in Figure 4.14. The displays that subjects judged in experiments one and two were different from those in experiment three, but the task — judging what percent the attribute of one object was of another — was the same. Hence, the comparison of the three experiments in Figure 4.14 is reasonable.

The error measures in Figure 4.14 are consistent with the theoretical discussion given earlier in this section. As suggested by Stevens' Law, length judgments are more accurate than area judgments, and as suggested by Weber's Law, judgments of position along identical, nonaligned scales are more accurate than length judgments. We saw earlier that angle and slope judgments are biased; thus it is not surprising that their error measures are greater than those for the length and position judgments, which are not biased.

Figure 4.15 shows the distance effect in experiment three. The filled circles show the error measure from Figure 4.14; recall that this measure combines the two closest positions. The open circles show the error measure at the third position *minus* the error measure at the two closest positions. In all cases the differences are positive, so the error increases in going from the two closest positions to the third position.

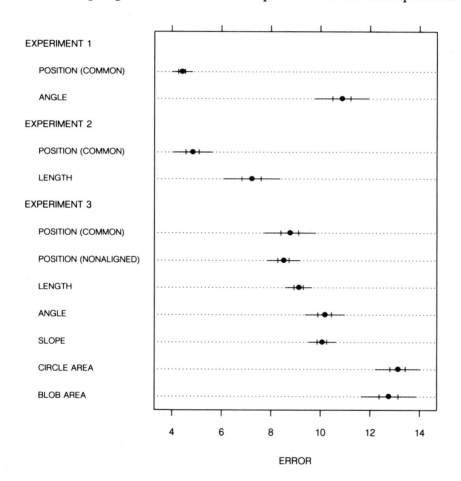

Figure 4.14   ERRORS. Measures of the errors of the elementary tasks for experiments one, two, and three are shown. The two-tiered error bars are 50% and 95% confidence intervals for the measures.

Thus increasing the distance between judged graphical elements can increase the error of the judgment, and as Figure 4.15 shows, by amounts that are nontrivial.

Earlier in this section, a formula was given for the bias that would occur in the judging of slope ratios if angles were being judged instead. In experiment three, subjects made 30 judgments of ratios of slopes.

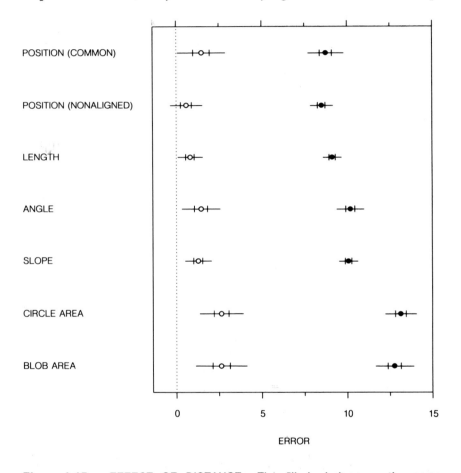

Figure 4.15   EFFECT OF DISTANCE. The filled circles are the error measures for experiment three, which are also shown in Figure 4.14. The unfilled circles are the increases in the measures resulting from an increased distance of the judged objects from the standard. The two-tiered error bars are 50% and 95% confidence intervals.

Figure 4.16 graphs estimates of the bias for the 30 judgments in the experiment against the theoretically derived biases; each of the thirty estimates is an average across subjects. The magnitudes of the actual biases are not as large as those derived theoretically, but this is to be expected because the derivation is based on an assumption that the slope judgments are *purely* angle judgments. What we expect is that slope judgments are only influenced by the angles; this is strongly supported by the high correlation of 0.66 that exists between the actual and theoretical biases.

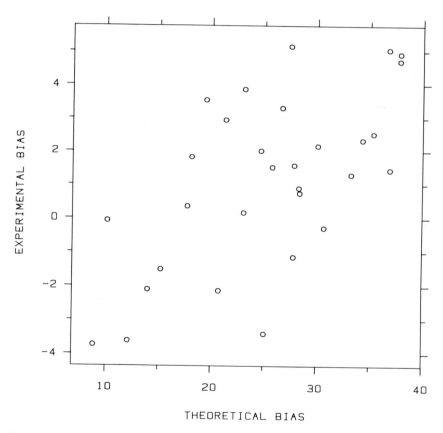

THEORETICAL BIAS

Figure 4.16   THEORETICAL AND ACTUAL BIAS OF SLOPE JUDGMENTS. The measures of biases of the 30 slope judgments from experiment three are graphed against the theoretical biases computed from assuming angles with the horizontal are judged instead of slopes. The high correlation suggests that angles do contaminate slope judgments.

Summary and Discussion

Graphical perception has been investigated by applying the theory of visual perception and by experiments in graphical perception. The theory and experimentation gave us information about the accuracies with which we perform the elementary graphical-perception tasks. The experimentation showed that accuracy decreases as the distance between judged graphical elements increases.

Table 4.3 presents an ordering of the elementary tasks from most accurate to least accurate. The ordering applies to the visual decoding of a quantitative variable, such as the frequency of radio waves, and not to a categorical variable, such as radio manufacturer. Some aspects of the ordering are based on informal experimentation with graphical data display; these aspects will be discussed shortly. There are several ties in the ordering, such as slope and angle; there is not enough information at this time to distinguish the accuracies of these tied tasks.

Table 4.3   ORDERING OF THE ELEMENTARY TASKS. The elementary graphical-perception tasks are ordered from most accurate to least accurate. The ordering is based on the theory of visual perception, on experiments in graphical perception, and on informal experimentation. An important principle of data display is that we should encode data on a graph so that the visual decoding involves tasks as high in the ordering as possible.

1. Position along a common scale
2. Position along identical, nonaligned scales
3. Length
4. Angle — Slope
5. Area
6. Volume
7. Color hue — Color saturation — Density

Several qualifications need to be made about the ordering. One involves slope judgments. We saw that as the angle of a line segment with the horizontal approaches $\pi/2$ radians, the error of slope judgments becomes extremely poor. Thus the position of slope judgments in the ordering is for slopes of segments whose angles with the horizontal are not too close to $\pi/2$; for example, the angles of the slopes did not exceed 1.34 radians (76.5°) in the third experiment in graphical perception described in this section, and slope judgments had about the same accuracy as angle judgments.

Another qualification involves the two types of position judgments, which are the most accurate tasks in Table 4.3. In the third experiment, the position judgments had nearly identical error measures. Nevertheless, position along a common scale is ranked ahead of position along identical, nonaligned scales for two reasons: The error measure for position along a common scale is considerably lower in experiments one and two (see [35] for a full discussion), and informal experimentation in which the same data are graphed in two ways suggests that position along a common scale is more accurate (see the next section). However, the ranking of the two position tasks should be regarded as needing more experimental verification.

Color hue, color saturation, and density have been put in last place in the ordering. This is based solely on informal experimentation with these methods. Color hue does not even have an unambiguous natural measure that we can use to encode data. As we saw in Section 5 of Chapter 3, using different colors or different densities can be very effective for showing a categorical variable, but they do a poor job of conveying the relative magnitudes of the values of a quantitative variable.

4.4 APPLICATION OF THE PARADIGM TO DATA DISPLAY

The basic principle of data display that arises from the ordering of graphical-perception tasks in Table 4.3 is the following: *encode data on a graph so that the visual decoding involves tasks as high as possible in the ordering.* Two qualifications must immediately be made. First, the principle does not provide a complete prescription for making a graph but rather provides only a rough guide. Second, *detection* and *distance* are mitigating factors that must be balanced with the goal of moving as high as possible in the ordering. The application of these ideas to graphing data will be illustrated in this section by many examples.

Slope Judgments: Graphing Rate of Change

The top panel of Figure 4.17 shows smoothed yearly average atmospheric CO_2 concentrations from Mauna Loa, Hawaii [75]. The raw data were smoothed by the lowess procedure described in Section 4 of Chapter 3. To visually compare the levels of two CO_2 concentrations at two times we can make judgments of positions along a common scale, the vertical scale.

In addition to decoding the values of the concentrations in this example, we want to decode the *rate of change* of the concentrations; we want to know if the amount of increase through time is itself increasing and by how much. Suppose the CO_2 concentration in year i is $c(i)$, then the rate of change from year i to a later year j is

$$\frac{c(j) - c(i)}{j - i} \; .$$

This number can be decoded visually by judging the slope of a line through the points for years i and j. For the year-to-year changes in CO_2, that is, when $j = i + 1$, we can judge the slopes of the line segments that are drawn on the graph; this provides an assessment of very *local* rate of change. For changes over time periods greater than a year we must judge mentally superposed lines, or *virtual lines* as David Marr [94, pp. 81-86] and Kent A. Stevens [117] call them.

In the top panel of Figure 4.17 the visual impression is that the slopes of the connecting lines are nearly constant from 1959 to about 1964 and are also constant but higher from about 1966 to 1980. This would mean that the local rate of increase is constant during the first time interval and constant but higher during the second time interval.

Judgment of slope is in fourth position in the order of graphical-perception tasks; we cannot expect to make slope judgments with as much accuracy as judgments of position along a common scale. In the bottom panel of Figure 4.17, local rate of change is graphed directly. The vertical scale is the yearly change in CO_2; for example, the value for 1966 is the 1967 CO_2 concentration minus the 1966 concentration. Now the yearly changes can be decoded by making judgments of position along a common scale. Now we can see that our assessment of local rate of change from judgments of slope in the top panel was not particularly accurate; local rate of change is indeed nearly constant from 1959 to 1964, but from 1966 to 1980 it fluctuates and increases overall by about 35%. The judgments of positions along a common scale have provided a more accurate assessment of the pattern than the slope judgments.

The ordering of elementary graphical-perception tasks and our explicit thinking about graphical perception have led to an important data-display principle: If the local rate of change of graphed values is of importance, then graph local rate of change directly on a juxtaposed panel, as in Figure 4.17. This allows the values to be decoded by the more accurate judgments of position along a common scale instead of slope judgments.

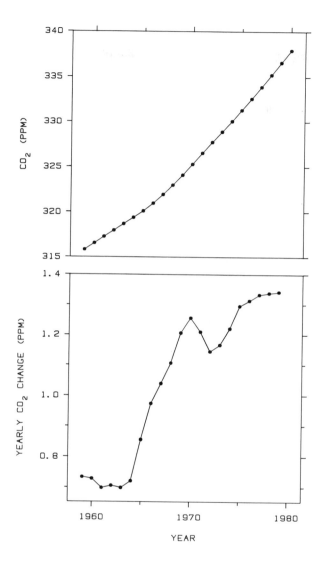

Figure 4.17   SLOPE AND POSITION JUDGMENTS. The top panel graphs smoothed yearly average CO_2 concentrations from Mauna Loa, Hawaii. To visually decode the rate of change of CO_2 we must make slope judgments; the visual impression is that local rate of change is constant from 1966 to 1980. In the bottom panel the yearly changes are graphed. Now local rate of change can be decoded by judgments of position along a common scale, which are more accurate than slope judgments, and now we can see rate of change is not constant from 1966 to 1980 but rather increases by about 35%.

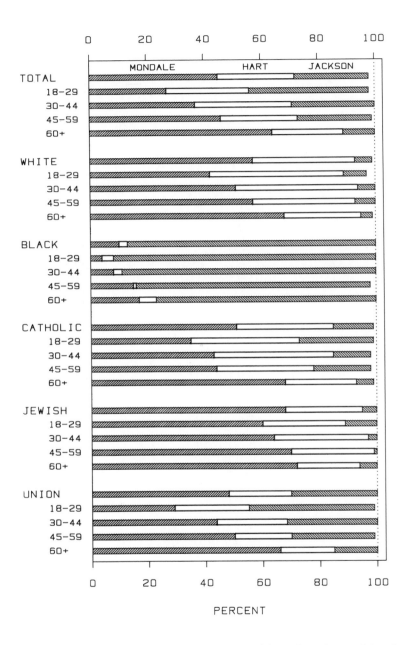

Figure 4.18   LENGTH JUDGMENTS. A divided bar chart is used to show the percentage of the vote for three candidates in the 1984 New York Democratic primary election. Because the Mondale values have a common baseline we can compare them visually by judging positions along a common scale. The Hart values, or the Jackson values, must be decoded by length judgments, which are not as accurate. It is difficult, for example, to see the Hart age effect.

Length Judgments: Divided Bar Charts

Length judgments play a fundamental role in Figure 4.18. The data are the percentages of the vote for each of three candidates — Mondale, Hart, and Jackson — in a sample of 2016 voters leaving polling places in the 1984 New York State Democratic primary [103]. Figure 4.18 is a *divided bar chart* that shows the percentages for four age groups and six categories of voters. The percentages for the three candidates do not add to 100 in all cases because of rounding of the reported data, voting for others, or omitted answers.

The Mondale bars in Figure 4.18 all have a common baseline at the left of the graph, so both the lengths of the Mondale bars and the positions of the right ends of the bars encode the Mondale vote. This means we can utilize the most accurate elementary task — judgment of position along a common scale — to visually compare the different values of the Mondale data. We cannot do this for the Hart or the Jackson values; neither has a fixed baseline and so we must rely on just length judgments.

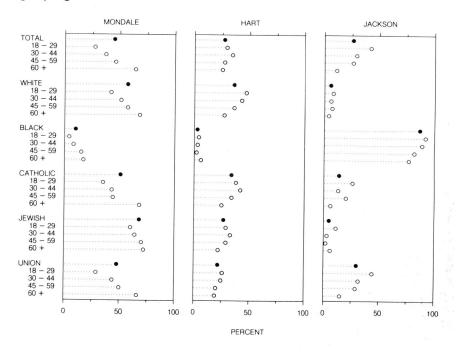

Figure 4.19   POSITION JUDGMENTS. The data from Figure 4.18 are graphed by a two-way dot chart. Now the Hart values, or the Jackson values, can be decoded by judgments of positions along a common scale. Now we can see that the 30-44 age group is Hart's strongest for several of the voter groups. To compare the values of different candidates we make judgments of positions along nonaligned, identical scales.

To compare the three percentages for the three candidates in a particular age-voter group in Figure 4.18, we also must make judgments of length. For example, we can see that the Jewish vote in the 18-29 age group is highest for Mondale, next highest for Hart, and lowest for Jackson.

Figure 4.19 is a two-way dot chart of the voting data. Each panel of the graph shows all ages and voter groups for one candidate. The three panels provide common baselines for the data of all candidates, not just Mondale. Now the data for each candidate can be compared by judgments of position along a common scale, which is two steps higher in the ordering than the length judgments that are required in Figure 4.18. Now the three values for the three candidates for a particular voter group and age group can be decoded visually by judgments of position along nonaligned, but identical scales, which is one step higher in the ordering than length judgments.

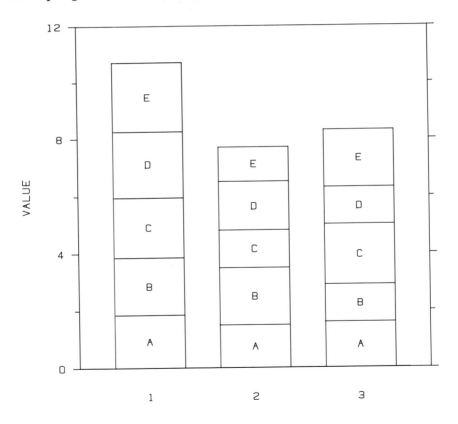

Figure 4.20   LENGTH JUDGMENTS. To visually compare the values of items in group 1 we must make length judgments. We cannot readily order these values from smallest to largest.

The invocation of more accurate elementary graphical-perception tasks in Figure 4.19 allows us to see patterns in the data that are not apparent in Figure 4.18. For example, Figure 4.19 shows there was a Hart age effect. The 30-44 age group was often Hart's strongest; when it was not, the 18-29 age group was usually the highest. This is the yuppy effect [65] — young, urban professionals identifying with Hart. But in Figure 4.18 the Hart age effect is not readily apparent and can be missed easily because of the reduced accuracy of the length judgments.

Figure 4.20 further illustrates, with made-up data, the poor performance of divided bar charts. The five values in group 1 must be compared by length judgments. Try to order them from smallest to largest. It is not a particularly easy task. In Figure 4.21 the data from Figure 4.20 are graphed by a grouped dot chart. Now all values can be decoded visually by making judgments of position along a common

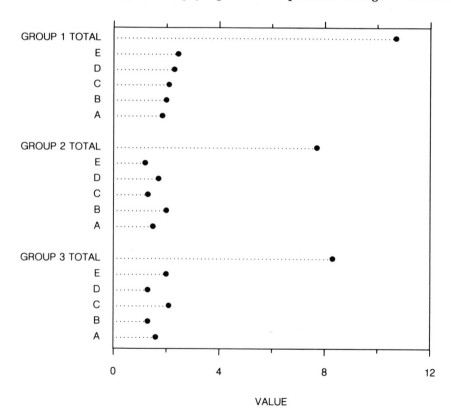

Figure 4.21   POSITION JUDGMENTS. The values from Figure 4.20 are graphed by a grouped dot chart. Since the values of items in group 1 can be compared visually by judgments of positions along a common scale it is easy to see the order from smallest to largest is A to E.

scale, and it is now easy to see that the order in group 1 from smallest to largest is A to E.

It is never necessary to resort to a divided bar chart and put up with the less accurate length judgments, because any set of data that can be shown by a divided bar chart also can be shown by a graphical method that replaces the length judgments of the bar chart by position judgments, but does not sacrifice meaning or organization. Figures 4.18 to 4.21 illustrate replacement by a dot chart. The next example illustrates replacement by a Cartesian graph with superposed data sets.

Figure 4.22 is a divided bar chart that shows yearly issues of three types of corporate securities from 1950 to 1981 [16, p. 59]. To visually decode the totals and the values for public bonds, we can make judgments of position along a common scale. But to study the values for private bonds and for stocks we must make length judgments.

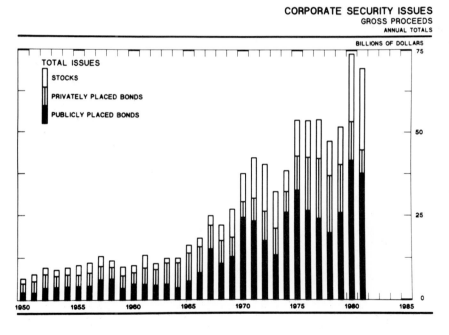

Figure 4.22   LENGTH JUDGMENTS. We must make length judgments to compare the stock values through time or to compare the private bond values through time or to compare the three values — stocks, private bonds, and public bonds — at a particular point in time.
Figure republished from [16].

Furthermore, to compare the three values for a given year we must make length judgments. Figure 4.23 is a graph that allows all values to be compared by judgments of position along a common scale. Logarithms of the data are graphed since it is natural to think about factors and percents for these data. Now we can study more effectively the movement of stock issues, the movement of private bond issues, and the three values of the three series for a particular year.

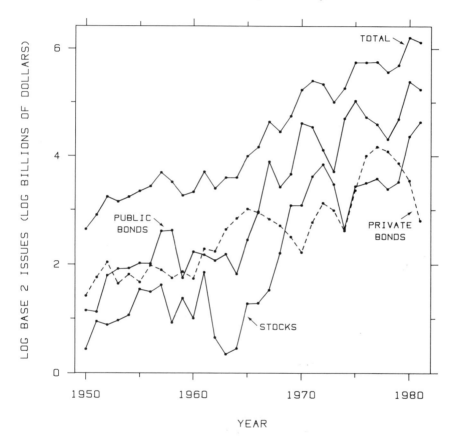

Figure 4.23 POSITION JUDGMENTS. The data from Figure 4.22 now can be decoded by judgments of positions along a common scale. Our perception of trends through time and of the relative values of stock issues, private bond issues, and public bond issues is now more accurate than in Figure 4.22. A divided bar chart always can be replaced by a graphical method that requires only position judgments.

Angle Judgments: Pie Charts

Data that can be shown by pie charts always can be shown by a dot chart. This means that judgments of position along a common scale can be made instead of the less accurate angle judgments. Fortunately, pie charts are little used in science and technology [27], but they are a staple of business and mass media graphics. Figure 4.24 is a pie chart with made-up data. Try to order the five values from smallest to largest. It is not easy to do. In Figure 4.25 the same values are graphed with a dot chart, and now it is easy to see the order is 1 to 5.

Cognition

In Section 4.1 we saw that in studying graphs we also perform cognitive tasks: reading values off scales and doing mental arithmetic and quantitative reasoning. It turns out that in converting from length, angle, and slope judgments to either of the two position judgments, we enhance our performance of the cognitive tasks because scale reading becomes easier. For slope judgments there is no scale at all. For length judgments we must judge two scale values, instead of just one, and do a mental subtraction. For angle judgments we could employ a polar, or circular, scale but this would also require two reads and a subtraction. Thus a beneficial spin-off of changing to position judgments is enhanced performance of the cognitive tasks.

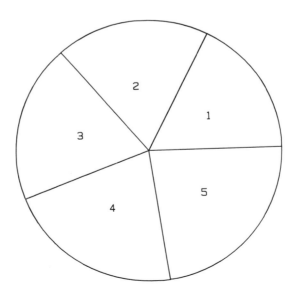

Figure 4.24   ANGLE JUDGMENTS. It is difficult to order the values encoded on this pie chart from smallest to largest.

Distance and Detection

Before continuing any further with the discussion of improving graphs by moving higher in the ordering of elementary graphical-perception tasks, it is important that we consider illustrations of the role of distance and detection. These two factors must be taken into consideration and balanced with the goal of moving higher in the ordering.

The experimentation described in Section 4.3 showed that as the distance of two graphical elements increases, our ability to visually decode the values encoded by the elements can decrease. This is illustrated by the Mondale values marked (1), (2), and (3) on Figure 4.26, which graphs the primary election data again. Our visual system can

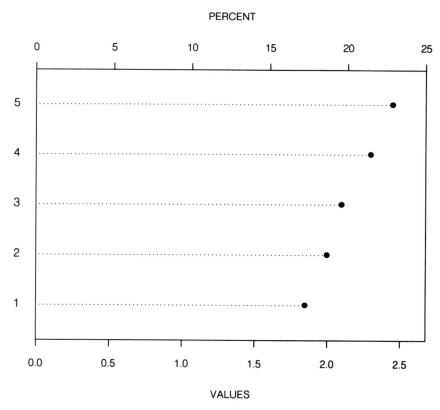

Figure 4.25 POSITION JUDGMENTS. The data from Figure 4.24 are shown by a dot chart. The values can be visually decoded by judgments of position along a common scale, which are more accurate than angle judgments, and now it is obvious that the order is 1 to 5. A pie chart always can be replaced by a dot chart, replacing angle judgments by more accurate judgments of positions along a common scale.

immediately determine that (2) is greater than (1), even though their difference is small, because the values are graphed next to one another. Try to judge visually which of (1) and (3) is the bigger. The task is very difficult. The answer is that (3) is greater than (1); in fact, (3) = (2) so (2) − (1) = (3) − (1). (1) and (2) are far easier to judge then (1) and (3) because the first pair are vertically much closer. These values are used purely for illustration, and it is not suggested that we need to differentiate such close values in order to understand the data in this example. The important point is that the distance principle illustrated is a general one that applies to all judgments.

One might, on the basis of the ordering of graphical-perception tasks, suggest the following new design of Figure 4.26: Since any two values for two different candidates must be compared by judgments of position along identical but nonaligned scales, arrange the three panels vertically so they all share a common scale; then all comparisons of

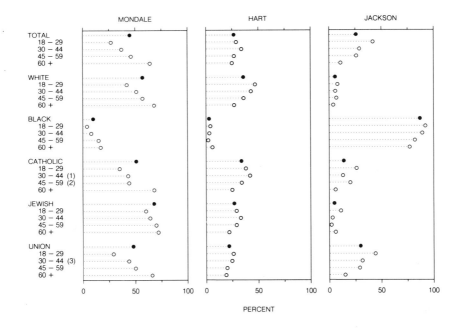

Figure 4.26 DISTANCE AND DETECTION. As the distance of two graphical objects increases, the accuracy of a visual comparison decreases. We can easily see in this figure that (2) is greater than (1); it is difficult to see that (3) is greater than (1), even though (2) = (3), because of the greater vertical distance. One of the strengths of this graph is that we can easily detect — that is, see by nearly effortless scanning — the three vote percentages of the three candidates for each voter-age combination.

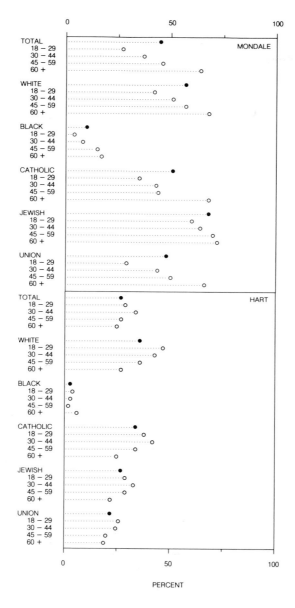

Figure 4.27   DISTANCE AND DETECTION. The Hart and Mondale data from Figure 4.26 are graphed on the same scale. While we have replaced judgments of position on nonaligned, identical scales by judgments of position along a common scale, the graph is not as effective as Figure 4.26 because we cannot easily detect the candidate percentages for each voter-age combination.

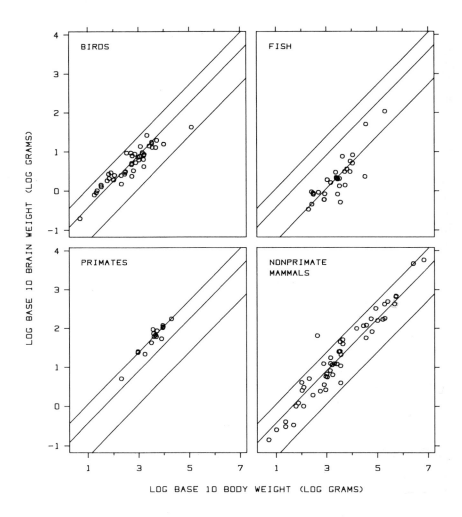

Figure 4.28 DETECTION. Detection must be considered carefully in designing a data display and must be balanced with the goal of moving as high in the ordering as possible. If we graphed the four groups of data in the same data region, all brain weights (or all body weights) would be on a common scale, but it would be impossible to detect each group of points.

values can be made by judgments of positions on this common scale. Figure 4.27 shows such an arrangement, but only for Mondale and Hart. This new display does *not* convey the data better than Figure 4.26. Let us see why.

While there is no experimental evidence as yet to back it up, the following seems like a reasonable conjecture: Once two quantities graphed along the same scale are sufficiently far apart in the direction perpendicular to the scale, the visual judging of the two quantities is no more accurate than judging them on identical, nonaligned scales. Thus the three-panel design of Figure 4.26, which requires us to make some judgments along identical but nonaligned scales to compare values of different candidates, does not reduce substantially the accuracy of our visual decoding compared with Figure 4.27.

In fact, the design in Figure 4.26 is more effective than the single-scale one of Figure 4.27 because of detection. In Section 4.2 we defined the detection of a group of graphical elements to mean that our visual system can see the elements either simultaneously or by nearly effortless scanning. In Figure 4.26 we can focus our visual system easily on the candidate percentages for a particular voter-age combination just by scanning horizontally. This focusing task is easier than in Figure 4.27 because of the horizontal organization in Figure 4.26.

The most common problem of detection is visual discrimination of different graphical elements in the data region of a graph; this problem was treated at length in Sections 4 and 5 of Chapter 3. In Figure 4.28, brain and body weights are graphed for four groups of animal species [40] by juxtaposing four panels. The juxtaposition forces us to make many judgments of positions along identical, nonaligned scales; for example, we carry out this task to compare brain weights of primates and birds. It would be advantageous if we could superpose all groups on the same panel, because then all brain weights, or all body weights, could be compared by judgments of positions on the same scale.

However, were we to superpose, at least in black and white, the graph would be an uninterpretable mess since the extensive overlap would make it impossible to *detect* the different groups. (In Section 5 of Chapter 3 we were able to superpose these data sets when color was used.)

Thus the important principle of detection is the following: Our visual system must detect the requisite graphical elements before the elementary graphical-perception tasks can be performed; thus detection must be carefully considered in designing a data display and must be balanced with the goal of moving as high in the ordering as possible.

Let us look at one more example illustrating distance and detection. Figure 4.29 shows data from WNCN, an FM radio station in New York City that plays classical music. The data were collected to resolve a debate about which composer is played the most on the station; one advocate was sure it was Beethoven and another was sure it was Johann Sebastian Bach. To resolve the debate a survey was conducted using the WNCN monthly program guide, *Keynote*, for the months of August 1984 and September 1984. The number of performances of pieces for each composer aired during this time period was counted. (Actually, the count is only for longer pieces since compositions less than about ten minutes are not included in the section of the guide that was used.) Repeat performances of a composition were counted; for example, Beethoven's Ninth Symphony was performed three times, so Beethoven got a count of three. The number of performances for all composers with more than 10 are shown in Figure 4.29. Almost as if to make both advocates happy, Bach and Beethoven tied for first place with 165 performances each.

Figure 4.29 shows some interesting information in addition to who was first. The very most popular composers are way ahead of the rest of the field. Fifth place Tchaikovsky, whom most would think of as quite a popular composer, is beaten by Bach and Beethoven by a factor of about 2.25, and tenth place Schumann is beaten by the winning pair by a factor of about four. Mozart has about 50% more performances than

Haydn, even though their compositions, to many ears, are similar. It is surprising to see Aaron Copland with so many performances. As the list shows, few 20th century composers get much exposure in classical music circles which, it would seem, makes the word "classical" appropriate.

Figure 4.30 shows the composer data, but arranged this time with composers in alphabetical order. As in Figure 4.29, we can compare all values by judgments of positions along the common horizontal scale. But for most purposes, Figure 4.29 is more informative than Figure 4.30. When we study a distribution of values such as the composer performances, we want to know what is large, what is medium, and what is small. The organization in Figure 4.29 allows us to easily *detect* the large, medium, and small values. We cannot do this nearly as effectively in Figure 4.30 because each of these sets of values is scattered throughout the graph. For example, in the above discussion of the data, we focused on the values of the top five composers and carefully compared them visually from Figure 4.29. This comparison was made easier by the five values being grouped together, which allows easy detection; in Figure 4.30 the five values are vertically spread out over most of the graph and are harder to detect as a group. Furthermore, the five values can be compared more accurately in Figure 4.29 because their distances in the vertical direction are generally smaller than in Figure 4.30. (Fortuitously, though, Johann Sebastian Bach and Beethoven are again next to one another in Figure 4.30, so we still can see easily that they tie for first place.)

Detection: Superposed Curves

There is a special but prevalent problem of detection associated with curves superposed in the same data region. The problem is pernicious because it is not one of lack of detection, which we would notice immediately, but rather one of detecting the wrong information, which usually goes unnoticed.

NUMBER OF PERFORMANCES

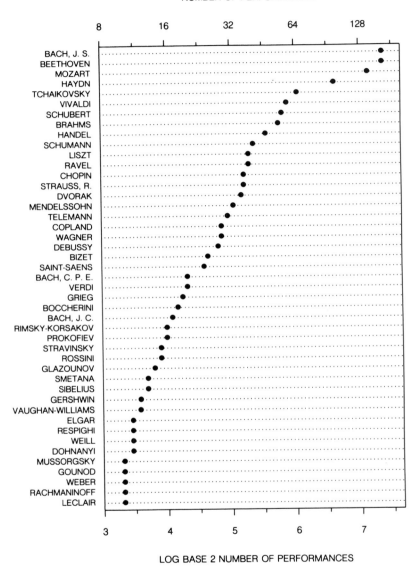

LOG BASE 2 NUMBER OF PERFORMANCES

Figure 4.29   DETECTION. The graph shows the number of compositions of 45 composers played on WNCN during August and September 1984. The data can be decoded by judgments of positions along a common scale. Because the values are ordered on the graph it is easy to detect which are small, which are medium, and which are large.

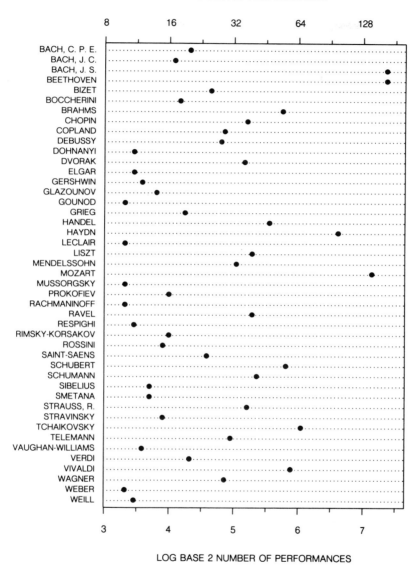

NUMBER OF PERFORMANCES

Figure 4.30   DETECTION.   The data from Figure 4.29 are now in alphabetical order by composer. Even though the values still can be decoded visually by judgments of positions along a common scale, the graph is not as effective as Figure 4.29 because we cannot as easily detect the small, medium, and large values.

Figure 4.31 illustrates the problem; the graph in the figure was published by William Playfair in 1786 [108]. The data, which were discussed in Section 1 of Chapter 1, are the values of imports and exports between England and the East Indies. To visually decode the import data we can make judgments of positions along a common scale; the same is true for the export data. Another set of important quantities on this graph is the amount by which imports exceeds exports; Playfair shaded the region between the import and export curves to highlight these values. To decode these values we must make length, or distance, judgments; we must judge the *vertical* distances between the two curves.

The problem is that when the slopes of two curves change by large amounts it is exceedingly difficult for our visual system to decode the data encoded by the vertical distances between the curves. For example, in Figure 4.32, which shows made-up data, the vertical distances between the curves are equal, but the visual impression is that the curves become closer in going from left to right. The problem is that our visual system cannot *detect* vertical distances; our visual system tends to detect minimum distances, which in Figure 4.32 lie along perpendiculars to the tangents of the curves. As the slope increases the distance along the perpendicular decreases, so the curves look closer as the slope increases.

This problem of detection very much affects our visual decoding in Figure 4.31. For example, during the period just after 1760 when both curves are rapidly increasing, the visual impression is that imports minus exports is not large and does not change by much. This is not the case. In Figure 4.33 the two curves are graphed in the top panel, and in the bottom panel imports minus exports are graphed directly. From the bottom panel we can decode imports minus exports by much more accurate judgments of position along a common scale, and it is clear that the behavior just after 1760 is quite different from how it appears in the top panel; there is a rapid rise to a peak and then a decrease, which is not at all apparent in the top panel.

Superposing two or more curves is one of the most common graph forms in science and technology. If it is important to compare the two vertical-scale values of two superposed curves for each value on the horizontal scale, then it is usually very helpful to graph the differences also, as in Figure 4.33. If many curves are superposed then it is impractical to graph all pairwise differences, and the only solution is for graph authors and graph viewers to fully appreciate that judged differences can be very inaccurate.

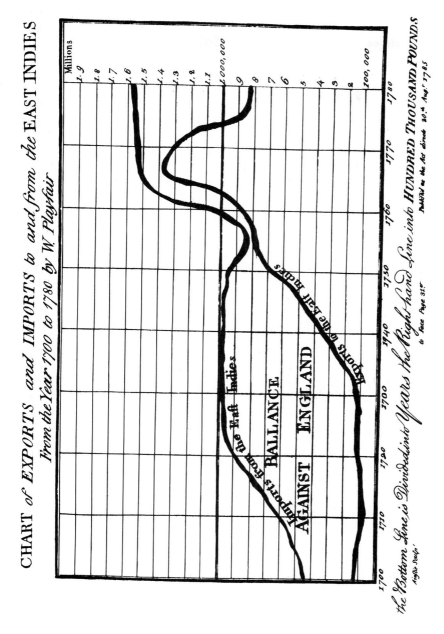

CHART of *EXPORTS* and *IMPORTS* to and from the EAST INDIES
From the Year 1700 to 1780 by W. Playfair

Figure 4.31   DIFFERENCES OF CURVES. This is a graph published by William Playfair in 1786. It is difficult to detect the vertical distances between the two curves, which encode imports minus exports.

Furthermore, we certainly do not want to create needless judgments of vertical distances between curves. Unfortunately, this is done in Figure 4.34 [16, p. 55], a familiar method for graphing time series; the bottom curve shows the private domestic nonfinancial data, the second curve shows the sum of the private domestic nonfinancial data and the commercial bank data, and each successive curve shows the sum of the previous sum and a new series. Thus the four series whose labels have arrows emanating from them must be decoded visually by judging vertical distances between two curves. The previous discussion has shown that we cannot expect to get even a roughly accurate appreciation of the behavior of these four series.

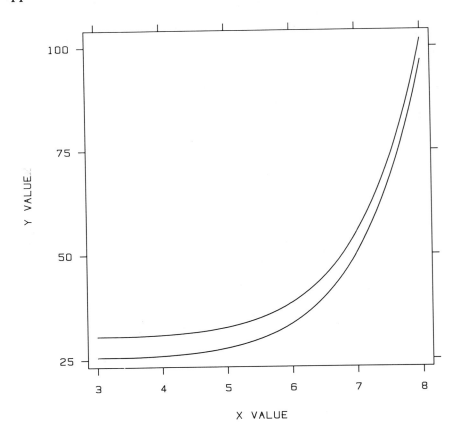

Figure 4.32   DETECTION. The vertical distances between the curves are equal but the visual impression is that the curves become closer in going from left to right; our visual system tends to judge minimum distances, which lie along normals to the curves.

Figure 4.35 uses made-up data to illustrate a minor variation of this same detection problem. The goal in the top panel is to judge the vertical distances of the points from the curve, which is no easier than judging curve differences. The visual impression from the top panel is that the points are closer on the right than on the left. The graph of residuals — data point values minus curve values — in the bottom panel shows the opposite is true.

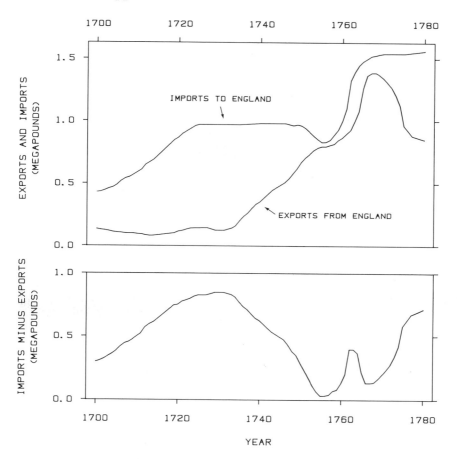

Figure 4.33   DIFFERENCES OF CURVES If it is important to compare the values of two curves with widely varying slopes, it is usually helpful to graph the differences also. The top panel of this graph shows the Playfair data from Figure 4.31. In the bottom panel, imports minus exports are graphed directly and their behavior, particularly around 1760, is quite different from the visual impression given by the top panel.

Area

Figure 4.36 is the graph of William Playfair [109] that was analyzed in Section 1 of Chapter 3. The populations of European cities around 1800 are encoded by the circle areas. Playfair may have been the first person to make a graph that directly encoded the data by area.

A common assumption about area judgments is unfortunately not always true. Darrell Huff [62, p. 69] writes, regarding two money bags that show two incomes: "Because the second bag is twice as high as the first, it is also twice as wide. It occupies not twice but four times as much area on the page. The numbers still say two to one, but the visual impression, which is the dominating one most of the time, says the ratio is four to one." Arthur H. Robinson and Randall D. Sale in a widely-read cartography textbook argue that map projections preserving areas are important; they write [112, p. 223]: "The mapping of some types of data specifically requires that the reader be given a correct visual impression of the relative sizes of the areas involved." Huff, Robinson, Sale and others have assumed that when people study areas, it is area they perceive and visually decode. We saw in Section 4.3 that this is

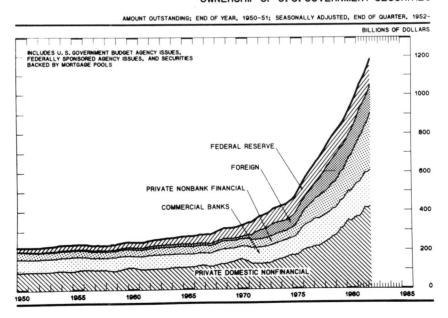

OWNERSHIP OF U. S. GOVERNMENT SECURITIES

AMOUNT OUTSTANDING; END OF YEAR, 1950–51; SEASONALLY ADJUSTED, END OF QUARTER, 1952–

Figure 4.34   CURVE DIFFERENCES. It is virtually impossible to decode the curve differences on this graph, despite the shading.
Figure republished from [16].

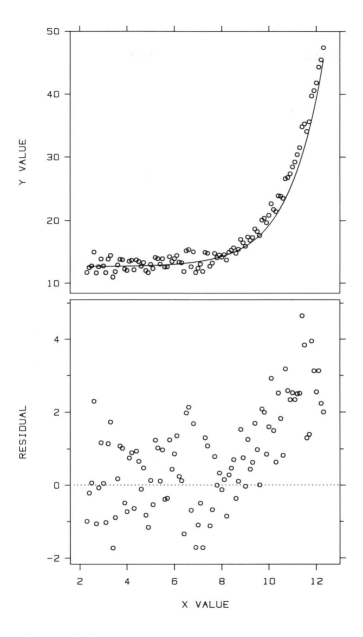

Figure 4.35   POINTS AND A CURVE. The same problem of detection occurs when we try to judge the vertical distances of points from a fitted curve. On this graph the deviations of the points on the left appear greater than those on the right. The graph of the residuals in the bottom panel shows the opposite is true.

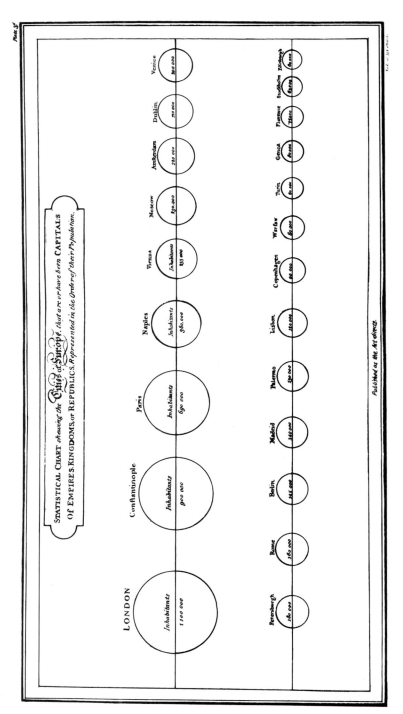

Figure 4.36   AREA JUDGMENTS. On this graph of William Playfair, which was published in 1801, circle areas encode populations of European cities. Area judgments are biased and are considerably less accurate than length and position judgments.

not always so; if people are shown two areas whose magnitudes are a_1 and a_2, and are asked to judge the ratio of a_1 to a_2, then most will judge on a scale

$$\left(\frac{a_1}{a_2}\right)^{\beta}$$

where $\beta < 1$. S. S. Stevens reports 0.7 as a typical value for β [119]. If the ratio is 4, as it is for Huff's example, then the judged area ratio when $\beta = 0.7$ is $4^{0.7} = 2.64$.

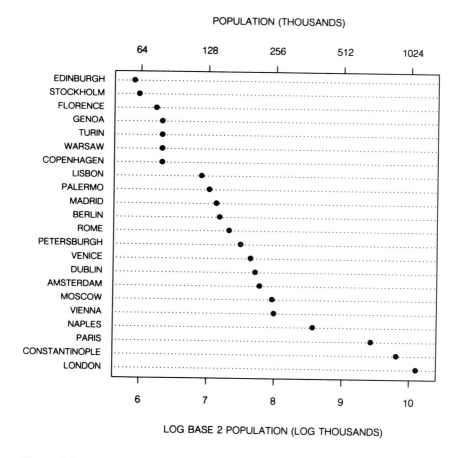

POPULATION (THOUSANDS)

LOG BASE 2 POPULATION (LOG THOUSANDS)

Figure 4.37   POSITION JUDGMENTS. The data from Figure 4.36 are graphed by a dot chart with a log scale. Now the data can be visually decoded by judgments of positions along a common scale and we can more accurately judge the populations than in Figure 4.36.

One might argue that the solution is to take the areas to be proportional to the data to the $1/0.7 = 1.43$ power, to counteract the bias. The problem is that there is no universal β; the value depends on the person making the judgment and on what is being judged [32].

The sensible solution to the problem of area judgments is to avoid them. Area is very low in the ordering of elementary tasks. A display of quantitative information that required area judgments almost always could be redesigned to replace the area judgments by position or length judgments and not degrade detection or the organization of the graph. (Maps are one exception.) Figure 4.37 is a dot chart of the Playfair population data using a log scale. Now the data can be decoded by judgments of position along a common scale and our perceptions are far keener than in Figure 4.36. For example, it is hard from Figure 4.36 to detect much of a change in the circle areas from Petersburgh to Lisbon, but Figure 4.37 shows that the populations vary by a factor of about $2^{0.5} = 1.4$.

The difficulty of area perception leads to an intriguing thought about maps. Maps are excellent graphical tools for conveying the positions, arrangements, and boundaries of geographical entities. Figure 4.38 is a map of the 48 contiguous U.S. states; it is an Alber conic projection, which preserves areas [112]. We can see states that are north and states that are south, or what is east and what is west, or how far it

Figure 4.38   AREA JUDGMENTS. Judging areas of geographical regions on maps is inaccurate and gives false impressions. For example, Florida (FL) appears larger than Georgia (GA) because the former is an elongated state with a large perimeter.

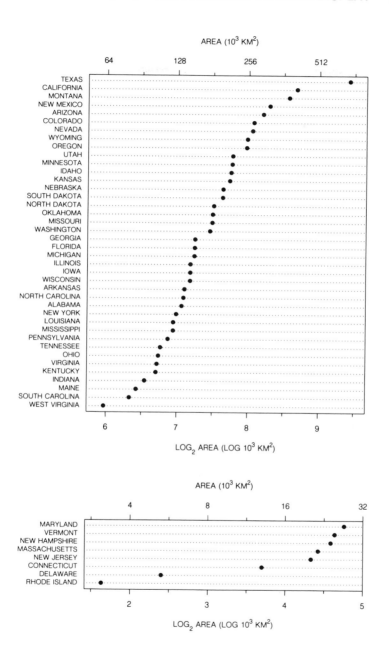

Figure 4.39   POSITION JUDGMENTS. The areas of the 48 U.S. States on the map of Figure 4.38 are shown by a dot chart. The graph gives a considerably more accurate visual decoding of state area. For example, it is now clear that the area of Florida is actually somewhat less than that of Georgia.

is from New York to California. But for the isolated task of judging just the relative areas of the states — and not, for example, how the areas depend on geographical location — we are no better off than trying to judge population from Playfair's circle graph. In fact, we are worse off because we must judge the areas of regions that are very different in shape.

Most of us undoubtedly have formed our judgments of the sizes of states of the U.S. from maps. This means most of us have an inaccurate concept of state areas. Figure 4.39, which graphs the state areas on a log scale, can give us a far more accurate impression of state sizes than a map. On the map of Figure 4.38 the visual impression is that Florida (FL) is considerably bigger than Georgia (GA). Figure 4.39 shows that Georgia is actually slightly bigger. Florida looks bigger on a map because it is a highly elongated state with a perimeter that is considerably larger than that of Georgia. Other states with appendages, such as Oklahoma (OK) and Idaho (ID), appear larger in area than they actually are. For example, Idaho looks much bigger than Kansas (KS), but Figure 4.39 shows they are very nearly equal in area.

Density and Length: Statistical Maps

Density, or amount of black, is also very low in the ordering of elementary graphical-perception tasks. Unfortunately, shading is used extensively on *statistical maps* to show how quantitative information varies geographically, which requires density judgments. Figure 4.40 is an example showing murders per 10^5 people in 1978 in 48 U.S. states [52]. Grids with different spacings encode the data; the spacings are a complicated function of the data that was chosen in an attempt to match encoded values with people's perceived values for this method of shading.

There are serious problems with statistical maps using shading. One is the low accuracy of the visual decoding; the best we can hope for is to perceive the correct order of the values. By referring to the key we can get a rough idea of numerical values, but the constant looking back and forth and matching patterns with the key is cumbersome and makes the graph, in reality, a table, but not a very accurate one. The reader is invited to judge from Figure 4.40 how much more the murder rate is for Florida than for New Jersey; it is a difficult task.

The shading in Figure 4.40 is visually imposing and when we study the graph our visual system sees definite, strong patterns. For example, the states appear to form geographically contiguous clusters. *We should not mistake this strong stimulus for getting an accurate impression of the data.* Much of what is visually imposing is misleading. Part of the reason why the clustering occurs so strongly is the reduction in the accuracy of the perceived quantitative information; values group together because we cannot differentiate them visually. Thus the encoding of the data by shading provides a kind of visual data reduction scheme in which noise is reduced and a signal comes through. Unfortunately the signal is of poor quality. For example, the deep South states (Texas, Louisiana, Mississippi, Alabama, and Georgia) deserve to cluster together as forcefully as the New England states (Connecticut, Rhode Island, Massachusetts, Vermont, New Hampshire, and Maine) but do not because our sensitivity to differences at the high end of the scale appears to be greater than at the low end of the scale. The range of the deep South values is 3.2, and the range for New England is 2.7, which is close to the deep South range. Furthermore the largest deep South value (Louisiana) is 1.4 units larger than the next largest value in its cluster, and the smallest New England value (New Hampshire) is 1.3 units less than the next smallest value in its cluster; but Louisiana appears to stand out in its cluster much more forcefully than New Hampshire does in its cluster.

The second serious problem with shading is that the states are treated very unequally because of the changing areas. The total amount of black inside a state's borders encodes, approximately,

$$\frac{\text{number of murders}}{\text{number of people}} \times \text{area} \ .$$

The result is that large states are very imposing and some small states nearly disappear.

The framed-rectangle graph, discussed in Section 6 of Chapter 3, can show data on a statistical map with far more accuracy and treats the states equally. This is illustrated in Figure 4.41, which shows the murder rates. Now the data can be decoded visually by judging positions along identical, nonaligned scales, because the frame and tick marks around each solid rectangle serve as scale lines. Now it is easy to see that the rate for Florida is about twice that of New Jersey.

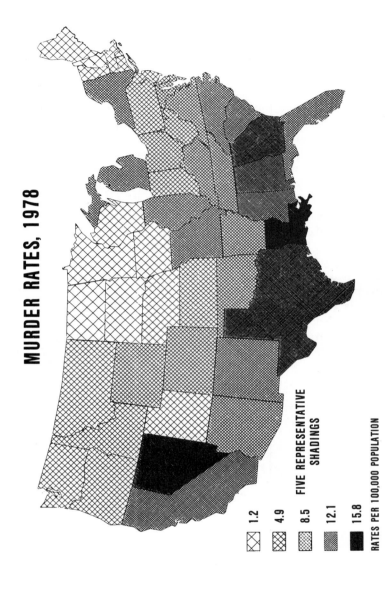

MURDER RATES, 1978

FIVE REPRESENTATIVE
SHADINGS

1.2

4.9

8.5

12.1

15.8

RATES PER 100,000 POPULATION

Figure 4.40   DENSITY JUDGMENTS.   Shading is often used to encode data on statistical maps, which requires density judgments to visually decode the data.   This figure is an example in which murder rates per 10^5 people in the U.S. are shown.   It is difficult to decode anything but the order of the values without constant reference to the key.   Also, the changing areas of the states makes the large states more visually imposing than the small states.
Figure republished from [52].   Copyright 1982 by the American Statistical Association.

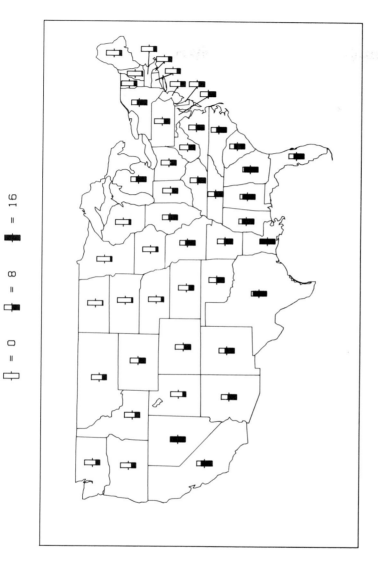

Figure 4.41 POSITION ALONG NONALIGNED, IDENTICAL SCALES. A framed-rectangle graph is used to show the murder rates from Figure 4.40. Now the rates can be decoded visually by judgments of positions along identical, nonaligned scales, which are much more accurate than shading judgments. Furthermore, the graphical elements representing the data do not have the radical change in visual impact that the elements in the shading method have.

Another method for showing geographical data is the *located-bar chart* [97, pp. 216-218]: the lengths of bars encode data at different geographical locations. This is illustrated in Figure 4.42 for the murder rate data. The graph does not perform as well as the framed-rectangle chart; as we saw in the discussion of Weber's Law in Section 4.3, the pure length judgments of bars are not as effective as the judgments of positions along the identical scales formed by the frames of the framed-rectangle chart.

Residuals

In Section 1 of Chapter 3 the usefulness of graphing residuals in various settings was demonstrated. Often, a graph of residuals will increase the resolution of the deviation of the data from a graphical reference, such as a curve or a line. But in addition, by graphing residuals directly, length judgments are replaced by the more accurate judgments of position along a common scale. An example will now be given that illustrates this.

Earlier, we discussed data on the number of compositions that were heard on radio station WNCN in New York City during August and September of 1984 for each of 45 composers. How reproducible are the results? For example, were Bach and Beethoven first during October and November of 1984? To help answer this question the sample was split; in Figure 4.43 the number of August performances is graphed against the number of September performances. The graph shows the points lie surprisingly close to the line $y = x$, which means the number of performances from one month to the next is reasonably stable.

From Figure 4.43 we can extract only a limited amount of information about the magnitude of the change in number of performances from August to September. Let x_i be the number of September performances and let y_i be the number of August performances. The vertical deviation of (x_i, y_i) from the line $y = x$ is $y_i - x_i$. (The horizontal deviation is $x_i - y_i$.) Thus to visually decode the differences, $y_i - x_i$, we must make length judgments.

Figure 4.44 was made to allow a more effective visual decoding of the August to September changes. The display is the Tukey sum-difference graph that was discussed in Section 1 of Chapter 3; the differences, $y_i - x_i$, are graphed against the total number of performances, $y_i + x_i$. Now the $y_i - x_i$ can be decoded by judgments of position along a common scale instead of length judgments.

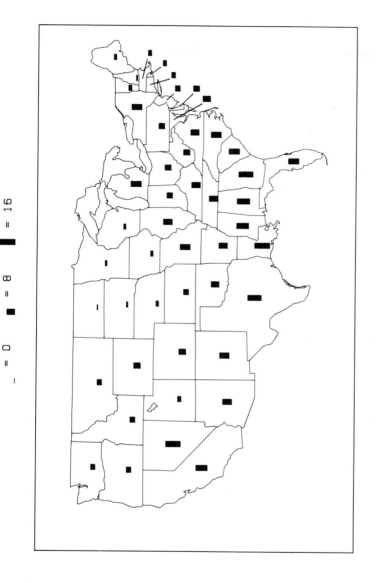

Figure 4.42 LENGTH. A located-bar chart is used to show the murder rates. Now, to decode the data we must make length judgments, which are not as accurate as the judgments of positions along identical non-aligned scales that we make in visually decoding the data in Figure 4.41.

Figure 4.44 shows that the composers with more performances tend to be more variable; for example, Vivaldi had 13 fewer performances in August than in September. Kurt Weill, a composer with a small number of performances, has a large positive difference because he had 11 performances in August and none in September. Weill was a featured composer on WNCN during August; the program guide *Keynote* ran a story on his life and many of Weill's pre-Broadway pieces were played.

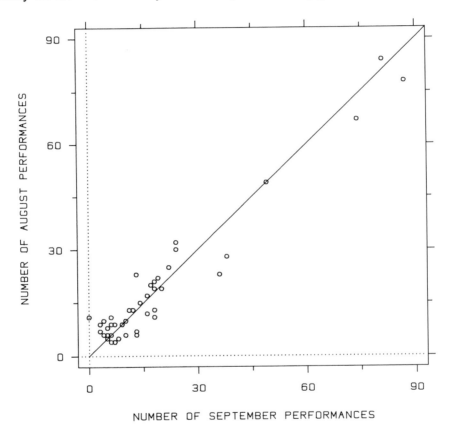

NUMBER OF SEPTEMBER PERFORMANCES

Figure 4.43 COMPARISON WITH *Y* = *X*. The numbers of August and September performances of 45 composers on WNCN are graphed. The purpose is to see how close the numbers are for each composer; to decode the August numbers minus the September numbers we can judge the vertical deviations of the points from the line *y* = *x*, which requires making length judgments.

Dot Charts and Bar Charts

Dot charts have been used extensively in the book to graph data in which the values have labels associated with them. Figure 4.45, which we saw in Section 4.3, is an example. The graphed values are the measures of accuracy for elementary graphical-perception tasks in three experiments. The two-tiered error bars show 50% and 95% confidence intervals.

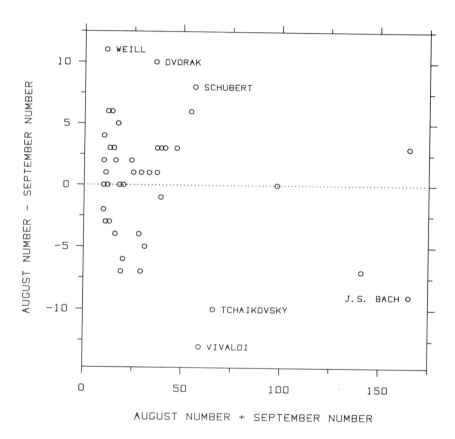

Figure 4.44   GRAPHING RESIDUALS. The changes from August to September in the number of performances can be more effectively studied on this figure, which is a Tukey sum-difference graph. The differences now can be decoded visually by judgments of positions along a common scale. In general, one of the strengths of graphing residuals is that we replace length judgments by judgments of positions along a common scale.

Ordinary *bar charts*, which sometimes can be used to show labeled data, have not been used so far in this book. (A *divided* bar chart was illustrated earlier in the chapter.) Dot charts are used instead because they are a more flexible display; they do not require a meaningful baseline on the scale line. Figure 4.46 shows the data of Figure 4.45 graphed by a bar chart with a scale that is the same as in Figure 4.45. The *lengths* and *areas* of the bars encode the data values *minus* the baseline value, which is between 3 and 4. Thus the bar lengths and

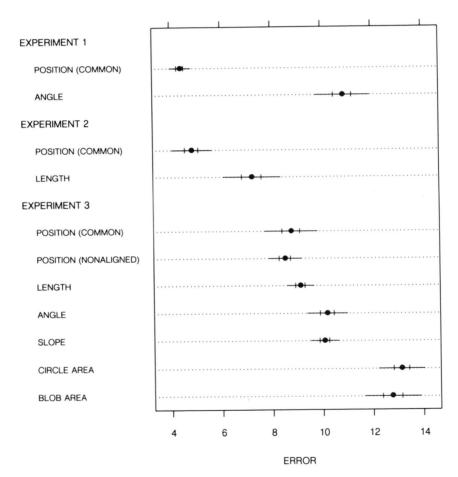

Figure 4.45   DOT CHARTS AND BAR CHARTS. A dot chart is used in this figure to graph data with a label for each value. Dot charts are more effective than bar charts since they can be used in a much wider variety of circumstances.

areas are meaningless, arbitrary numbers; we could just as well have the bars emanate from the right side of the graph. With dot charts we accommodate a meaningless baseline by making the dotted lines go all of the way across the graph, as in Figure 4.45; this visually deemphasizes the portion between the data dot and the left baseline. With the bar chart of Figure 4.46 the only remedy is to move the baseline to zero so that bar length and area encode the data, but this would waste space and degrade the resolution of the values.

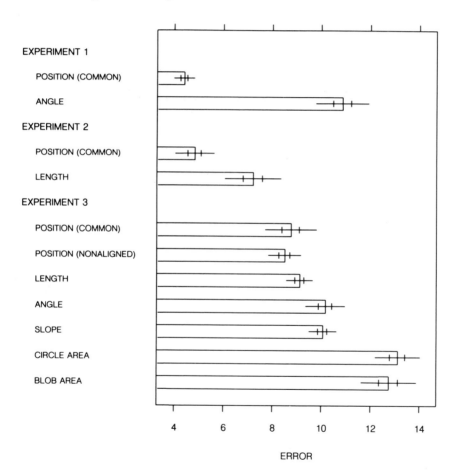

Figure 4.46   DOT CHARTS AND BAR CHARTS. A bar chart shows the data graphed by a dot chart in Figure 4.45. A bar chart should not be used in this way; the bar lengths and areas are meaningless since they encode the data minus an arbitrary number somewhere below four.

Summation

The paradigm of graphical perception developed in Sections 4.1 to 4.3 arises, in part, from formal, scientific studies: applications of the theory of visual perception and experiments in graphical perception. In a sense, the material in this section provides a partial test of the validity and applicability of the paradigm. The paradigm has been applied to many graphical methods; some methods are altered, and others are discarded and replaced by new methods. The reader can compare the old and new methods to judge the success of the paradigm.

Past studies in graphical perception [82, 83] generally have been hampered by the lack of a paradigm to explain results and to guide thinking. Thomas S. Kuhn [84, p. 16] points out that while "fact-collecting has been essential to the origin of many significant sciences, anyone who examines, for example, Pliny's encyclopedic writings or the Baconian natural histories will discover that it produces a morass." Much of the experimental work in graphical perception has been aimed at finding out how two graphical methods compare, rather than attempting to develop basic principles. Without the basic principles, or the paradigm, we have no predictive mechanism and every graphical issue must be resolved by an experiment. This is the curse of a purely empirical approach. For example, in the 1920s a battle raged on the pages of the *Journal of the American Statistical Association* about the relative merits of pie charts and divided bar charts [41, 42, 47, 63]. There was a pie chart camp and a divided bar chart camp; both camps ran experiments comparing the two charts using human subjects, both camps measured accuracy, and both camps claimed victory. The paradigm introduced in this chapter shows that a tie is not surprising and shows that both camps lose because other graphs perform far better than either divided bar charts or pie charts.

The material of this chapter is a first step in the formulation of a paradigm for graphical perception. As more experimental results are gathered the paradigm will evolve, as paradigms in science inevitably do.

REFERENCES

[1] Abbott, E. A. (1952). *Flatland; A Romance of Many Dimensions*, 6th edition, New York: Dover Publications.

[2] Alvarez, L. W., Alvarez, W., Asaro, F., and Michel, H. V. (1980). "Extraterrestrial cause for the Cretaceous-Tertiary extinction," *Science*, **208**: 1095-1108.

[3] Anderson, E. (1957). "A semigraphical method for the analysis of complex problems," *Proceedings of the National Academy of Sciences*, **43**: 923-927. Reprinted (1960) in *Technometrics*, **2**: 387-391.

[4] Andrews, D. F. (1972). "Plots of high-dimensional data," *Biometrics*, **28**: 125-136.

[5] Bacastow, R. B. (1976). "Modulation of atmospheric carbon dioxide by the Southern Oscillation," *Nature*, **261**: 116-118.

[6] Bacastow, R. B., Keeling, C. D., and Whorf, T. P. (1981). "Seasonal amplitude in atmospheric CO_2 concentration at Mauna Loa, Hawaii, 1959-1980," paper presented at the Conference on Analysis and Interpretation of CO_2 Data, World Meteorological Organization, Bern, Sept. 14-18.

[7] Baird, J. C. (1970). *Psychophysical Analysis of Visual Space*, New York: Pergamon Press.

[8] Baird, J. C. and Noma, E. (1978). *Fundamentals of Scaling and Psychophysics*, New York: John Wiley & Sons.

[9] Becker, R. A. and Chambers, J. M. (1984). *S: An Interactive Environment for Data Analysis and Graphics*, Monterey, California: Wadsworth.

[10] Becker, R. A. and Cleveland, W. S. (1984). "Brushing a scatterplot matrix: high-interaction graphical methods for analyzing multidimensional data," AT&T Bell Laboratories Technical Memorandum.

[11] Bentley, J. L., Johnson, D. S., Leighton, T., and McGeoch, C. C. (1983). "An experimental study of bin packing," *Proceedings, Twenty-First Annual Allerton Conference on Communication, Control, and Computing*, 51-60, University of Illinois, Urbana-Champaign, Oct. 5-7.

[12] Bentley, J. L., Johnson, D. S., Leighton, F. T., McGeoch, C. C., and McGeoch, L. A. (1984). "Some unexpected expected behavior results for bin packing," *Proceedings of the Sixteenth Annual ACM Symposium on Computing*, 279-288, New York: The Association for Computing Machinery.

[13] Bentley, J. L. and Kernighan, B. W. (1985). "GRAP — a language for typesetting graphs: tutorial and user manual," Computing Science Technical Report No. 114, Murray Hill: AT&T Bell Laboratories.

[14] Bertin, J. (1973). *Semiologie Graphique*, 2nd edition, Paris: Gauthier-Villars. (English translation: Bertin, J. (1983). *Semiology of Graphics*, Madison, Wisconsin: University of Wisconsin Press.)

[15] Bloomfield, P. (1976). *Fourier Analysis of Time Series: An Introduction*, New York: John Wiley & Sons.

[16] Board of Governors of the Federal Reserve System (1982). *1982 Historical Chart Book*, Washington, D.C.: Federal Reserve System.

[17] Bridge, J. H. B. and Bassingthwaighte, J. B. (1983). "Uphill sodium transport driven by inward calcium gradient in heart muscle," *Science*, 219: 178-180.

[18] Bruntz, S. M., Cleveland, W. S., Kleiner, B., and Warner, J. L. (1974). "The dependence of ambient ozone on solar radiation, wind, temperature, and mixing height," *Symposium on Atmospheric Diffusion and Air Pollution*, 125-128, Boston: American Meteorological Society.

[19] Buck, B. and Perez, S. M. (1983). "New look at magnetic moments and beta decays of mirror nuclei," *Physical Review Letters*, 50: 1975-1978.

[20] Burt, C. (1961). "Intelligence and social mobility," *British Journal of Statistical Psychology,* **14**: 3-23.

[21] Chambers, J. M., Cleveland, W. S., Kleiner, B., and Tukey, P. A. (1983). *Graphical Methods for Data Analysis,* Monterey, California: Wadsworth (hard cover), Boston: Duxbury Press (paperback).

[22] Chatterjee, S. and Chatterjee, S. (1982). "New lamps for old: an exploratory analysis of running times in Olympic games," *Applied Statistics,* **31**: 14-22.

[23] Cheh, A. M., Skochdopole, J., Koski, P., and Cole, L. (1980). "Nonvolatile mutagens in drinking water: production by chlorination and destruction by sulfite," *Science,* **207**: 90-92.

[24] Chernoff, H. (1973). "The uses of faces to represent points in k-dimensional space graphically," *Journal of the American Statistical Association,* **68**: 361-368.

[25] Clayburn, J. A. P., Harmon, R. S., Pankhurst, R. J., and Brown, J. F. (1983). "Sr, O, and Pb isotope evidence for origin and evolution of etive igneous complex, Scotland," *Nature,* **303**: 492-497.

[26] Cleveland, W. S. (1979). "Robust locally weighted regression and smoothing scatterplots," *Journal of the American Statistical Association,* **74**: 829-836.

[27] Cleveland, W. S. (1984). "Graphs in scientific publications," *The American Statistician,* **38**: 261-269.

[28] Cleveland, W. S. (1984). "Graphical methods for data presentation: full scale breaks, dot charts, and multibased logging," *The American Statistician,* **38**: 270-280.

[29] Cleveland, W. S., Devlin, S. J., and Terpenning, I. J. (1982). "The SABL seasonal and calendar adjustment procedures," *Time Series Analysis: Theory and Practice 1,* 539-564, Anderson, O. D., ed., Amsterdam: North Holland Publishing Company.

[30] Cleveland, W. S., Freeny, A., and Graedel, T. E. (1983). "The seasonal component of atmospheric CO_2: information from new approaches to the decomposition of seasonal time series," *Journal of Geophysical Research,* **88**: 10934-10946.

[31] Cleveland, W. S., Graedel, T. E., Kleiner, B., and Warner, J. L. (1974). "Sunday and workday variations in photochemical air pollutants in New Jersey and New York," *Science,* **186**: 1037-1038.

[32] Cleveland, W. S., Harris, C. S., and McGill, R. (1982). "Judgments of circle sizes on statistical maps," *Journal of the American Statistical Association*, **77**: 541-547.

[33] Cleveland, W. S. and McGill, R. (1984). "Graphical perception: theory, experimentation, and application to the development of graphical methods," *Journal of the American Statistical Association*, **79**: 531-554.

[34] Cleveland, W. S. and McGill, R. (1984). "The many faces of a scatterplot," *Journal of the American Statistical Association*, **79**: 807-822.

[35] Cleveland, W. S. and McGill, R. (1985). "Graphical perception and graphical methods for analyzing and presenting scientific data," *Science*, **229**: 828-833.

[36] Cleveland, W. S. and Terpenning, I. J. (1982). "Graphical methods for seasonal adjustment," *Journal of the American Statistical Association*, **77**: 52-62.

[37] Coffman, E. G., Jr., Garey, M. R., and Johnson, D. S. (1983). "Approximation algorithms for bin packing — an updated survey," *Algorithm Design for Computer System Design*," 49-106, Ausiello, G., Lucertini, M., and Serafini, P., ed., New York: Springer-Verlag.

[38] Conway, J. (1959). "Class differences in general intelligence: II," *British Journal of Statistical Psychology*, **12**: 5-14.

[39] Craves, F. B., Zalc, B., Leybin, L., Baumann, N., and Loh, H. H. (1980). "Antibodies to cerebroside sulfate inhibit the effects of morphine and β-endorphin," *Science*, **207**: 75-76.

[40] Crile, G. and Quiring, D. P. (1940). "A record of the body weight and certain organ and gland weights of 3690 animals," *The Ohio Journal of Science*, **15**: 219-259.

[41] Croxton, F. E. (1927). "Further studies in the graphic use of circles and bars II. Some additional data," *Journal of the American Statistical Association*, **22**: 36-39.

[42] Croxton, F. E. and Stryker, R. E. (1927). "Bar charts versus circle diagrams," *Journal of the American Statistical Association*, **22**: 473-482.

[43] Davies, O. L., ed., Box, G. E. P., Cousins, W. R., Himsworth, F. R., Kenney, H., Milbourn, M., Spendley, W., and Stevens, W. L. (1957). *Statistical Methods in Research and Production*, 3rd edition, New York: Hafner Publishing Co.

[44] Diaconis, P. and Freedman, D. (1981). "On the maximum deviation between the histogram and the underlying density," *Zeitschrift für Wahrscheinlichkeitstheorie*, **57**: 453-476.

[45] Diaconis, P. and Friedman, J. H. (1980). "M and N plots," Technical Report No. 15, Stanford, California: Department of Statistics, Stanford University.

[46] Dorfman, D. D. (1978). "The Cyril Burt question: new findings," *Science*, **201**: 1177-1186.

[47] Eells, W. C. (1926). "The relative merits of circles and bars for representing component parts," *Journal of the American Statistical Association*, **21**: 119-132.

[48] *Encyclopaedia Britannica* (1970). "Meteorites," Vol. 15, 272-277, Chicago: Encyclopaedia Britannica.

[49] Feynman, J. and Crooker, N. U. (1978). "The solar wind at the turn of the century," *Nature*, **275**: 626-627.

[50] Fillius, W., Ip, W. H., and McIlwain, C. E. (1980). "Trapped radiation belts of Saturn: first look," *Science*, **207**: 425-431.

[51] Frisby, J. P. and Clatworthy, J. L. (1975). "Learning to see complex random-dot stereograms," *Perception*, **4**: 173-178.

[52] Gale, N. and Halperin, W. C. (1982). "A case for better graphics: the unclassed choropleth map," *The American Statistician*, **36**: 330-336.

[53] Gould, S. J. (1979). *Ever Since Darwin: Reflections in Natural History*, New York: W. W. Norton & Company.

[54] Gould, S. J. (1983). *Hen's Teeth and Horse's Toes*, New York: W. W. Norton & Company.

[55] Gregory, R. L. (1966). *Eye and Brain*, New York: McGraw-Hill Book Company.

[56] Grier, J. W. (1982). "Ban of DDT and subsequent recovery of reproduction in bald eagles," *Science*, **218**: 1232-1235.

[57] Hansen, J., Johnson, D., Lacis, A., Lebedeff, S., Lee, P., Rind, D., and Russell, G. (1981). "Climate impact of increasing atmospheric carbon dioxide," *Science*, **213**: 957-966.

[58] Hearnshaw, L. S. (1979). *Cyril Burt, Psychologist*, Ithaca, New York: Cornell University Press.

[59] Hewitt, A. and Burbidge, G. (1980). "A revised optical catalog of quasi-stellar objects," *The Astrophysical Journal Supplement Series*, **43**: 57-158.

[60] Houck, J. C., Kimball, C., Chang, C., Pedigo, N. W., and Yamamura, H. I. (1980). "Placental β-endorphin-like peptides," *Science*, **207**: 78-80.

[61] Huber, P. J. (1983). "Statistical graphics: history and overview," *Proceedings of the Fourth Annual Conference and Exposition*, 667-676, Fairfax, Virginia: National Computer Graphics Association.

[62] Huff, D., pictures by Geis, I. (1954). *How to Lie with Statistics*, New York: W. W. Norton & Company.

[63] von Huhn, R. (1927). "Further studies in the graphic use of circles and bars I. A discussion of Eells' experiment," *Journal of the American Statistical Association*, **22**: 31-36.

[64] Hunkapiller, M. W. and Hood, L. E. (1980). "New protein sequenator with increased sensitivity," *Science*, **207**: 523-525.

[65] Huntley, S., with Bronson, G. and Walsh, K. T. (1984). "Yumpies, YAP's, yuppies: who they are," *U.S. News & World Report*, April 16.

[66] Iqbal, Z. M., Dahl, K., and Epstein, S. S. (1980). "Role of nitrogen dioxide in the biosynthesis of nitrosamines in mice," *Science*, **207**: 1475-1477.

[67] Jastrow, J. (1892). "On the judgment of angles and position of lines," *American Journal of Psychology*, **5**: 214-248.

[68] Jerison, H. J. (1955). "Brain to body ratios and the evolution of intelligence," *Science*, **121**: 447-449.

[69] Judge, D. L., Wu, F.-M., and Carlson, R. W. (1980). "Ultraviolet photometer observations of the Saturnian system," *Science*, **207**: 431-434.

[70] Julesz, B. (1965). "Texture in visual perception," *Scientific American*, **212**(2): 38-48.

[71] Julesz, B. (1971). *Foundations of Cyclopean Perception*, Chicago: University of Chicago Press.

[72] Julesz, B. (1981). "Textons, the elements of perception, and their interactions," *Nature*, **290**: 91-97.

[73] Kamin, L. (1974). *The Science and Politics of I.Q.*, Potomac, Md.: Erlbaum.

[74] Karsten, K. G. (1925). *Charts and Graphs*, New York: Prentice-Hall.

[75] Keeling, C. D., Bacastow, R. B., Whorf, T. P. (1982). "Measurements of the concentration of carbon dioxide at Mauna Loa Observatory, Hawaii," *Carbon Dioxide Review: 1982*, 377-385, Clark, W. C., ed., New York: Oxford University Press.

[76] Keely, C. B. (1982). "Illegal migration," *Scientific American*, **246**(3): 41-47.

[77] Kerr, R. A. (1983). "Fading El Niño broadening scientists' view," *Science*, **221**: 940-941.

[78] Kleiner, B. and Hartigan, J. A. (1981). "Representing points in many dimensions by trees and castles," *Journal of the American Statistical Association*, **76**: 260-276.

[79] Kolata, G. (1984). "The proper display of data," *Science*, **226**: 156-157.

[80] Konner, M., and Worthman, C. (1980). "Nursing frequency, gonadal function, and birth spacing among !Kung hunter-gatherers," *Science*, **207**: 788-791.

[81] Kovach, J. K. (1980). "Mendelian units of inheritance control color preferences in quail chicks *(Coturnix coturnix japonica)*," *Science*, **207**: 549-551.

[82] Kruskal, W. H. (1975). "Visions of maps and graphs," *Auto-Carto II, Proceedings of the International Symposium on Computer Assisted Cartography*, 27-36, Kavaliunas, J., ed., Washington D. C.: U. S. Bureau of the Census and American Congress on Survey and Mapping.

[83] Kruskal, W. H. (1982). "Criteria for judging statistical graphics," *Utilitas Mathematica*, **21B**: 283-310.

[84] Kuhn, T. S. (1962). *The Structure of Scientific Revolutions*, Chicago: University of Chicago Press.

[85] Kukla, G. and Gavin, J. (1981). "Summer ice and carbon dioxide," *Science*, **214**: 497-503.

[86] Lawless, J. F. (1982). *Statistical Models and Methods for Lifetime Data*, New York: John Wiley & Sons.

[87] Levy, R. I. and Moskowitz, J. (1982). "Cardiovascular research: decades of progress, a decade of promise," *Science*, **217**: 121-129.

[88] Littler, M. M., Littler, D. S., Blair, S. M., and Norris, J. N. (1985). "Deepest known plant life discovered on an uncharted seamount," *Science*, **227**: 57-59.

[89] Lyman, C. P., O'Brien, R. C., Greene, G. C., and Papafrangos, E. D. (1981). "Hibernation and longevity in the Turkish hamster *Mesocricetus brandti*," *Science*, **212**: 668-670.

[90] Maclean, I. E. and Stacey, B. G. (1971). "Judgement of angle size: an experimental appraisal," *Perception and Psychophysics*, **9**: 499-504.

[91] Maglich, B., ed. (1974). "First chemical analysis of the lunar surface," *Adventures in Experimental Physics*, Delta Volume, Princeton, NJ: World Science Education.

[92] Maheshwari, R. K., Jay, F. T., and Friedman, R. M. (1980). "Selective inhibition of glycoprotein and membrane protein of vesicular stomatitis virus from interferon-treated cells," *Science*, **207**: 540-541.

[93] Margon, B. (1983). "The origin of the cosmic x-ray background," *Scientific American*, **248**(1): 104-119.

[94] Marr, D. (1982). *Vision*, San Francisco: W. H. Freeman and Company.

[95] Mauk, M. R., Gamble, R. C., and Baldeschwieler, J. D. (1980). "Vesicle targeting: timed release and specificity for leukocytes in mice by subcutaneous injection," *Science*, **207**: 309-311.

[96] Mayaud, P. N. (1973). *A Hundred Year Series of Geomagnetic Data: 1868-1967*, Paris: International Union of Geodesy and Geophysics.

[97] Monkhouse, F. J. and Wilkinson, H. R. (1971). *Maps and Diagrams*, London: Methuen & Co.

[98] Mostafa, A. E.-S., Abdel-Kader, M., and El-Osmany, A. (1983). "Improvements of antijam performance of spread-spectrum systems," *IEEE Transactions on Communications*, **31**: 803-808.

[99] National Center for Health Statistics (1983). *Monthly Vital Statistics Report, August*, Washington, D.C.: U.S. Government Printing Office.

[100] National Science Board, National Science Foundation (1983). *Science Indicators 1982*, Washington, D.C.: U.S. Government Printing Office.

[101] Newbrun, E. (1982). "Sugar and dental caries: a review of human studies," *Science*, **217**: 418-423.

[102] New Jersey State Lottery Commission. *Pick-it Winning Numbers*, Trenton, New Jersey.

[103] *The New York Times/CBS NEWS POLL* (1984). April 5, p. B10, New York: The New York Times Company.

[104] Orth, C. J., Gilmore, J. S., Knight, J. D., Pillmore, C. L., Tschudy, R. H., and Fassett, J. E. (1981). "An iridium abundance anomaly at the palynological Cretaceous-Tertiary boundary in northern New Mexico," *Science*, **214**: 1341-1343.

[105] Paonessa, G., Metafora, S., Tajana, G., Abrescia, P., DeSantis, A., Gentile, V., and Porta, R. (1984). "Transglutaminase-mediated modifications of the rat sperm surface in vitro," *Science* **226**: 852-855.

[106] Pearman, G. I. and Hyson, P. (1981). "The annual variation of atmospheric CO_2 concentrations observed in the Northern Hemisphere," *Journal of Geophysical Research*, **86**: 9839-9843.

[107] Penzias, A. A. and Wilson, R. W. (1965). "A measurement of excess antenna temperature at 4080 Mc/s," *Astrophysical Journal*, **142**: 419-421.

[108] Playfair, W. (1786). *The Commercial and Political Atlas*. London.

[109] Playfair, W. (1801). *Statistical Breviary*, London.

[110] Program, Lowess (1979). FORTRAN program available from the publisher.

[111] Ramist, L. (1983). Personal communication.

[112] Robinson, A. H. and Sale, R. D. (1969). *Elements of Cartography*, 3rd edition, New York: John Wiley & Sons.

[113] Sagan, C. (1977). *The Dragons of Eden: Speculations on the Evolution of Human Intelligence*, New York: Random House.

[114] Scott, D. W. (1979). "On optimal and data-based histograms," *Biometrika*, **66**: 605-610.

[115] Smith, E. J., Davis, L., Jr., Jones, D. E., Coleman, P. J., Jr., Colburn, D. S., Dyal, P., and Sonett, C. P. (1980). "Saturn's magnetic field and magnetosphere," *Science*, **207**: 407-410.

[116] Smith, E. M., Meyer, W. J., and Blalock, J. E. (1982). "Virus-induced corticosterone in hypophysectomized mice: a possible lymphoid adrenal axis," *Science*, **218**: 1311-1312.

[117] Stevens, K. A. (1978). "Computation of locally parallel structure," *Biological Cybernetics*, **29**: 19-28.

[118] Stevens, K. A. (1981). "The visual interpretation of surface contours," *Artificial Intelligence*, **17**: 47-73.

[119]   Stevens, S. S. (1975). *Psychophysics,* New York: John Wiley & Sons.

[120]   Strunk, W., Jr. and White, E. B. (1979). *The Elements of Style,* 3rd edition, New York: Macmillan Publishing Co.

[121]   Stuiver, M. and Quay, P. D. (1980). "Changes in atmospheric carbon-14 attributed to a variable sun," *Science,* **207**: 11-19.

[122]   Trainor, J. H., McDonald, F. B., and Schardt, A. W. (1980). "Observations of energetic ions and electrons in Saturn's magnetosphere," *Science,* **207**: 421-425.

[123]   Tufte, E. R. (1983). *The Visual Display of Quantitative Information,* Cheshire, Connecticut: Graphics Press.

[124]   Tukey, P. A. and Tukey, J. W. (1981). "Graphical display of data sets in 3 or more dimensions," *Interpreting Multivariate Data,* 189-275, V. Barnett, ed., Chichester, U. K.: John Wiley & Sons.

[125]   Tukey, J. W. (1977). *Exploratory Data Analysis,* Reading, Massachusetts: Addison-Wesley Publishing Co.

[126]   Tukey, J. W. (1984). *The Collected Works of John W. Tukey,* Monterey, California: Wadsworth.

[127]   Turco, R. P., Toon, O. B., Ackerman, T. P., Pollack, J. B., and Sagan, C. (1983). "Nuclear winter: global consequences of multiple nuclear explosions," *Science,* **222**: 1283-1292.

[128]   U.S. Bureau of the Census (1975). *Historical Statistics of the United States: Colonial Times to 1970,* Bicentennial Edition Part 2, Washington, D. C.: U.S. Government Printing Office.

[129]   U.S. Bureau of the Census (1982). *Statistical Abstract of the United States: 1982-1983,* Washington, D. C.: U.S. Government Printing Office.

[130]   U.S. Bureau of the Census (1983). *1980 Census of Population. Vol. 1, Characteristics of the Population,* Washington, D.C.: U.S. Government Printing Office.

[131]   U.S. Bureau of the Census (1983). *Statistical Abstract of the United States: 1984,* Washington, D.C.: U.S. Government Printing Office.

[132]   Vetter, B. M. (1980). "Working women scientists and engineers," *Science,* **207**: 28-34.

[133]   Wahlen, M., Kunz, C. O., Matuszek, J. M., Mahoney, W. E., and Thompson, R. C. (1980). "Radioactive plume from the Three Mile Island accident: xenon-133 in air at a distance of 375 kilometers," *Science,* **207**: 639-640.

[134] Weber, E. H. (1846). "Der Tastsinn und das Gemeinfühl," *Handwörterbuch der Physiologie*, **3**: 481-588, Wagner, R., ed., Braunschweig: Vieweg.

[135] Wilk, M. B. and Gnanadesikan, R. (1968). "Probability plotting methods for the analysis of data," *Biometrika*, **55**: 1-17.

[136] Willoughby, D. P. (1974). "Running and jumping," *Natural History Magazine*, **83**: 69-72.

[137] *The World Almanac & Book of Facts 1983*, New York: Newspaper Enterprise Association.

[138] *The World Almanac & Book of Facts 1985*, New York: Newspaper Enterprise Association.

[139] Yagi, N. and Matsubara, I. (1980). "Myosin heads do not move on activation in highly stretched vertebrate striated muscle," *Science*, **207**: 307-308.

GRAPH INDEX

TEXT INDEX